DEVELOPMENT AND DISPLACEMENT OF WOMEN IN SOUTHEAST ASIA

DEVELOPMENT AND DISPLACEMENT OF WOMEN IN SOUTHEAST ASIA

S Pandey

MD PUBLICATIONS PVT LTD
NEW DELHI
www.mdppl.com

Published by :

MD Publications Pvt Ltd
"MD House", 11, Darya Ganj,
New Delhi - 110 002
Phone : +91-11-45355555
E-mail : contact@mdppl.com
Website: www.mdppl.com

ISBN: 978-81-7533-357-4

Published and Prined by Mr. Pranav Gupta on behalf of **MD Publications Pvt Ltd** at Mohit Enterprises, Delhi.

PREFACE

South-East Asia is the most heavily populated and amongst the poorest regions in the world. It faces enormous social, economic and health challenges, including pervasive inequality, violence, political instability and high burden of diseases. In South-East Asia, most of the societies are predominantly patriarchal. The cultural norms prevailing in South-East Asia perpetuate the subordinate position of women socially and economically.

It is generally accepted that employment generally has a beneficial effect on psychological health. It brings interest and fulfillment, structure and sense of control as well as income, social status and social contacts. Women in South-East Asia have fewer opportunities for paid jobs, which affects their mental well-being.

There is little doubt that trade liberalization has had a profound effect on the well-being of women in Southeast Asia. Not all of these impacts are negative, however. Indeed, the opening up of the region's economies, at both national and regional levels, has brought about opportunities in the form of new employment, which may allow them to access higher incomes and improve their status in the society. Given their increasing role in the economies of Southeast Asia, however, women are often the major victims of economic openness. Poor women, in particular, remain vulnerable to economic policy changes that occur in the region. Unfortunately, trade policies are often gender-blind and ignore women's interests and aspirations.

Even in the new millennium, women in South Asia are deprived of their socio-economic and legal rights. They live in a system where religious injunctions, tribal codes, feudal traditions and discriminatory laws are prevalent. They are beset by a lifetime social and psychological disadvantage, coupled with long years of child bearing. They often end up experiencing poverty, isolation and psychological disability. In some urban regions of South-Asian countries, women's social roles have changed to some extent. They have now comparatively more opportunities for education, employment and enjoyment of civil rights within society. However, the de-stereotyping of the gender roles which have been traditionally assigned by our society is still far away.

The United Nations plays an important role in helping governments of the region provide assistance to internally displaced populations. With the exception of India, Myanmar and Bangladesh, where governments have declined offers of international assistance for people displaced by conflict, the UN addresses internal displacement in all countries. The cluster approach has now been rolled out in eight countries out of ten, but only in five of them (Afghanistan, Nepal, Pakistan, Sri Lanka and Timor-Leste) were the needs of conflict-induced IDPs a regular item on the agenda of the protection clusters, mainly because of the sensitivities of governments (as in the Philippines) or their refusal to acknowledge the existence of such groups (as in Indonesia and Myanmar).

I am very grateful to Mr. Pranav Gupta, Director of MD Publications Pvt Ltd, New Delhi, for his kind cooperation and support for this book.

S Pandey

CONTENTS

1

Asian Women Entrepreneurs

Growing women's entrepreneurship in Asia is emerging as an alternative to the male-dominated corporate culture and patriarchal social structure; the economic and political contribution made by Asian women entrepreneurs is expected to exert significant influence in shaping a new business model in Asia in the 21st century. In fact many international organizations have recognized Asian women's potential to generate economic wealth as well as general social welfare. After the adoption of the Jakarta Declaration for the Advancement of Women in Asia and the Pacific in 1994 and the Beijing Declaration and the Platform for Action in 1995, the UN's focus on economic performance and gender has helped other organizations, such as Asian Development Bank, World Bank and OECD, pay greater attention to the issue.

They are finding out how to provide women with access to necessary resources - information, capital and a social network - to establish their own medium to small size businesses. In addition to the obvious economic benefits, having more Asian women who own businesses can diminish gender inequality, increase political representation and change the business management style and giving some importance to balancing career and family responsibilities.

The increasing prominence of Asian women entrepreneurs since the 1990s has raised a lot of debate about their characteristics and management styles, which many believe are significantly different from those of their male counterparts. For instance, Abdul Rashid (1995) demonstrates that women entrepreneurs are less motivated by financial reasons, such as money and economic necessity, than the men. Lee and Choo (2001) find that women face specific challenges in the form of family commitments and sex-role conflicts. Women have also been shown to be especially good at cultivating interpersonal relationships but poor at planning, organizing and controlling. However, research on these women is still very much at an infant stage.

There is a wide range of strategic issues which requires more in-depth scrutiny, particularly that pertaining to their styles of leadership. Given that innovation is one of the most critical functions of entrepreneurship, an attempt is made in this study to examine female leadership in the context of cultivating innovativeness in business organizations. The study is carried out in Peninsular Malaysia, where approximately 15% of businesses are owned by women. Although small in numbers, this segment of the Malaysian business population serves huge social and political purposes, as discussed in the following section.

WOMEN ENTREPRENEURS IN MALAYSIA

Malaysian women's participation in commerce may exist in any of the four categories of employment status, i.e. as an employer, an employee, an own-account worker or an unpaid family worker. The Malaysian Labour Force Report documents that out of the total working female population in 2003, 77.5% were paid employees, 11.7% were own-account workers and 9.6% were unpaid family workers. Only 1.2% were categorized as employers. For men, the percentages were higher for the employers and own-account workers categories but lower for employees. The fact that the number of unpaid female family workers is almost five times higher than the males' is particularly disturbing.

One possible reason for this is that Malaysian women are being exploited and made to work for free by their own family members. Based on that scenario, it is believed that some women become entrepreneurs to secure financial independence. But financial independence alone cannot explain women's decision to set up their own business; after all 77.5% of Malaysian working women find financial independence by being employed. So what are the real motives for entrepreneurial intention among these women? Although previous research shows that the most common appear to be intrinsic such as self-satisfaction and interest in business, a deeper analysis suggests that there may be social and political factors too. As voters, Malaysian women compose about half of the total eligible population.

In the elections, it is no secret that women both in the ruling party and the opposition play the biggest role in house-to-house campaigns and getting right down to the grassroots. For the government, empowering women with opportunities in education and career is therefore critical to ensure their political support. Since career opportunities in the government and corporate sectors are limited, women are encouraged to become business players. They are given training, funding, and counseling as incentives and business networks are provided through affiliation with political parties. In addition, business equity has been used as a measure of social justice since the era of the New Economic Policy.

For UMNO, the Malay component of the ruling coalition, raising Malay equity symbolizes its success as the champion of Malay rights. Unfortunately the young Malay male population suffers from a horde of social ills - from dropping out of school to illegal racing to drug abuse - and UMNO finds itself turning more and more to its womenfolk as role models. According to the Malaysian Labour Force Report (Department of Statistics, 2004), out of the total number of women employers, a clear majority are located in urban areas and aged between 30 and 49 years. Almost half are Malays, followed by 40% Chinese, and 5% Indians. In another study, it is established that Malaysian women entrepreneurs are most likely to be in the service industries, have prior working experience and small i.e. with fewer than 20 full-time employees and earning less than RM100,000 per annum. Their businesses are mainly funded by personal savings, and most are either sole proprietorships or partnerships. They also tend to concentrate on local markets, with less than 10% going international.

ENTREPRENEURSHIP AND INNOVATION

Entrepreneurship, as an area of research, began in France approximately three hundred years ago. In the earliest stage of its conception by Richard Cantillon, a noted French economist in the 1700s, entrepreneurship was associated with the risk involved in a business transaction where the costs were known but the profits were not. In the 18th century, Jean Baptiste Say and Francis Walker further distinguished the entrepreneur from a venture capitalist; the former was viewed as a capital user while the latter, a capital provider. The concept of entrepreneurship continued to widen and became more articulated in the 19th and 20th centuries when it was used to explain a lot of economic phenomena; market expansion, rapid technological development and the booming of small-and-medium industries were mostly attributed to entrepreneurship.

Entrepreneurs were considered important too because of their ability to develop competitive strategies which were vital not only to the firm but also the nation, as suggested by Adam Smith in his 1776 book, *The Wealth of Nations*. Due to this purported social significance of entrepreneurship, the quest for a genuine profile of the entrepreneur gained more momentum in Western literature in the mid 1900s. In particular, there were considerable discussions on the traits and functions of an entrepreneur. McClelland (1961), one of the most prominent scientists to have studied the entrepreneurial psyche proposed that an entrepreneur was someone who was proactive, achievement-oriented and committed.

In *Can Capitalism Survive?* Joseph Schumpeter (1952) argued that the function of an entrepreneur was to reform or revolutionize the pattern of production by exploiting new or untried technology and processes. The notion of the entrepreneur as an innovator is thus believed to have been conceived by Schumpeter. Since then, innovative skills have generally been accepted as one of the critical attributes of successful entrepreneurs. Some of the most profitable companies in the world have associated their growth with innovation, which they perceive as the ability to change and reinvent themselves as a way to exploit opportunities.

In the words of Bill Gates, the founder and CEO of Microsoft Corporation:

The Role of Leadership in Innovation

Many classical theorists on innovation argue that innovation is triggered and driven by certain individuals in the society who have the necessary characteristics to make it happen. This perspective is supported by latter thinkers such as Bennis and Nanus (1985) and Nam and Tatum (1997) who also believe that entrepreneurs are the ones primarily responsible for initiating changes and novelties in the society. The explanation offered for the theory is that entrepreneurs possess certain traits such as risk-propensity and ambitiousness that induce them to strive for better and greater things. Entrepreneurs are held responsible too for educating the society on the need for new ways of life and solutions to life's problems.

This the entrepreneur may achieve by destroying the present equilibrium and creating a new one through novelties – a process described by Schumpeter (1934) as "creative destruction". Although the individualist perspective of innovation has been criticized as overly narrow and simplistic, the notion of leaders as agents of change has accepted wide acceptance among management scholars. Research indicates that innovation thrives within certain organizational cultures - such as a learning orientation and an open attitude towards risk - which are shaped by their leaders. Likewise, a leadership high in Power Distance has been suggested to have an adverse effect on innovativeness and vice versa. However, existing typologies of leadership style do not adequately describe the female perspective. For instance, leaders are said to be either result-oriented or people-oriented but the truth is that women, especially Asian women, often get results by being people-oriented. Thus there appears to be a need to identify a more accurate typology of leadership styles among Malaysian women entrepreneurs, particularly one which relates to innovation.

Study Framework and Methodology

The objective of the study is to examine how women entrepreneurs lead their employees and influence other stakeholders towards building an innovative organizational culture. Due to the intended depth of the analysis, a qualitative approach is considered more suitable. Ten women entrepreneurs are identified and personally interviewed based on a series of open- ended questions. These women are deliberately chosen from all over Peninsular Malaysia to represent various industries and personal backgrounds.

Each interview takes place at the respondent's business premise and lasts for approximately an hour. In some cases, a brief tour of the premise is also provided which gives the author a first hand opportunity to observe some of the innovations implemented by the entrepreneurs. Their responses are then content-analysed to generate a typology of female leadership styles within the context of business innovation.

DISCUSSION OF RESULTS

1. Their age ranges from late twenties to early fifties; 2. Two received tertiary education, seven higher secondary, and one lower secondary; 3. Four of them are in consumer services, one in business services, two in distribution and three in manufacturing; 4. Five have been operating for less than 5 years, three for 5 to 10 years and two for more than 10 years; 5. Five of them are based in the Central region, two are in the East Coast states, two in the South, and one in the North. Based on their qualitative responses, four distinct styles of female leadership are identified. These styles, referred here as the "Mother", the "Teacher", the "Boss" and the "Chameleon", are described as follows.

The "Mother"

This style reflects a family-oriented approach in the management of business innovation. The four women who fall into this category, namely PI2, PI7, PI8 and PI9, view their employees and other stakeholders as their extended families. They are extremely protective of others, and often get involved in the personal affairs of those they perceive to be under their care. These women frequently use phrases such as "help each other out like brothers and sisters", "they respect me like their own mother", and "I scold them if they do anything wrong".

In their organizations, innovation is often treated with caution. Each time the entrepreneur decides to embark on a new project, she tries it out herself first. When she is absolutely sure of its success, she demonstrates in detail to others how exactly she wants things to be done and takes great care to minimize the chances of failure. She also has very little reservation about asking for personal favors from suppliers and customers.

The "Teacher"

The style displayed by PI1 and PI10 closely approximates that of an educationist. The women believe in the good of academic qualification, training and continuous upgrading of skill and technology. PI1 tells of her latest recruit, a Chemistry graduate, who is hired as her food technologist and quality controller. And PI10 apologises at the outset of the interview that she only has an hour before having to rush off to Singapore for a workshop on childhood education.

The women have a very open attitude towards the learning process, and regards mistakes as a natural part of it. They encourage their employees to try out new things on their own and the organizations often develop new ideas by trial-and-error. Computerisation and automation are integrated within the process flow to improve quality and maintain standards. They even educate their customers on the benefits of innovation.

The "Boss"

This particular style describes the entrepreneur's emphasis on the formalization of innovation. Novelties are adopted as official business targets tied to the employees' performance evaluation and remuneration packages. Instructions are given in a precise, orderly manner and changes are carried out systematically.

The "Chameleon"

This style reflects the entrepreneur's tendency to be situational. She believes in adopting different approaches to different individuals and circumstances. According to her, to be effective, an entrepreneur needs to understand the exact needs and wants of various stakeholders and strive to fulfill each in many different ways. Innovation is perceived as merely a means to an end, and not something which should be actively encouraged. PI3 says she visits government and business clients with two different sets of product catalogue, because she knows that each has a different budget. Therefore, even though she knows which product is the best, she feels that there is no point in educating the customer about the product simply because the budget will not allow for it. In the case of PI4, she carries products from four parent companies and adjusts her presentation package and style according to the customer. She does not see anything wrong with the practice because she is not legally bound to any one of them.

The study demonstrates that female leadership styles do not neatly fit into existing typologies commonly associated with modern leaders. There is enough evidence gathered in the interviews suggesting that women entrepreneurs are not simply either result-oriented or people-oriented; instead they often derive results by being people-oriented. This may be explained by the theory of social conditioning which argues that because society conditions women to be gentle and nurturing, they behave as such. Thus it is possible that even women in leadership positions assume roles which are more socially acceptable such as "mother" and "teacher" so that the society will be more tolerant and accepting towards their leadership.

This behaviour is likely to be more pervasive in a masculine society where gender differentiation is high than in a feminine society which advocates gender equality. Of course, due to the limited number of samples, it would be presumptuous to conclude that the study's findings can adequately explain female leadership styles in every setting. As leadership is a highly cultural variable, it is believed that different cultural group will have a different tendency towards a particular style.

For instance, in highly masculine societies such as Japan, most women entrepreneurs may adopt the "Mother" and "Teacher" styles whereas in feminine societies no clear-cut relationships may be observed since women are freer to express their true identities. It is also important to determine which style is more effective for women entrepreneurs: Is the organization more innovative when she behaves in a specific manner? To make reasonable conclusions, obviously more data is required.

Hence it is recommended that quantitative studies involving larger samples be conducted to ascertain the following:

1. The relationship between culture and leadership style.
2. The effect of leadership style on organizational innovation. In so doing, other criteria including the validity and reliability of the leadership style scale will first have to be met.

Future studies may also raise additional issues such as the measure of organizational innovation in women-owned enterprises. In 2001, 24 women became the founding members of the Bangladesh Women Chamber of Commerce and Industry (BWCCI). BWCCI has been successful in removing traditional social and political barriers to women's participation in the economy and supporting women entrepreneurs. With the support of local and international partners and stakeholders, BWCCI has continued to increase its role in nurturing Bangladeshi business women. Perhaps the most telling indicator of the organization's success has been a tremendous growth in its dues-paying membership - from the original 24 in 2001 to 1,500 by the end of 2008 - clear evidence of the value of the services BWCCI provides.

Yet BWCCI has been able to provide much more than practical training on running and organizing a business. Its advocacy efforts have resulted in a number of policy victories, including changes in the national bank policy that have allowed for 10 percent of funds dedicated to small and medium-sized enterprises (SMEs) to be earmarked for women-owned businesses and to be loaned at lower rates and without collateral. In addition to the concrete benefits of policy change, BWCCI has been able to give women a political voice by listening to their concerns and distilling these into policy priorities. BWCCI helps struggling women by providing them with opportunities for job and wealth creation. Tangible benefits like greater business opportunities for its members come alongside intangible benefits, including a more positive perception of women in business.

The social barriers that remain a source of male bias in lending are beginning to come down, as more and more women become economically and politically successful. BWCCI's efforts are also self-reinforcing. Advocating policy changes in support of women in business increases its own membership ranks. A larger membership creates a greater opportunity to exchange expertise and business ideas. A more vibrant market attracts new entrants, who, should they join the business association, bring in more ideas and more information that help formulate future reform initiatives. This section assesses the regional context in which BWCCI and other women's business associations operate. Afterward, a closer look at BWCCI provides the details of its dramatic success.

WOMEN'S BUSINESS ASSOCIATIONS IN SOUTH ASIA

Women have long been marginalized in political, economic, and social endeavors. Exclusion from civic and political life and limited access to education and intellectual development have precluded women's economic independence. Women's progress towards independence can be loosely compared to a nation's march towards self-determination, prosperity, access to education, and democratic institutions. Globally, countries with a strong private sector, free market economies, and democratic policymaking have made significant strides in bringing greater opportunities and freedoms to their female populations. A similar trend is underway in South Asia. Civil society has emerged as a vibrant agent for advocacy and reform on behalf of women.

The pressure for transparency in public and private institutions is aiding women's progress in the economic and political arena. In a region that houses one quarter of the world's population and half of the world's poor, South Asia is also faced with conflict and threats of weapons of mass destruction, terrorism, narcotics, illiteracy, and corrupt institutions. Further, despite rapid global economic growth during the 1990s, South Asian countries still have some of the lowest per capita incomes in the world. In addition to being socially marginalized, the plight of women has been exacerbated by poverty, and precarious political realities. Bangladesh and Nepal are afflicted by political uncertainty and teeter on the brink of violence, while Afghanistan, Pakistan, and Sri Lanka are beleaguered by war. Despite being the only country in the region with stable democratic structures and an active civil society, India shares many systemic problems that beset the rest of the region.

Increasing women's political engagement is directly connected to elevating women's economic and social status. Despite local efforts to increase women's political involvement, women remain poorly represented in local and national governments. Support for empowerment Programmes that promote women's networks and solidarity around issues related to their economic independence must be a priority for South Asian governments. Women's business associations have championed this cause.

THE ROLE OF WOMEN'S BUSINESS ASSOCIATIONS IN SOUTH ASIA

Policymakers must recognize that women participating in the economy boost community development and improves the general welfare of the public. While most developing countries have established initiatives to develop and promote micro-credit institutions, SMEs do more to generate employment opportunities, create economies of scale, and boost export growth because they deliver these benefits directly to individuals. Since women's role in the formal economy is fairly limited in South Asia, the need for women's business associations is essential. These business groups can encourage entrepreneurship by providing women opportunities for effective advocacy regarding access to finance, markets, information, and training. Business associations can provide business-to-business networking events, business development services, policy reform, credit facilities, technical assistance, and mentoring Programmes.

These support mechanisms help women grow their businesses from micro to small or even medium-sized enterprises. In many South Asian countries, female business leaders have created their own business associations, which are often elite enclaves that primarily benefit the founders. These founders frequently come from privileged backgrounds and thus have access to power, influence, and sources of wealth generation. Associations of this sort tend to revolve around building the image of the founders. On the other hand, many other women's business associations have evolved into viable institutions, complete with qualified, trained staff who address community issues and provide mentoring services. Some associations, often those that receive support from local chambers of commerce, non-governmental organizations (NGOs), or development organizations, including the United States Agency for International Development (USAID) and the International Finance Corporation, have developed to a point where they can successfully participate in public- private dialogue and influence public policy.

FORMAL AND INFORMAL BARRIERS

While differences abound in geography, language, demographics, and economic conditions, women residing across South Asia face common difficulties and obstacles to joining the formal economy.

Poverty

Perhaps most detrimental to women's entrepreneurial motivations is the pervasive poverty of region, which limits economic opportunities for women. Women must struggle to simply survive, let alone secure the resources necessary to start a business. When opportunities are available, they are often offered to men instead of women. For example, about half the population in Bangladesh lives on just $1 per day, and women are among the very poorest in the country, a trend of marked "feminization of poverty." Still, several South Asian countries have made progress in combating severe poverty, such as Pakistan, which has successfully decreased poverty levels by 10 percent since 2001.

Education

Another common hindrance to women in these countries is limited, or even non-existent, access to education. For example, while the literacy rate of men in Afghanistan is about 43 percent, that of women is just 14 percent. Likewise, although the male literacy rate stands at 72 percent in India, female literacy is just 44 percent. Almost 50 percent of the total Nepalese population over age 15 is literate, but the literacy rate for all women is just 35 percent.

Women in Pakistan also suffer from a low level of practical literacy and little to no knowledge of English - the language in which business is very often conducted. This lack of access to educational and training opportunities seriously hinders South Asian women from developing the skills and acquiring the knowledge essential to entrepreneurship. Creating structures that help women to gain economic and political empowerment is the only way to break systemic discrimination and deprivation cycle.

Conflict

The instability inherent in several countries in this region also serves to undermine women's economic development, as women are often more vulnerable in conflict situations. Incessant war can leave a vacuum when men are off fighting or deceased. Women are thus left alone to cope with raising families and generating sufficient income to provide food and shelter. Since women face unfavorable odds in finding gainful employment, starting their own business can provide a valuable opportunity for women to support their families.

In Afghanistan, protracted armed conflict has resulted in massive internal displacement and high refugee flows. Similarly, the unresolved civil conflict between the *Liberation Tigers of Tamil Eelam* and the Sri Lankan Government has resulted in an environment inhospitable to economic growth or even basic subsistence. If (or when) these countries do achieve some sort of non-violent stability, studies have shown that post-conflict societies face a 44 percent chance of relapse within the first five years of peace. Supporting entrepreneurship can help mitigate causes of discontent while collective action through business associations could help repair lingering schisms within local communities.

Social and Cultural Gender Roles

Cultural gender stereotypes hinder the socio- economic progress of women in South Asia. Most countries in this region are characterized by a patriarchal social structure, in which women do not have access to the same opportunities and freedoms as men. Women's social and economic marginalization often prevents them from escaping abuse, obtaining justice, or seeking opportunity. Although the risks and types of abuse may relate to a woman's ethnicity, religion, age, class, caste, sexual orientation, or national origin, gender itself often subjects women to an unequal status.

Prevalent forms of gender- based violence in the region include domestic violence, marital rape, female infanticide, sexual harassment, trafficking, and forced marriage. Despite economic growth and increased access to services and credit markets, deeply entrenched social norms and biased legal systems still undermine women's opportunity. Women's labor force participation in South Asia is the lowest in the world. Even as female labor participation increases, women remain at risk of sexual harassment, poor working conditions, pregnancy- based discrimination, and being passed over in career promotions. Women have limited decision- making power at all levels, and routinely receive less pay than men for the same work. Religious and social constraints, such as restricted freedom of movement, early marriages, stigmatization of widows, and denial of basic human freedoms, also limit women's ability to participate in the economy to varying degrees across the region.

Social and cultural expectations are a particularly daunting barrier to women's entry into business. Between 2001 and 2003, only 7.4 percent of businesses in Bangladesh were owned by women in contrast to 20 percent in India and 39 percent in Southeast Asia. The average female worker in Sri Lanka still earns 66 percent less than her male counterpart. Nepalese traditions (regarding men and women) do not always allow for great social or economic mobility. Professions are often determined by the caste system, and the workforce is largely segregated, resulting in entire communities that have little or no access to education or training. With poor property rights, Nepalese women are economically dependent on men.

Although women constitute 43 percent of the labor force, they are confined to low-paying jobs with little opportunity for advancement, in positions such as clerical or administrative assistants. At the same time, of all economically active women in Nepal, about three- quarters are self-employed, and in the past two decades, significant progress has been made in entrepreneurship development among both rural and urban women. A large number of Sri Lankan women work in the informal sector, especially in agriculture. In urban areas in Pakistan, women play an active role in the informal service sector by filling the lowest- paid jobs. Across the region, women are limited to a set range of occupations defined by cultural norms, including teaching, nursing, and garment production.

Marriage responsibilities, an inability to raise even the minimum equity fund for a loan, lack of confidence, gender stereotypes, and unsupportive husbands all serve to keep women away from economic independence and income generation. Despite these pervasive gender stereotypes, and in part due to necessity, South Asian women are moving beyond customary occupations into traditionally male livelihoods. The women of Bangladesh have traditionally engaged in agro-based businesses or cottage industries, such as stitching and embroidery, cane and bamboo weaving, raising poultry, and dairy farming, but more women are now entering production lines in the garment industry, producing costume jewelry, supplying dry and fresh flowers to hotels and restaurants, catering food, establishing educational institutions, and setting up fashion design houses.

Political and Civil Rights

Unequal property and inheritance rights render women economically dependent on patriarchal systems. Even though the civil codes guarantee women's property rights, these laws are often poorly, if at all, enforced. In many cases, the codes are rendered nearly meaningless by the dictates of personal status laws and customary practices, which deny women rights to own and inherit property. Women in South Asia typically do not possess political rights equivalent to men. Ironically, the region is noted for its many female heads of state at the same time as women have limited opportunities for political participation. Women remain a minority among Sri Lanka's parliamentarians and ministers, despite the fact that the country boasts the world's first elected female head of state (in 1960).

Moreover, women lack representatives who might effectively further their interests - especially in business issues. Several countries have undertaken efforts to address their unequal political situation. Since the reinstatement of Nepal's parliament in April 2006, a number of important pro-women legislative and policy measures have passed. The Gender Equality Bill was passed and the Citizenship Act was amended to allow Nepalese women to pass on their citizenship to their children. With the current drafting of the Nepalese Constitution, female constituent assembly members, civil society groups, and parts of the private sector are advocating before Parliament to ensure that women's issues be included in the Constitution.

Although there is usually a time lag between the passage and implementation of laws, each small step is greeted joyously by women and their advocates. After years of the near-complete exclusion of women from social, economic, and public life in Afghanistan, the new constitution of 2004 grants equal rights and duties before the law to both men and women, and prohibits discrimination among its citizens. Two seats per province are reserved for women in the national assembly. Yet, women who run female literacy projects, raise awareness about sexual and domestic violence, or work in the government continue to receive death threats and suffer from attacks on their homes and offices. Recently, even girls attending school have been targeted in the southern regions of the country.

While each country in the region has its own set of challenges in relation to women's entrepreneurship, women's business associations have had success across South Asia in advancing women's interests. These groups facilitate and encourage change in national policies on behalf of their members, and provide assistance in business conduct and development. This section provides a brief overview of some key groups in each country.

Afghanistan

In Afghanistan, informal women's groups supported numerous women working at home under the Taliban. Formal NGOs began appearing in 2003, as women started bringing their businesses into public. While focused on different areas of economic empowerment, each organization below has had success in redefining the role of women in Afghan society. The Afghan Women's Business Association (AWBA) enables women looking for the expansion of their businesses to engage in policy dialogue with the government and the media, voice their concerns, and enhance their public image. AWBA also develops links between women's businesses, finds international markets for their products, ensures participation in national and international trade fairs, and helps in securing credit for members' business growth and expansion.

The Afghan Women's Business Council (AWBC) receives support from the Afghan Government and comprises established individual businesswomen, NGOs, sector startups, and entrepreneurs. The council offers advocacy, training, and research facilities, and provides a forum for women to support each other and to speak to the government about a better business environment and greater access to markets. The council facilitates linkages between national, regional, and international trade partners. The Afghan Women's Business Federation (AWBF) was founded in 2004 through a cooperative effort of the USAID-funded Women's Enterprise Development project, the Ministry of Commerce, 18 women's business organizations (including AWBA and AWBC), CIPE, and NGOs such as Aid Afghanistan. AWBF gives businesswomen the support network necessary to develop business skills, helps them realize their potential, and helps them access to funding sources. AWBF membership now stands at 55 associations supported by more than 20 full-time staff.

Bangladesh

Bangladesh is an example of innovators successfully creating new realities on the ground. Grameen Bank, founded by the Nobel Prize laureate Professor Muhammad Yunus, has reversed conventional banking practices by removing the need for collateral and created a banking system based on mutual trust, accountability, participation, and creativity. It provides credit to the poorest of the poor in rural Bangladesh, without any collateral. As of September 2008, it has 7.58 million borrowers, 97 percent of whom are women. With 2,530 branches, Grameen Bank provides services in 83,178 villages, covering more than 99 percent of the total villages in Bangladesh. Now the bank is making inroads into serving SMEs, taking its successful model to the next level. This model has been adapted in other developing countries around the world.

The Women Entrepreneurs Association of Bangladesh (WEAB) was established and registered with the Ministry of Commerce in 2000, under the auspices of the Federation of Bangladesh Chambers of Commerce and Industry. One of its major victories was the creation of a platform to help businesswomen establish themselves in competitive fields traditionally dominated by men. WEAB has also developed a support system for women entrepreneurs to help them improve their product quality, market their products, meet changing market demands, and access training on technical know-how, design, and development. The Bangladesh Women Chamber of Commerce and Industry (BWCCI) has encouraged entrepreneurial women to venture into the information technology, media, and publications fields in addition to traditional women's business sectors such as beauty, fashion, health products, and handicrafts.

The women of BWCCI have also provided institutional support, guaranteed loans, and supported advocates for women in business at the regional and national levels. The organization continues to work with CIPE to promote both rural and urban women entrepreneurs in the national policy reform process and facilitate women's greater democratic participation. BWCCI's early work in Bangladesh focused on strengthening internal election monitoring (for business associations) and expanding the participation, leadership development, and influence of women and youth in politics and civil society. These efforts have since expanded to include the Five Estates of Democracy Initiative (Five Estates) - private industry, labor, NGOs, the media, and political parties. By working with the International Republican Institute to empower the Five Estates, BWCCI hopes to create a more representative and responsive democracy, with a focus on the women of Bangladesh. Such initiatives are conducive to the creation of a bold and entrepreneurial spirit among women.

Bhutan

In light of the other political and economic challenges faced by this remote country, women's issues have never been a priority in Bhutan. The female population of Bhutan suffers the same issues of subordination and discrimination suffered by women in most other South Asian nations. The National Women's Association of Bhutan (NWAB) was established by the government in 1981 as an NGO charged with the responsibility of improving socio-economic conditions of women throughout the country. NWAB was primarily devoted to the advancement of women in agreement with resolutions adopted at the United Nations conference in

Nairobi in 1985 and the Convention on the Elimination of All Forms of Discrimination against Women. NWAB has worked to promote economic opportunities, develop women's entrepreneurial capacity and raise awareness of women's rights and potential. It aims to provide access to capital, markets, and support to women entrepreneurs.

India

India's diversity is illustrated by the fact that within its 28 states and 7 union territories, there are over 2,000 ethnic groups and several hundred languages spoken by its citizens. Each state has its own chamber of commerce and industry, set up to create advocacy opportunities and public- private cooperation. Most parent associations have either exclusive woman's divisions or women representatives specifically dedicated to women's entrepreneurship issues. The success of these ancillary enterprises varies by the length of their operations, the strength of their leadership, and Programmatic focus. India, with its long colonial history, has an organized system of free enterprise and trade associations, a distinct advantage over other South Asian nations. The Federation of Indian Chambers of Commerce and Industry (FICCI) has empowered Indian businesses to bolster their competitiveness and enhance their global reach.

The FICCI currently has a nationwide membership of nearly 1,500 corporations and over 500 chambers of commerce and business associations. The federation espouses the shared vision of Indian businesses and speaks directly and indirectly for over 250,000 business units. The FICCI Ladies' Organization was established in 1983 to facilitate women entrepreneurs' efforts in finding pro-active business solutions through research, interactions at the highest political level, and global networking. The Association of Women Entrepreneurs (AWE) was established in 1993 and initially worked with women who were already engaged in some economic activity and sought to improve their effectiveness and sustainability. AWE's goal is to enhance women's business skills and make their work more productive. The association's guiding mantra is to tap new potential markets and provide networking opportunities to its members.

Nepal

The Federation of Woman Entrepreneurs Associations of Nepal (FWEAN) was formed as the national chapter of the Woman Entrepreneurs Associations of Nepal. FWEAN has worked to place women entrepreneurs into mainstream national development through the establishment of chapters in Nepal's districts to strengthen and sustain the established chapters, and bring women entrepreneurs under a single umbrella organization to represent their interests. FWEAN was established as a non-governmental, non-political, and non-profit organization and it is currently the only national body representing women-owned SMEs in the trade, commerce, industry, and tourism sectors.

FWEAN advocates for policies and Programmes concerning women's issues for national socio- economic development and builds linkages and affiliations at the regional and international level, with a focus on the economic empowerment of women. The federation also helps to increase economic opportunities for women and enhance the business skills of potential and existing woman entrepreneurs. The organization gives priority to local women interested in working for self- sustainability through enterprise development, especially conflict-affected women, minority women, and poor women.

Pakistan

In Pakistan, the women's movement has shifted from reacting to government legislation to focusing on three primary goals: securing women's political representation in the National Assembly, working to raise women's social awareness (particularly about family planning), and countering suppression of women's rights by defining and articulating positions on current events in order to raise public awareness. Pakistan's 2006 Trade Organisations Ordinance, issued by the government after a year- long consultative process initiated by CIPE Pakistan, has resulted in the formation and growth of a more representative associations that can advocate more effectively fo economic reform. Under the new law, women are able to form their own associations without male sponsorship. Each of the four provinces in Pakistan boasts its own women's chamber of commerce, and two have succeeded in achieving full legal registration. All work toward the same goal of encouraging entrepreneurship and economic independence among Pakistan's female population.

The Women's Chamber of Commerce and Industry (WCCI) was first registered as the Pakistan Association of Women Entrepreneurs in 1986 in Karachi and is an honorary member of the Federation of Pakistan Chambers of Commerce and Industry, which also boasts a standing committee on women entrepreneurs. In 2002, WCCI emerged in its current form and is awaiting accreditation. The organization was founded by a successful businesswoman, its executive committee has 22 members, and it claims about 300 active members. Services for members include advisory and mentoring Programmes, training, access to micro- credit, business development Programmes, and access to domestic and international markets. WCCI works primarily with clothing manufacturers and fashion designers in urban areas, and also with small rural entrepreneurs in the production of embroidered and stitched linens and other finished home textiles.

The Punjab Women Chamber of Commerce and Industry (PWCCI) is based in the city of Lahore, and was established in 2002 to promote and develop women's entrepreneurship in Punjab. The chamber has been licensed by the government and encourages women entrepreneurs belonging to all tiers of society to come together to voice their concerns and to seek assistance in research and development. PWCCI provides a forum for debate and discussion, the opportunity to interact with both local and international counterparts, and a community of support for female entrepreneurs. PWCCI was founded by a past member of the executive committee of the Lahore Chamber of Commerce and Industry (LCCI) who went on to become the head of the committee on women entrepreneurship of the Federation of Pakistan Chambers of Commerce and Industry. LCCI was established by the businessmen and industrialists of Northern India in 1923.

While the chamber has about 18,000 members, only 500 of them are women - but this number is growing rapidly. LCCI membership services include organizing training sessions for its members, helping arrange credit from banks, and establishing relations with lawyers, bankers, and tax advisors. The chamber seeks to create opportunities for businesswomen by putting up local exhibitions or facilitating participation in trade fairs and exhibitions abroad and champions the cause of Punjab's women entrepreneurs through their advocacy efforts to policy-makers. The Women's Resource Center (WRC) is an entity within LCCI that is attracting new members at a rapid pace. As women increasingly make their presence felt in the business sphere, the WRC has provided them an opportunity to meet and discuss various opportunities and challenges.

The department functions as the secretariat for women's business activities and coordinates with the relevant governmental agencies and departments to facilitate their development and implementation. Its location within the parent LCCI gives the WRC the opportunity to advocate directly to the men running the association and effecting groundbreaking changes that favor women. The Standing Committee of the WRC in Lahore tackles issues like raising funds through bank loans and developing contacts with various government departments and agencies to promote and facilitate business transactions. It educates its members about the techniques and strategies of national and international marketing. The committee also formulates proposals for the national budget, with the goal of increasing involvement of women entrepreneurs in national economic activities.

Sri Lanka

The Women's Chamber of Industry and Commerce (WCIC) first opened its doors in 1985, operating as a non-profit organization committed to helping urban and rural women in their entrepreneurial skills. Recently, WCIC launched the

Women in Business (WIB) Trade Fair and Exhibition at the Sri Lanka Exhibition and Convention Centre to support local and international women entrepreneurs, allowing women to exhibit their products, sell and accept firm orders for supply, sell on a retail basis, enter into long-term joint ventures, and obtain ideas on product diversification, quality improvement, and cost cutting methods. WIB serves to establish new market links and provide maximum exposure to women entrepreneurs, particularly from rural areas. There are several other women's business associations operating in Sri Lanka.

For more than half a century, the Asia Foundation has been a leader in helping women to realize their potential. The foundation's Women's Programme strengthens families and societies by developing women's leadership, strengthening women's organizations, advocating women's rights, ensuring women's personal security, and creating new political and economic opportunities. In order to combat extreme poverty, illiteracy, and issues related to civil conflict, the Asia Foundation provides vocational training and education, enabling women to become economically self-reliant. Programmes are diverse and flexible, empowering women to challenge the multiple causes and consequences of their marginalization and discrimination, and are customized and targeted to the Sri Lankan context.

The foundation also works to create equitable conditions where women can prosper as entrepreneurs and where women workers can hold employers and government accountable for workplace treatment of women. The foundation's Programmes assist women to overcome legal and regulatory barriers and challenge discriminatory practices by providing them with legal aid and equipping them with political organizing, negotiating, and networking skills that can make them effective advocates for policies that will create more jobs and ensure equal access to future opportunity.

Regional

A regional association, the Association of Lady Entrepreneurs of Andhra Pradesh (ALEAP), was established in 1993 by like-minded women entrepreneurs who wanted to train, guide, support, and enhance other women. The association empowers women through their efforts to formally establish SMEs, giving women legal rights to their property. ALEAP has built up a strong support network among government and non-governmental organizations alike, and works with them to provide the expertise and training in entrepreneurship development in India as well as in Sri Lanka.

The Asia Foundation has provided vocational training and education to more than 2,300 trafficking survivors and those at risk of being trafficked and enabled these women to become economically self-reliant. With support from Give2Asia, the Asia Foundation's philanthropic partner, the foundation trains trafficking victims with the skills to become mechanics and drivers – traditionally male occupations. The Asia Foundation helps their newly-trained mechanics to establish "one-stop shops" for motorcycle and electronic repairs. These small shops also provide employment for other women. By helping women become gainfully employed and in turn employ others, this Programme reduces the risk of further trafficking.

ASSOCIATION STRUCTURE AND GOVERNANCE

For any of these organizations to be successful, they need to be professionalized, with credible and effective governing boards and CEOs. There is an immediate need, for dividing quotidian operations from more strategic ones as well as creating clearly demarcated areas of operation and responsibility. Most established parent organizations (which are often male-dominated) already have these structures in place. Women's institutions remain underdeveloped in most emerging economies, yet have huge potential. Further, as these associations grow in size and importance, it is essential to establish effective governance structures based on successful models, rather than on the personalities that are often at the head of the organizations.

The fact that all 24 board members of the Dhaka Chamber of Commerce and Industry (DCCI) are male speaks volumes. However, its women's entrepreneurship development

Programme became the first private sector effort in Bangladesh to focus on the obstacles faced by women in business. CIPE and the National Endowment for Democracy (NED) supported this Programme by providing business skill training, financial counseling and access to technology. DCCI is still working on key advocacy issues to improve women's participation in the economy, reducing barriers to entry, and increasing access to information. The Women Entrepreneurs Association of Bangladesh serves women all over Bangladesh, including North Bengal.

Established in 2000 under the aegis of the Federation of Bangladesh Chambers of Commerce and Industry, it is creating a platform to help businesswomen establish themselves in competitive fields traditionally dominated by men. After the opening up of the Indian economy, closely preceding the establishment of the World Trade Organization, eight state-level SME associations formed the Federation of Indian Small and Medium-Sized Enterprises (FISME) in 1995. Today, as an umbrella organization of SMEs, FISME has affiliated associations in most Indian states. FISME is a network that reaches more than 100,000 SMEs through state-level SME associations and sectoral associations. Industries representing all major sectors are also invited to take direct membership.

The Association of Chambers of Commerce of India and Ceylon (ASSOCHAM) started with 13 chambers as its original members, under the auspices of the British. These were joined by the Indian Merchants' Chamber of Bombay, then in its 80th year, in 1987. New governing articles of the association for ASSOCHAM were worked out and the membership structure of the chamber was categorized into promoter chambers, patron members, ordinary members, and corporate associates. For the first time, ASSOCHAM also opened itself up for overseas membership.

RESULTS AND OUTCOMES

Business associations play a vital role in the advancement of women's entrepreneurial efforts in South Asia. From influencing legislation in support of women, to providing business skills training and facilitating access to finance and markets, a multi- dimensional approach is slowly but surely producing the desired results. The following examples represent the kind of change that is occurring. In one CIPE initiative in Afghanistan, over 200 women were trained in basic and advanced entrepreneurship skills, which facilitated the expansion and creation of dozens of businesses.

Women's Enterprise Development also organized women's trade exhibitions, trade missions, and matchmaking Programmes that created both jobs and trade expansion opportunities for women entrepreneurs. With funding from USAID, CIPE helped the Afghan Women's Business Federation (AWBF) to establish itself as a provider of Programmes and services for its member associations and directly to thousands of Afghan women throughout the country. Members of the Women Entrepreneurs Association of Bangladesh have gained market access in Canada, India, Malaysia, Nepal, the United States, the United Kingdom, and neighboring Arab countries.

Small, medium-sized and large companies meet, exchange ideas and expertise, and participate in national and international trade fairs and exhibitions. They are provided loan facilities to start and maintain small and medium-sized enterprises. Members' newfound independence has bolstered their confidence in the contributions they can make to the country. The Bangladesh Women Chamber of Commerce and Industry (BWCCI) successfully advocated for the first National SME Women Entrepreneurs Forum in 2006. At the opening, the Prime Minister also announced the creation of a separate bank to serve the needs of Bangladeshi women entrepreneurs.

This was a much-needed initiative since bank policies limit access to finance by women entrepreneurs. As a result of BWCCI's efforts, the central bank has also changed its policies to include women's needs reserving 10 percent of all SME loans for women, reducing the interest on loans to women from 20 percent to 5-10 percent, and allowing up to $22,000 in loans without collateral to encourage business development and expansion. BWCCI also works in rural business communities across the country. The Bangladeshi Government has established a National SME Forum under the SME Foundation of the Ministry of Industry to promote women's participation in formal economic sectors. In India, the Association of Women Entrepreneurs (AWE) successfully holds weekly fairs and has set up the Savings and Credit Society that can award up to Rs. 35,000 ($700) each to of its nearly 500 members.

AWE also initiates various training Programmes and courses. Organizations such as the Federation of Indian Chambers of Commerce and Industry Ladies Organization (FLO), established 25 years ago to promote women's entrepreneurship, holds regular workshops, runs a business consultancy cell, and facilitates networking through periodic meetings. FLO has a broad agenda that includes supporting self-help groups in rural India. Younger women in Pakistan are making strides in their endeavor to attain economic independence, pursuing a variety of entrepreneurial ventures in the wider market. Home-based businesses related to the fashion and the beauty industries are the most popular among upper and middle class entrepreneurs, especially among married women or those living in more rigid social enclaves. Independent business opportunities for women in the less privileged classes are less abundant.

There is some non-governmental organizational activity in both urban and rural areas to provide development assistance and training as well as some micro-credit facilities, but much still remains to be done to lift them out of their state of dependence and disempowerment. The Lahore Women's Resource Center organizes business orientation Programmes, workshops, and lectures for the guidance of both established and new women entrepreneurs with a view to enhancing quality consciousness. It helps organize local product exhibitions and coordinates and facilitates trade delegations of its members to international markets. Once these indigenous women's business associations mature and find their optimal governance potential, options for women entrepreneurs should grow exponentially.

CIPE partnered with Pakistan's business community and the Pakistani Ministry of Commerce to help create a new law to promote competition between chambers of commerce and associations (and thus raise the quality of services offered). The 2006 Trade Organisations Ordinance was instrumental in weeding out 30 defunct chambers through re-registration requirements. It created the first-ever legal opportunity for women to form chambers and business associations. On a provincial basis, up to five women's business organizations were prime candidates for licensing under the new ordinance.

RECOMMENDATIONS FOR WOMEN'S BUSINESS ASSOCIATIONS

In order to build the capacity of various local trade associations, support units, and resource organizations within the women's business community, the following factors must be embedded in the culture of the association:

- Development, training, and marketing efforts for women-run businesses, with a special focus on small and medium enterprises.
- Facilitation of loan acquisition for women entrepreneurs though banking institutions.
- Finding market linkages for women producers domestically and abroad.
- Encouraging governments to support girls' education, thus enhancing the social position of women and inspiring other women to enter the entrepreneurial field.
- Organizing women into membership-based trade unions, cooperatives, and associations.
- Influencing public policy through advocacy and the enactment of women-friendly national rules and regulations.
- Advocating for an equitable legal regime, including inheritance laws as well as political and business quotas.
- Capital formation in their own names, either individually or collectively, in their groups and organizations.
- Social security provisions for women, including access to health care, childcare, insurance, housing, and old age benefits.

Women contribute significantly to family business

operation, even if in an unpaid capacity. Yet, families and academic studies underestimate these efforts. On the other hand, many enterprises defined as being run by women are in fact controlled by men, who oversee operations and decision- making. Programmes intended to reach women entrepreneurs can succeed only in the event that associations attempting to aid women are aware of this paradox. Familial and social conditioning that reduces the confidence, independence, and mobility of women can be overcome through education and leadership training. A similar challenge is that women in South Asia are perceived as supplementary income providers. Since women are not considered to require a full day's wage for a full day's work, they are frequently subject to large-scale exploitation. To combat these entrenched views, associations should ease women's transition into independent professional work.

While families routinely provide financial and emotional support to sons, they rarely extend such assistance to daughters. Appropriate training is still the key to a successful entrepreneurship Programme. The teaching profession constitutes a large component of the service sector in South Asia, and employs many women. However, neither financial institutions nor banks extend financing for setting up, equipping, or running schools. Still, educational institutions can influence companies' decisions to locate in a certain place, and can thus have an impact on local growth potential. Businesses are unlikely to establish offices in cities where quality educational facilities are not available. Emphasizing funding for creating competitive, private schools makes both economic and social sense.

Another challenge for women entrepreneurs is marketing. In the initial stages of running a business, women may lack both the time and confidence to seek out and develop markets. Even when otherwise in control of an enterprise, women often depend on male relatives in this area. Marketing involves mobility and confidence in dealing with the external world, both of which women have been discouraged from developing by social conditioning. The long- term strategy of a successful association should be to build marketing skills in women entrepreneurs from the very beginning to enable them to promote their products more effectively and without dependence on others.

A final concern for women entrepreneurs is stagnation in growth, caused in large part by the demands of household duties, mobility problems, and limitations to expanding space and staff. Moreover, women who do succeed and grow their businesses beyond home-based enterprises often face hostility and resentment within their family circles. Providing training and counseling to stagnated association members would greatly facilitate growth and vibrancy. For associations, stagnant members are simply an obstacle to a brighter future, while enthusiastic, growing members can become effective ambassadors to seek out new members and set out on new initiatives.

CASE STUDY: THE BANGLADESH WOMEN CHAMBER OF COMMERCE AND INDUSTRY

The overall level of economic growth and development of Bangladesh – a country with a per capita GDP of $500 – is largely shaped by small and medium-sized enterprises (SMEs). The 2003 National Private Sector Survey of Enterprises in Bangladesh, co-financed by USAID, revealed that micro, small, and medium-sized enterprises employed more than 31 million people, contributed 25 percent of GDP, and constituted more than 90 percent of industrial enterprises in Bangladesh. At the same time, women constitute less than one percent of all entrepreneurs in Bangladesh.

The traditional view of women in Bangladesh often confines them to the home, hindering their entry into the SME sector. The obstacles awaiting those who do venture into the marketplace are difficult to overcome: social stereotypes, lack of access to finance, lack of business experience, and undeveloped skills, to name a few. Yet, without the active participation of women in regular economic activities, a dynamic and sustainable economy that leads to poverty alleviation is impossible. To facilitate women's entry into the economy and the overall development of Bangladesh, the Bangladesh Women Chamber of Commerce and Industry (BWCCI) came into being as an association devoted exclusively to facilitating the advancement of female entrepreneurs.

POLITICAL WILL TO EMPOWER WOMEN

The Bangladesh Government views SMEs as vehicles for quality of life improvement, economic growth, and poverty alleviation of the common people. The government put forth its Poverty Reduction Strategy Paper, which includes the following goals: employment generation, nutrition, maternal health, quality education (at primary, secondary, and vocational levels), sanitation and safe water, criminal justice, and local governance. The implementation of poverty alleviation Programmes is a systematic and continuous effort in Bangladesh. The framework for an equitable business environment does exist.

The Constitution of Bangladesh grants equal rights to women and men in all spheres of public life [Article 28(1) and 28(3)2]. The Constitution also mandates women's active and meaningful participation in all spheres of public life [Article-10]. In 1984, Bangladesh ratified the United Nations Convention on the Elimination of All Forms of Discrimination against Women, and the government continues to initiate institutional and policy measures for women entrepreneurs, such as the creation of a separate ministry on women's affairs and several other Programmes.

Social Culture and the Business Environment

Dr. Kaniz N. Siddique, member of the Gender and Poverty Reduction Strategy Paper Group, published a review of women's advancement and rights issues in the *National Strategy for Accelerated Poverty Reduction*. He reported that, due to existing inequalities between men and women, women are subject to discrimination and injustice. In the social structure of Bangladesh, young girls and women are sometimes viewed as burdens.

Removing this stigma is necessary before the contributions of women can be fully recognized. Yet of course, women's contributions are essential at multiple levels. First, women undertake various domestic activities for members of the family and community. Second, they assume a variety of expenditure and savings activities, which contribute to the economic well-being of the family. Third, women participate in income-generating activities through their entry into the formal [and informal] labor market.

A survey carried out by BWCCI and CIPE in 2007, "A Situation Analysis of Women Entrepreneurs in Bangladesh," showed that women's participation in the formal economy has not freed them from the traditional roles and responsibilities associated with family life. Entry into the economy actually results in a double workload, consisting of traditional household responsibilities as well as the new economic task. There is indication that, despite this trend, female entrepreneurs are able to open to the challenge and often run their businesses successfully. Most women surveyed reported being satisfied by current business conditions and described the overall business atmosphere as increasingly conducive to women, an improvement many women credit to BWCCI.

BIRTH OF BWCCI

The initiative to form a chamber of commerce devoted exclusively to the advancement of female entrepreneurs was that of Selima Ahmad. Ahmad is a successful businesswoman with longstanding experience in the private sector, and was honored in 2001 with the title of Best Woman Entrepreneur in Bangladesh. She was well aware of the need for a national body that represented the interests of female entrepreneurs and supported their initiatives. Ahmad recognized that female business owners could assist in the modernization Bangladesh's economy by creating jobs, stimulating competition, inspiring innovation, and providing a valuable source of income; they just needed a representative organization to strengthen and encourage these initiatives.

With Ahmad's understanding of business and the plight of women in a patriarchal and impoverished society, she has been able to guide entrepreneurial talent and organize financial and marketing resources so that women can fully realize their potential to make significant contributions to Bangladesh's economy. To this end, Ahmad established BWCCI in June 2001. BWCCI was the country's first trade body working exclusively for women's economic and social empowerment. The BWCCI strategy is clearly defined by its mission: to become the leader of economic development of women entrepreneurs.

The main goals of the chamber were formulated according to its strategy:

- Create a strong platform for women's economic and social empowerment.
- Undertake initiatives to remove existing economic, social, and cultural obstacles blocking female participation in all areas of public life.
- Work as a catalyst to undertake policy measures by the government in order to create a gender-friendly business environment.
- Support female entrepreneurs in marketing their products and services by developing a broad based business network at the local, national and international level.
- Help women entrepreneurs obtain access to financing and other services provided by public and private institutions.
- Build the professional capacity of women entrepreneurs, particularly rural women.

BWCCI registered with the government under the Ministry of Commerce as a non-profit, non- partisan organization with the aim of supporting women entrepreneurs through training, loan guarantees, advocacy, fair trade participation, and global and domestic market exposure. In 2008, BWCCI was formally recognized by the Federation of Bangladesh Chambers of Commerce and Industry, the national umbrella group of all chambers and trade organizations in Bangladesh. BWCCI is also registered with the Joint Stock Company of the Bangladesh Government and has consultative status with the United Nations Economic and Social Council.

Growth of the Organization

Due in large part to government policies, a favorable change in the Bangladesh women's business environment is evidenced by BWCCI's recent growth – membership increased from the 24 founding members in 2001 to 1,500 members in 2008. BWCCI members cover the entire socio- economic spectrum, and are engaged in traditional pursuits such as food, beauty, fashion, health products, and handicrafts, as well as such non- conventional ventures as information technology, media, and publications. Over the past seven years, BWCCI has acted as a nucleus to assist, activate, inform, and organize Bangladesh's women entrepreneurs and help them assimilate into the global economy.

It is a vibrant and accessible platform for women in business. From its inception, BWCCI recognized that profound changes cannot be achieved in isolation in Bangladesh. In order to more effectively advance reform, BWCCI developed relationships at the regional, national, and international levels to develop the conditions for female entrepreneurs to prosper. Building partnerships with organizations, informal groups, and committed visionaries enabled BWCCI to increase the support base for projects and more broadly spread female entrepreneurship. BWCCI benefited from the multiplying effect of other Programmatic information sources.

For example, the president of BWCCI is a member of the Gender and Poverty Reduction Strategy Paper Group (GPG), initiated by a local consultative group that includes 38 members working on women's advancement and gender equality. GPG consistently supports BWCCI initiatives among its members. At the national level, BWCCI cooperates with various ministries in developing and implementing activities for women's economic empowerment and entrepreneurial development. The Ministry of Industry's SME Department has started capacity- building Programmes all over Bangladesh. Through these Programmes, a total of 3,000 women-owned SMEs will be trained in business skills in 2008.

Three hundred members of BWCCI have already received training under this Programme. The Ministry of Industry has also formed a committee to ensure the relevancy and proper execution of this Programme. This type of cooperation of government bodies allows BWCCI to inform and influence national- level policymakers. On the international level, BWCCI's partners deliver professional and financial support in the field of institutional capacity-building, development of management and executive staff, strategic planning, and advocacy. Since 2005, the CIPE-supported Promoting Women Entrepreneurs through Advocacy Programme has contributed greatly to the institutionalization of BWCCI as an advocacy organization and increased women's participation in the economy.

Successful Programmes

From the beginning, BWCCI has paid particular attention to developing Programmes in cooperation with international organizations and donors, drawing on these organizations' expertise and lessons learned. The women of BWCCI required training on how to start and manage businesses, in addition to learning about the necessity of an active economic and social life. It was also necessary to introduce these women to advocacy techniques and activities. BWCCI actively participated in a range of successful Programmes resulting in a greater capacity, an improved image in society, and its recognition by public bodies as the country's leading representative of female entrepreneurship.

Programme: Promoting Women Entrepreneurs through Advocacy (PWEA)

Through a concise, three-tiered advocacy Programme, the ultimate goal of this effort is to create a gender-friendly environment for women entrepreneurs, where it is easy to start and grow a business. One of the primary activities of the project was the formation of advocacy groups at the local level. These advocacy groups facilitate focus group discussion, organize seminars, conduct advocacy meetings with policymakers, and develop policy papers for policymakers, NGOs, civil society organizations, trade organizations, and academia. Six sectoral focus groups and six district focus groups were created under the PWEA Programme.

These focus groups were made up of female entrepreneurs who had worked as advocates for local rural women. These entrepreneurs aimed to have an inclusive discussion that shared the experiences of women entrepreneurs, explored their problems, consulted stakeholders to identify the problems of women entrepreneurs, and publicizes suggestions and recommendations for women's promotion in business. In addition to the focus group discussions, four pressure groups, established at the divisional level, focused on project design, media, regulatory bodies, and finance in order to advocate and negotiate with the policymakers. Each group, consisting of six women entrepreneurs and led by a member of the board of directors, organized brainstorming sessions to discuss vital issues of advocacy and explore possible strategies for change. In this phase, BWCCI organized advocacy meetings with public and private institutions.

More than 20 meetings with 157 total participants were organized with key representatives of various public and private institutions. These meetings allowed BWCCI to present their agenda while obtaining important policy commitments from these people. Six district-level advocacy groups made up of five to seven women entrepreneurs each aimed at influencing public institutions, local government, local media, and financial institutions to improve the business environment for women at the local level. BWCCI also organized 28 cross-sectoral meetings at the national level and 39 at the local level. During these meetings, the central advocacy team focused on the proper implementation of policies published in the Bangladesh Bank's circular. The circular presented the bank's refinancing scheme for women-owned SMEs.

The central advocacy team petitioned the bank to open a department specifically designed for women entrepreneurs to help in the implementation of this policy. The project also organized six divisional seminars on women's entrepreneurial development. These seminars attracted 516 total participants, including policymakers, women entrepreneurs, international donors, business associations, journalists, academics, bankers, and civil society representatives. Based on these discussions, each seminar concluded with the formulation of a set of recommendations. About 150 participants from across the spectrum of Bangladeshi life participated in a cumulative seminar, "Strengthening Capacity of Women Entrepreneurs," in Dhaka. Two roundtables with the media focused on the pending national budget and the Bangladesh Bank circular's promotion of a refinancing scheme for women-owned SMEs. In addition, this seminar featured eight interactive and informal discussions for women entrepreneurs from rural areas with new start-ups. Over 100 women had the opportunity to discuss relevant issues such as access to finance, training, market access, social security, company registration, trade licenses, and business networking. From these roundtables, BWCCI developed and submitted five memorandums to local mayors in an effort to follow up on seminar activities.

BWCCI also sent policy papers on access to finance, along with relevant recommendations, to appropriate public institutions with the intent to reinforce participants' concerns and demands. BWCCI's advocacy contributions to women's position in the economy covered a wide spectrum of issues, brought significant attention to these themes, and promoted grassroots participation. Moreover, the project established strong relations among the BWCCI, local women entrepreneurs, NGOs, and public and financial institutions. The Bangladesh Bank issued a circular to its comprising banks, "Refinancing Scheme for Women's SME Loans," and adopted important provisions in support of women entrepreneurs, including earmarking 10 percent of its aggregate SME loan funds for female entrepreneurs at a lower interest rate (5-10 percent), and collateral free.

The Bangladesh Bank issued a second circular that requested commercial banks and financial institutions to open a desk for women entrepreneurs and that this be run by a female officer. The impact of this Programme has become visible in public policy. The National Women Development Policy of 2008, which calls for the recognition of women's equal right to economic resources and family property, also recommends that women constitute one third of the National Parliament. As a result of the Programme, the government assisted the SME Foundation in coordinating the first national Women's SME Trade Fair in February 2008. The government also facilitated a study by the SME Foundation on regulatory barriers and regulatory effect in order to develop national policy recommendations.

Additionally, the government created the "Better Business Forum" - with two female members at the request of the BWCCI - to improve the business environment. The government even organized a consultation workshop, at which the president of BWCCI presented the keynote speech, cn credit wholesaling and SME access to finance.

Research Programme: A Situation Analysis of Women Entrepreneurs in Bangladesh

BWCCI lacked first-hand baseline information on the situation of women entrepreneurs in Bangladesh, which hindered the proper inclusion of women's issues in policy measures. The lack of information inhibited female entrepreneurs from claiming their rights in a justified and structured fashion. Over two years, BWCCI, in partnership with CIPE, collected extensive information on the situation of female entrepreneurs in 11 districts across Bangladesh, especially rural women. This study reached nearly 1,500 stakeholders through 12 focus group discussions and 13 seminars, which were organized in six divisional cities and six district cities during the PWEA project.

The study also elicited recommendations and suggestions from stakeholders on strategies for addressing existing problems and promoting a gender-friendly business environment. Considering the overall objective, the study selected the following issues as thematic areas of this research initiative:

- Socio-demographic profile of women entrepreneurs.
- Profile and types of women-owned enterprises.
- Regulatory procedures including tax, value-added tax, and company registration.
- Training, capacity building, and human resources.
- Access to finance, according to the parameters in the Bangladesh Bank circular.
- Business management, including business planning, accounting, and bookkeeping.
- Product design and development, marketing, and business promotion.
- Social perspective of women entrepreneurs.
- Conditions and position of women entrepreneurs in family life, including their economic contributions to the family.
- Overall perceptions of the business environment.

Programme: Building Better Trainers

Another partnership Programme of BWCCI is the Building Better Trainers Programme, which is part of a five- year partnership agreement with Humber Institute of Technology and Advance Learning (HITAL). The project aims to reduce poverty and to decrease women's vulnerability by enabling them to establish, manage, and effectively grow their enterprises. BWCCI feels that it has a profound role to play in this respect and is building its capacity to provide quality services to members through a strong training unit. With sustainability in mind, four key elements of this project are drafting a curriculum on entrepreneurship development and small business management, developing Trainers who can effectively train women as entrepreneurs and small business owners, growing capacity to further develop and adapt new training products, and upgrading the BWCCI Business Support Center to provide higher quality support to women entrepreneurs.

Following completion of a needs assessment survey and selection of a core group of Trainers, the project focused on developing the Trainers and the curriculum for the first three years. In the fourth year, two BWCCI Trainers were sent to Canada for further skills development. During this time, the BWCCI Business Support Center purchased several computers at the chamber office, along with a technology and software training session, for the core training group of the BWCCI.

Programme: Training Delivery Programme (2004- 2009)

Another partnership was formed with the South Asia Enterprise Development Facility to increase training opportunities for BWCCI members. The Training Delivery Programme is an ongoing project aimed at alleviating poverty and reducing the vulnerability of women by helping Trainers build their capacity to design curricula, conduct training and needs assessments, and write case studies. This project also aims to develop the skills of women entrepreneurs and to increase market access in the divisional cities and district towns of Bangladesh.

The funding provided for this project enabled BWCCI Trainers to conduct sessions in and around Dhaka, covering business topics such as marketing, business development, accounting, and management. A total of nine training sessions took place, with 224 total participants. BWCCI now has a dedicated pool of Trainers who deliver training Programmes to members in Dhaka and other divisional areas. BWCCI is committed to ensuring the continuous improvement of these Trainers to ensure they adequately address the needs of women entrepreneurs.

Programme: Fostering International and Local Trade Programme (2004-2009)

Along with a need for training, a lack of market access poses a considerable obstacle for female entrepreneurs in Bangladesh. Women lack contacts to access local or global markets. They have insufficient knowledge about international product standards, and are financially and socially restricted in their ability to travel internationally. With the assistance of the Canadian International Development Association, the Soros

Economic Development Fund, and the World Bank, BWCCI has developed the Fostering International and Local Trade Programme, which provides its members with exposure to overseas buyers, facilitates networking with international trade organizations, and promotes a gender- friendly business environment.

BWCCI has encouraged its members to participate in trade fairs around the world, including fairs in Australia, Canada, Dubai, Hong Kong, India, Nepal, Spain, and the United States. Participation in these trade fairs has been an opportunity for women entrepreneurs to acquire knowledge about international product standards and improve their international market connections. Through such experiences, some members are now exporting to Belgium, Italy, and the United States. In 2007, 24 BWCCI members participated in six trade fairs around the globe, where they displayed and sold their products, received orders from international buyers, and conducted overseas market research.

Programme: Providing Market Facilities

Although these Programmes have provided expanded international opportunities to some, the lack of access to local markets is still a large obstacle to many BWCCI members. In response, BWCCI established the Providing Market Facilities: Arushi Retail Outlet Programme. This is a BWCCI-managed project that provides physical market space for BWCCI members in Dhaka. This outlet, which houses several restaurants and shops, has operated successfully for several years and provided the local community with eateries and fashion facilities.

Participating entrepreneurs also received training on successful business operation and management practices. An outlet user's committee was formed for monitoring and management. This Programme supplied stable employment opportunities, provided good wages for other poor women (in addition to the business owners and operators), and increased exposure of both BWCCI and the participating women entrepreneurs. Less tangible benefits included a more positive perception of female entrepreneurs, a feeling of economic empowerment, and a more ethical business culture.

OVERCOMING CURRENT CHALLENGES

Despite the contribution of the Promoting Women Entrepreneurship through Advocacy Project to improving women's economic status, BWCCI and female entrepreneurs still face a variety of challenges. BWCCI took advantage of its newly-gained intangible assets – increased grassroots participation, mass awareness of women's economic roles and need to incorporate women into the mainstream economy, increased organizational capacity in public advocacy, commitments from different national and local authorities to women's entrepreneurship development, and media support. By taking advantage of these assets, BWCCI also learned of problems women entrepreneurs face at the grassroots level, which include difficulty in access to trade licenses and company registration, lack of intellectual property protection, limited access to new technologies, difficulty in obtaining financing, insufficient training and skill development, lack of market access, and persistent gender discrimination.

BWCCI has recognized some key themes in the issues it will approach as it moves into the future: access to finance (particularly a proper execution of the central bank's refinancing scheme for women), product design and development through additional public resources and education, company registration and trade license reform, training and capacity development for female entrepreneurs (particularly for rural women), and simplified VAT procedures. Exports provide a world of opportunity for expansion for women entrepreneurs, and businesswomen must be nurtured in their international trade efforts. Internationalization of women's SMEs is also a theme for BWCCI. The organization plans to provide special support to women involved in export-oriented activities and advocate increasing budgetary allocations for their participation in international trade fairs.

THE FUTURE OF BWCCI

BWCCI is well positioned to maintain its efforts in creating a better future for female entrepreneurs in Bangladesh. BWCCI will continue advocating to reduce business barriers on behalf of thousands of women entrepreneurs in Bangladesh. The highly successful project with CIPE, Promoting Women Entrepreneurs through Advocacy, will continue to be a major activity of the organization. BWCCI will expand its advocacy efforts into different regions of Bangladesh and continue to engage in dialogue with key figures and policymakers at the regional and national level to establish a gender- friendly business environment. BWCCI will also strive to ensure that advocacy participants honor commitments from its previous projects. In the third phase of PWEA, BWCCI formed a coalition of national and local-level women's organizations.

This coalition developed a Women's National Business Agenda, which is currently pending presentation to decision-makers. Simultaneously, with broad support from NGOs and civil society, BWCCI will be developing new advocacy campaigns to unify the voice of women entrepreneurs and present a cohesive vision to the government. Looking to the future, BWCCI renews its strong commitment to self-improvement. The ongoing capacity-building projects will ensure that the organization can deliver the best services to women entrepreneurs while maintaining a high level of self-sufficiency. The partnership with HITAL will continue to strengthen the capabilities of BWCCI's Trainers and training unit.

BWCCI is committed to achieving the highest quality in other services, including the facilitation of fair trade participation. BWCCI will diversify and improve member skills through a new, two-year project currently under preparation with the Danish Government office in Bangladesh. The project will strengthen the capacity of women entrepreneurs at the local level by training them in accounting, fiscal regulations, and marketing. One additional future objective of BWCCI is to focus on institutional capacity building by increasing its office coverage in the country. BWCCI is continually searching for new project ideas and services to enhance the current effort of serving women entrepreneurs and is constantly seeking new ways to share these tools with members.

2

Changing Southeast Asia
Women in Emerging Civil Societies

Worldwide, the proliferation of civil society organizations (CSOs) is creating new opportunities for women to participate in and influence political processes and decision making bodies. Increasingly, citizens' groups are playing a crucial role in bringing women and other "powerless" groups and their concerns into the political process, enabling them to influence decisions, laws, and policies, and seek collective resolutions to problems. Organizations that have traditionally been involved in service delivery, including education, healthcare, and reproductive healthcare are now playing important roles in the policy arena, whether as community groups working to influence village development policy or as public interest organizations working to encourage broad citizen participation in formal and informal decision making processes. Working with and through local, national, regional, and international partner organizations, the Foundation's Women in Politics Programme explicitly seeks to build the capacity of CSOs to increase women's skills as effective leaders in and out of government; as informed, independent citizens and voters able to make their own self- directed choices; as agents for encouraging citizen participation and voicing the interests and concerns of women.

The Programme provides technical assistance, training, and support to CSOs working to increase women's involvement and influence in the public arena. In doing so, the Programme encourages a climate in which the government is accountable to the needs and demands of both their female and male constituents, while equipping women with the skills needed for involvement in all of the decision making processes that affect their lives. Operating in Asia, Africa, Latin America, and the Middle East through its Global Women in Politics Programme, a four-year partnership with the U.S. Agency for International Development, the Foundation plays an important role in facilitating sharing of models, strategies, tools and techniques developed in one country or region that can provide important lessons for organizations elsewhere.

The Foundation also directs an innovative Programme to increase women's economic and legal rights by giving women a practical understanding of how to use political process to access their rights and expand their economic opportunities. With enhanced skills and knowledge, women are increasingly recognizing the power of their number and are successfully seeking collective solutions to common problems. The Asia Foundation is committed to increasing women's effective political participation both as a critical means to achieving improvements for women in other areas and an important end in itself, advancing civil society and promoting democratic governance.

In Asia over the last decade, there have been enormous changes in virtually all societies from those that have no tradition of democracy such as China and Vietnam to new and emerging democracies such as Mongolia and Nepal, to older democracies that are undergoing devolution of power to the local level, such as the Philippines. Asia presents the whole spectrum of democratic development. We are seeing both a real change in the way that Asian societies are viewing these organizations as well as an important shift in the roles CSOs are playing. In some cases, the activities of CSOs are complementary to government services, while in other countries they have become a substitute for governments themselves; where governments are failing to act, civil society organizations are filling the gaps.

In many societies, it is women's organizations that are prime agents for societal change, demanding responsive and accountable decision making, more open and transparent processes, broad citizen participation that includes women, and expanded and equitable rights for all citizens, women and men. Our panelists today are going to discuss the state of development of civil society in their country, noting some of the trends, progress, and impediments to development of a civil society sector, particularly highlighting the roles of women's organizations.

PANELISTS

Zhang Ye directs our China Programmes from Beijing. Educated at Smith College and the Kennedy School at Harvard following undergraduate work in China, she is an expert on civil society organizations in China and a frequent writer and speaker on the topic. Kaori Kuroda, our assistant representative in Japan, is very active in the women's movement and the emerging civil society sector in Japan. Japan does not have the tradition of nongovernmental organizations like some other countries, such as the Philippines or Bangladesh. Kaori is going to discuss the situation in Japan now and comment on the factors that encourage or inhibit civil society sector development in her country.

Oyunbileg is a Programme officer in our Mongolia office. She manages Programmes on strengthening citizen's participation in public affairs. Her work with women's organizations involves monitoring their activities in the areas of voter education and accountability and transparency of government, as well as activities that focus on domestic violence, legal literacy and aid, and economic empowerment. Ruengrawee Ketphol is Programme manager for the Women's Political Participation Programmes for Thailand, Laos, and Vietnam in the Bangkok office.

She has been a central player in the Thai Women in the Constitution Network project, which was a very successful advocacy campaign to guarantee women's rights in the new constitution and is now involved in a nationwide education campaign to increase women's knowledge of their rights and use the constitution to reform discriminatory laws, policies, and practices. Zhang Ye will begin. This is an unusual year for almost every country in Asia, as well as China. Early on, like many other countries in East and Southeast Asia, China has had to deal with the regional monetary crisis.

Though China is not directly affected, Hong Kong's collapsing stock market and economic recession create a challenge for mainland China as well. In an effort to support Southeast Asia's economies, China made the commitment not to devalue its currency. Another significant development was China's National People's Congress election of a new central government with Zhu Rongji, a well-known reformer, as Premier. He came into office with a reform agenda to dramatically downsize government agencies and reconfigure state-owned enterprises on a large scale.

At the same time, the new government's economic goal for 1998 is to achieve 8 percent growth. As the nation began struggling with implementing a very difficult agenda, the record-breaking floods along the Yangtze River in China and the Songhua River in Northeast China caused thousands of deaths and left millions of people homeless. The government faced many problems on all fronts and felt inadequate to deal with such wide-scale natural disaster. Under these circumstances, nongovernmental organizations (NGOs) played essential roles in organizing and mobilizing citizens to counter the floods, and to deliver disaster relief.

China Charity Federation - one of the biggest NGOs in China - launched the first NGO-managed fund, which raised 600 million Yuan for disaster relief. In less than two months, between August and September, NGOs at various levels raised 1.7 billion Yuan with the help of other agencies - approximately $2 million. NGOs helped coordinate government agencies, enterprises, and volunteers to ensure that funds and materials were delivered to people in disaster areas. At the community level, volunteers organized and coordinated with one another to save lives, arrange children's boat schools in the south Yangtze River region, and relocate people and families to safer places.

While the floods have been detrimental to the whole nation, they aroused citizen consciousness and helped the nation unite while providing civil society an opportunity to play a crucial role to further develop. The development of China's NGO movement has been pioneered by China's women. The 1995 United Nations World Conference on Women greatly impacted China's women's movement, bringing 30,000 to 40,000 women from all over the world to Beijing.

The preparation process and the conference itself created a momentum for the Chinese, as well as the women of the world, to develop new tools, concepts, and teamwork to tackle common needs and problems. New concepts, such as gender perspective, advocacy, empowerment, and the process of networking among Chinese NGOs helped China's women to break out of the isolationism of traditional Marxist women's theory. Organizations are now able to use this new methodology to address women's basic needs as well as human rights issues.

Many new women's NGOs were established at the height of the women's conference, such as women's hotlines, university-based women's studies centers, and legal aid centers, which deal with violence against women, women's personal and property rights, and unemployment issues. These new organizations are more independent and autonomous than traditional Chinese NGOs. All of these events helped China to change rapidly and the institutional shift is dramatic.

Existing institutions, such as the All China Women's Federation - which was called a mass organization, but was also a quasi-governmental organization - were given the task in the early development of the People's Republic of China (PRC) to act as a "transmission belt" between the party, the government, and women. During the current transition period and the introduction of a market economy, the organization has to find a new niche, be more responsive to women's needs and the market economy. In particular, local women's federations increasingly find themselves in a situation requiring them to be more accountable to women.

At the same time, however, their budgets are being cut back considerably. These organizations generate income and rely on women they work with in the provinces in order to survive. These two elements -budget constraints and the need to be more responsive - have combined to cause an institutional change. Organizations like the All China Women's Federation and women's federations at the local levels now have to reconsider their roles - whether to serve only government policy or provide services and counseling to women and represent women's needs and voices. So increasingly we see the federations operating more like non-government organizations.

The Asia Foundation's China Programme focuses on building civil society. On the one hand, the Foundation is supporting or enhancing the enabling environment - helping legislators gain a broader, comparative perspective when they draft laws and regulations governing NGOs. We have supported groups to visit the United States and other Asian countries and will support another major conference in Beijing in the spring of 1999 to discuss laws and regulations governing NGOs in all countries. At the same time, the Foundation continues working with Chinese NGOs to increase their awareness of civil society.

For example, we work with a rural women's magazine to highlight micro-credit projects that advance women's economic opportunities. We also work with a women's hotline in Shaanxi Province that deals with violence against women. China stands a good chance of further developing its civil society, however long that process may take, and women will play a crucial role. It is through citizens' efforts that government, NGOs, and the business sector will find ways to work in partnership with one another.

Community development will establish a new kind of social welfare system - dependent on the effective intersection and combination of resources from government, NGOs, and enterprises. The United States, which has a long civil society tradition, funding resources, and a willingness to be involved in China's transition and development, has a lot to offer. The Japanese civil sector has grown significantly and has become increasingly visible during the 1990s. This phenomenon is attributable to both external and internal factors, including:

1. Emerging civil society has become a worldwide phenomenon.

2. The end of the Cold War.
3. Citizens are becoming increasingly frustrated with inability of governments to deal effectively with domestic and international problems. Although, historically speaking, Japanese have tended to trust their government, constant scandals and lack of accountability and transparency are creating an increasing sense of distrust. As a result, a consensus has been reached that government alone cannot address problems effectively.
4. The 1995 Hanshin earthquake created a very similar situation to China's experience with this year's floods. This tragedy led the ruling coalition government to review the legal environment for nonprofits.
5. The Law to Promote Specified Nonprofit Activities (the so-called NPO law), which will enhance and reshape Japan's civil sector, was created in March 1998. I would like to touch upon some of the background and the role and impact of citizens' advocacy in this legislation.

Despite the growth of the civil sector in the 1990s, infrastructure to support this sector has remained weak. For incorporation as a foundation, Article 34 of the Civil Code, the Nonprofit Public Interest Corporation Law (enacted in 1898), requires minimum basic capital of several million dollars and the approval of "competent government authorities." This approval system allows the government considerable discretionary authority and as a result, the majority of Japan's citizen-initiated organizations have remained unincorporated.

Although the need to review this civic law had been discussed among groups of academics, foundation officials, nongovernmental and nonprofit organizations (NGOs and NPOs) for years, the first attempt to recommend such a review was made in the late 1980s. A few other recommendations followed. In 1994, a broad-based coalition of citizens' organizations called "C's"-Coalition for Legislation to Support Citizens Organizations - was formed. C's prepared its own draft of the NPO law reflecting citizens' views that C's used to develop and implement an advocacy strategy.

Core members of C's participated in hundreds of small meetings organized by local citizens' groups to stress the importance of such a law; published a number of booklets to present and explain the drafts submitted by different political parties; and organized and hosted a number of open symposia and fora to which Diet members in charge of this particular bill were invited. The coalition also expanded its contacts to work with other civil society networks, including community-based networks, networks of artist organizations, international NGOs, welfare organizations, and others.

Such coalition building had never happened before - previously the different groups existed separately and seldom worked together. In addition, C's approached the Keidanren (Federation of Economic Organizations) and Rengo (The Japanese Trade Union Confederation) for the first time. At the same time, C's initiated research projects on accountability for nonprofit organizations and on how to increase membership for small organizations. An NPO bill submitted by the ruling parties in December 1996 still had burdensome requirements and controls imposed on citizens' groups.

Citizens' networks lobbied very hard for amendments to remove these restrictions, particularly with the newly established Democratic Party of Japan. An amended bill was finally submitted to the Diet and was passed in the House of Representatives in June 1997. It was further amended in favor of citizens and was finally passed into law by both Houses in March 1998. This law simplifies the incorporation process for nonprofit organizations and is a significant step in creating a more supportive legal environment for the expansion of civil society organizations in Japan. This law is unique in that it covers every detail of the documents to be required by the government, in an effort to eliminate any arbitrary power held by government officials.

As long as applications adhere to the law, an organization will receive legal nonprofit status. However, the legal environment for nonprofit organizations still has a long way to go. Although the new NPO law was passed as a special amendment to Article 34 of the Civil Code, there is no clear distinction between the NPO law and the existing 1898 law in terms of targeted organizations except for the fact that the new law defines 12 non-profit activities. I hope this unusual circumstance will eventually lead to a review of Article 34.

In addition, tax breaks are still under discussion. The issue of taxation was only mentioned in a resolution attached to the NPO law. It seems that a system is needed to provide nonprofits tax deductibility for donations, an important requirement for their survival and growth. While growing steadily, even though there has been significant discussion on the subject as well as media coverage, the nonprofit and civil sector is still small. Civil society has become a popular subject; people like to refer to civil society as a driving force for decentralization, deregulation, and social change for Japan. But the profile of NGOs and NPOs has been inflated, creating a gap between image and reality.

Nonprofit organizations still have many challenges ahead of them, including: a lack of funding sources; a lack of tax deductibility; a lack of professionalism; and insufficient citizen support are just a few. Now it is time to think about what else is needed to strengthen this sector. What kind of legal environment is sufficient? How do nonprofits increase membership? How do they attract supportive donors? Can they develop the capacity to play a truly constructive role in the resolution of issues?

These are all questions that must be addressed. Nonprofit organizations still have many challenges ahead of them, including: alack of funding sources; alack of tax deductibility; a lack of professionalism; and insufficient citizen support are just a few. Unlike other sectors in Japan, such as business or government, Japanese women play a very significant role in the NPO sector. Although good statistics are lacking because most NPOs are unincorporated, the 1996 JANIC (Japanese NGO Center for International Cooperation) directory indicates that 38 percent were founded or are headed by women.

This figure is quite large compared to the percentage of women managers in other fields, such as government officials, which was only 0.8 percent in 1995, or corporate general managers, which was only 1.5 percent in 1995. Adding domestic organizations involved in welfare, education, children, and consumer issues to this list, increases the number of NGOs and NPOs that are managed by women significantly. Nongovernmental organization (NGO) history in Mongolia began only six years ago.

The first independent organizations started in 1992, the year our new democratic constitution was established- so civil society is only as old as our constitution. The current number of NGOs in Mongolia is 800. In the last year, NGO sector growth has slowed (I think it increased only by 50), due to the re-registration required by the new NGO law passed in January 1997. Despite the great diversity of missions and goals among NGOs, the first concern has been to provide people with social protection and social security, two areas that were previously the sole responsibility of the state.

NGOs still cannot provide social services in the way that they would like, because they are still too weak and lack significant financial and human resources. Therefore, most NGOs are involved in pressuring the government by claiming people's rights-and there are too many rights to claim. Another characteristic of NGOs in Mongolia is that they were first established in very strong affiliation with political parties in the late 1980s and early 1990s. However, they quickly realized the nonpartisan nature of their work and broke from the political parties.

Nonetheless, they have not given up their interest in working in politics and in public policy areas. Women's NGOs were among the first established-they were first to lead the newly emerging civil society by promoting and raising awareness about democratic values and practices. Women's NGOs in Mongolia are not limited only to women's issues. Women's NGOs aim to help people adjust to the new order and to take advantage of it. Being weak in almost every regard does not prevent these organizations from educating people about civil society, the basics of the market economy, the rule of law, and citizen's rights and responsibilities.

In this effort, women's organizations were ahead of the government and much more efficient. For instance, the organization of an NGO campaign in support of the NGO law was remarkably strong. A number of organizations participated in the drafting of the bill. Many of these same groups joined to mobilize the entire NGO community in support of the bill. The coalition was able to secure the endorsement of the president of Mongolia, and ultimately convinced the parliament to adopt the bill in 1997. This movement marked the first NGO-initiated and drafted law in the country.

Until that time, The Asia Foundation was virtually the only major donor organization to provide much-needed support for the young NGOs, providing substantive expertise and technical assistance, opportunities to learn and gain experience, and training for NGO leaders. Examples of successful coalition building can be drawn from among women's NGOs. For instance, the first women's NGO coalition organized a successful campaign for women's representation in Parliament.

The number of women representatives in Parliament increased from three to seven in 1996. Another example is the National CEDAW (Convention for Elimination of All Forms of Discrimination against Women) Watch Network of seven women's NGOs established in 1997 with the goal of monitoring the government's implementation of the United Nations Convention, which Mongolia signed in 1981. The network is the first permanent NGO coalition and the first to take government oversight as its mandate.

It conducted a comprehensive analysis of the government's implementation of the U.N. Convention and presented it at a training of Trainors' workshop for women leaders and rural women activists. The National CEDAW Watch Network ensured rural women's input into the CEDAW monitoring agenda, encouraging rural women's participation in monitoring on the local level. Through the media, it is implementing an information campaign to raise awareness of the CEDAW concepts, to introduce the network and its activities, as well as to discuss how Mongolian laws and practices comply with the U.N. Convention and, if they do not, to introduce changes.

The natural evolution of NGOs in Mongolia has been from urban-based NGOs to rural-based branches in the provinces. These branches, while organizationally linked to their headquarters, are essentially independent both financially and Programmatically. That is, they focus their attention on issues of local concern, such as unemployment, lack of information, the need to encourage job creation, and income generation. To assist rural NGOs in their ability to address local issues, The Asia Foundation has supported internship Programmes for rural activists at the headquarters of the Women's Lawyers Association (WLA) and the Liberal Women's Brain Pool (LEOS), and enabled rural women's participation in almost every activity that took place over the last few years.

Capacity-building activities were specifically designed to strengthen institutional management of rural chapters so that they are prepared to organize and implement local Programmes effectively. While increasing public popularity and public respect for NGOs is occurring, most remarkable is the government's recognition of NGOs. A three-year effort of nonpartisan voter education activities by Women for Social Progress (WSP) resulted in a tripartite agreement between WSP, the Secretariat of the State Great Hural (Parliament), and the National History Museum. Under this agreement, WSP is responsible for informing citizens of what is going on in the government. This agreement ensures free access to parliamentary archives and other information.

That information is published and distributed nationwide in a newspaper called, *Trust and Effort*. The paper contains parliamentary voting records on specific issues of concern and comparisons of elected representatives' performance to positions in their campaign platforms. Another important WSP publication is an index to parliamentary proceedings. For years, Parliament did not publish its proceedings, and although the new government has done so after the 1996 elections, this document has had limited distribution. To allow broader usage of the proceedings, WSP prepared a manual for citizens on how to use them together with an index that serves as a direct reference.

The WSP chapter in Uvurhangai province also concluded an agreement with the local representative government to serve as an information bridge between citizens and government on the local level. But the WSP branch went one step further and convened the community, NGOs, and businesses, as well as local government officials, to hold a dialogue on local priority issues. Half of the recommendations of the local community dialogue were accepted by the local council and included in their agenda. Currently, they are having a more focused discussion on an issue of priority-the development of small and medium enterprises. Suggestions of this dialogue will be presented to the upcoming session of the local council.

The WSP community watches will follow the decisions of the local hural (council) and will convene again to develop an action plan on participation in the implementation of the local Programme. The WLA has completed the first long-term strategic plan and developed its first individualized plans-strong signs of improved institutional development and Programme implementation capability at the local level. The WLA and the Center against Violence (CAV) are leading another NGO campaign on legal advocacy for new legislation on domestic violence.

Through various mechanisms, the WLA and CAV are engaging and cooperating with all other NGOs. Together they drafted the bill and are implementing a strategy to advance the bill, as well as to prepare for the efficient enforcement of the law after its adoption. Another NGO that does not have a women's agenda but was initiated, founded, and is run by women is called the Center for Citizenship Education (CCE). The CCE is providing regular assistance to the country's new NGOs through training and information Programmes on institutional development, providing skills and knowledge to improve NGO participation in public affairs.

The Asia Foundation's support enables the CCE to reach rural NGOs through its regional seminars, consultancy and information services. There are, of course, numerous challenges that Mongolia's young civil society is facing, but despite its short history, the basic elements are in place and hopefully will lead to a sustainable and strong civil society in Mongolia. In one case, a recently unemployed young mother threw her four-year-old daughter out of a fourth-story window of the public hospital because the hospital staff told her that she had to pay $200 for her daughter's surgery. She was about to follow her daughter when someone rescued her, after which she gave an interview. She said that she did not know how to cope with the situation. Her husband had left her and disappeared for three days.

Although he promised to come back, he did not return and she feared that he would be like her friend's husband, who always ran away in critical moments. When the media interviewed the hospital's representatives, they said, 'We already told her that we would provide surgery free-of-charge for her daughter.' You can guess who told the truth. Another incident occurred two weeks after the new labor code became effective in mid-August. There was a protest by a pregnant woman holding a banner saying that she wanted to get her job back. She was laid off on the understanding that the new code stipulated that pregnant women could not work the night shift. This incident demonstrates a misinterpretation of the intent of the law.

Finally, there is the example of how the Thai people exercise their rights. The shrimp farmers and the rice farmers came to Bangkok to voice their opposing views. The shrimp farmers claimed their right of freedom of occupation but the rice farmers claimed the rights to live in a sound environment. Although the two groups disagreed, they were citing different chapters of the same constitution to defend their rights. In the last two or three years, demonstrations have increased in Bangkok. Last year, more than 700 demonstrations and strikes took place in Thailand, both in the major cities as well as in Bangkok.

This widespread discontent clearly illustrates that the central government was not helping to solve problems at the grassroots level. In the last couple of years, Thailand has tried to transform an open economy with assistance from the World Bank and the International Monetary Fund (IMF) through national economic and social development plans. Now, under the new Constitution, many provisions need to be implemented. Independent organizations working to protect people's rights, like the Office of the Ombudsman, human rights commissions, and administrative courts, need to be established.

These things are happening on the national level. In the past two years, as Thailand was drafting its new Constitution, there has been an emergence of women's coalitions. At least 35 women's organizations came together in an effort to incorporate into the new Constitution. Many innovative strategies were drawn from groups and individuals during the drafting process. Within the Women and the Constitution Project, although we never think in terms of lobbying, we take action proactively-to get into Parliament; to try to express ourselves; as representatives of the Women and the Constitution Network.

We have proposals, but we had to fight with the security guard to get into Parliament. By observing Parliamentary debates we tried to offer some support for members of the Constitutional Drafting Assembly who are sympathetic with women's issues. We went to a series of meetings working on the first draft of the Constitution and tried to exchange our proposals with other groups, such as the handicapped. We exchanged views and pledged support for each other. With environmental groups, for instance, we offered to support community rights and requested they support gender rights.

In the end, we finally succeeded: Chapter 30 of the new Constitution guarantees that women in Thailand have gender equality. Injustice and discrimination are illegal on the basis of gender and age. In addition, the government must implement and conduct affirmative action or measures to ensure that people can exercise the rights that have been guaranteed. Another accomplishment was in the area of domestic violence, which all women remember. We proposed including domestic violence protection in that chapter, but many male lawyers said there is already protection under family law and therefore we do not have to put it in the Constitution.

In one of the debates, broadcast live on TV and radio, the chairman of the Constitutional Drafting Assembly interrupted a female member by saying, 'Don't talk about that, it is too small an issue; reserve it for legislation, not for the Constitution.' But she said, 'We proposed this and it is on paper. This is very undemocratic if you do not allow me to speak on this topic.' She cried out and expressed herself emotionally, and many male members supported her- so we used whatever tactics that worked. As the core members of Women and the Constitution, we stormed into parliamentary sessions to watch the debates.

Only women's groups consistently monitored all the sessions until many males withdrew their opposition to this "women's" proposal. After the Constitution was promulgated, we continued educating people about their rights. We lack Trainors, however. Ten to fifteen of us had to go to 65 two-day workshops all over Thailand-from city to city and to villages near the jungle where there was never any kind of training before. We found that at first the women sat in the back, in the corners. In the past two years, as Thailand was drafting its new Constitution, there has been an emergence of women's coalitions.

At least 35 women's organizations came together in an effort to incorporate into the new Constitution. But on the second day, they stood up and said, 'thank you.' Some of them even said, 'We studied three years in school, but it was not as valuable as this two-day workshop.' We educated the women about the rights they have, what mechanisms they can utilize to access their rights, including certain courts that can provide protection of their rights. But there are some other mechanisms provided by the new Constitution that need to be established within two years, including a human rights commission, administrative courts, and others.

There are also some very good channels for accessing rights guaranteed in the Constitution. The other number that the participants loved were 50,000-50,000 eligible voters can sign petitions to propose legislation and also impeach or recall corrupt politicians.

Another topic we talk about in these workshops is how the electoral system has changed. There are two kinds of voting procedures for the 500 members of the House of Representatives. We focus on why you have to vote and what your power is when you mark the ballot. We also talk to them about decentralization. The Constitution specifies that local governments will be given more administrative power, can utilize national resources, and enhance their autonomy. Budgets and responsibility must be increased for local governments.

What we did was try to open a forum for local people to give input into what they need in the new local government code. They do not just need power. What they need more than that is accountable councilors and bureaucrats. Bureaucratic reform is necessary as well because the system is still very powerful and government officials think that local problems cannot be solved in communities. They still do not believe that people have power and are able to solve their own problems. The corruption issue was also addressed in the training.

At one of our training workshops, an elected official asked, 'What about the money that contractors give us? What do you call that kind of money-is that corruption? Is it a violation of law?' It has become customary that people receive "commission money," or corruption money. During the training, we used the phrase 'women, men, and the Constitution.' The content we presented to them had core elements on gender, equity, and participation. Why did we choose gender as the first subject?

The gender issue itself is provocative-it makes people angry. We also included men in the training and sometimes it was the first time that men realized that, 'Oh, we torture women, we victimize them.' Sometimes men did not realize that they did that, whether by nature or by culture. At the same time, we helped empower the participants. As a role play, we ask them to act out frequently cited stories. The first-most popular story was the abuse of power by the police-like false arrest and torture. The second-most popular story was about health services at the community or provincial level. When the poor and rich come to receive the same health services, the poor are discriminated against simply because they are poor.

The third topic that was very popular was domestic violence. It was obvious that many husbands, particularly drunk husbands, beat their wives and children. When the victim goes to report the incident to the police, the authorities say, 'This is a domestic affair, don't bother us.' This happens every day. After the workshop, some participants go back home to review the electricity bills, the telephone bills, or the water bills. They take the bills to officials and ask why the price doubled in one month, or why they were charged to reconnect the telephone when the line was never cut off.

Now they understand the Constitution, that government officials have a duty to provide services for the people and how they also have the right to sue government officials for abusing power. Had we done things like this before? The Women and the Constitution Project has networks throughout the country. I do not know who set up that network, but have injected new political issues into the group. If we look at the pyramid of power, we see that there were several networks there already. But what we have been trying to do is to build a pipe to link the grassroots level, to the national level, to the top, to the core organizations in Bangkok.

That pipe conveys messages, courage, and serves to strengthen one another. There are three tiers: local, provincial, and national, and we try to use the existing structures that have been established. The other Programme that we have been focusing on is decentralization. Over the last six years, The Asia Foundation Programme has been trying to increase the number of women in local governments. We believe that women are experts in gender issues-we do not have to worry too much whether women at the local level are gender-sensitive or not, because they always support social issues, education, income generation, etc.

What we worry about is the situation at the provincial and national levels-whether those women are sensitive to gender issues, because there are so many factors, such as families, parties, and money-factors that do not make women gender-sensitive at those levels. So we try to focus our resources at the local levels instead of the national level. We have been doing this very successfully. In the target area where candidate training was provided, the number of women who have been elected increased from 1 percent to 14 percent at the new local government unit.

With local decentralization, we have opened up forums for women and other local leaders to give feedback on local government legislation. We try to give them opportunities to network and form confederations or coalitions so their voices can be heard effectively in the legislative committees. We have also intruded into as many legislative committees as possible, and now the coordinator of the network sits on the local government legislative committee. I sit on the human rights legislative committee and others sit on the political reform committees. I think that our Programmes and strategies fit into three aspects of reform: the legal aspect, political aspect, and cultural aspect.

It may take years and years to reform cultural attitudes, but I think it is essential. We have to thank The Asia Foundation, because all these activities are solely funded by the Foundation. We hope that next year, assistance from Canada, Australia, and private organizations will support this Programme-a Programme that The Asia Foundation initiated. It was the first time that we had the pleasure of having the NGOs in our office. Although some of them did not respond to our invitation, those who came, in particular our friends from The Asia Foundation, gave us good insight into the tremendous changes going on in Thailand, as well as the opportunities.

We also have an effort financed by the Japanese government to further identify some of the needs for legal reform, because we need to promote the inclusion of gender in the overall legal reforms. The constitution was a major achievement, but now we need to put into practice some of the legislation that is required. I think the advocacy groups and the NGO networking is fundamental. The financial institutions sometimes have a very limited conduit of discussion with the public sector.

And we sometimes neglect the needs of civil society. How do you address the establishment of legal centers in China? We may need to learn from China to do that in other countries. China's NGOs are only starting to deal with the problem. Though the Chinese Constitution, women's laws, and marriage laws are all meant to protect women's rights, laws are abstract, not easy to implement, and access to legal services is lacking. At the same time, legal literacy is still a serious problem among women as well as men. Women's NGOs try to deal with all these problems. The legal aid centers of universities as well as women's hotlines all try to address women's rights issues.

They provide legal services and refer women to other service and counseling centers. Through media and publications, they make women's voices heard by society. At other levels, women's organizations that are engaged in development issues are trying to get more women involved in development Programmes and at the same time strengthen their institutional capacity so women's groups can have enough leverage to influence policy and eventually transform decision- making patterns.

How do men look at gender relations? To me, it comes through as a bit elitist-the types of advocacy groups that exist, although there are links to the grassroots level. At the grassroots level, how do men and women relate to each other in terms of some of the advocacy that you are doing? And number two, how much freedom do you have to do what you want? Do you have the freedom to do what you think is best without thinking of, perhaps, the political repercussions within the country? Or, are you being constrained by that? How do you connect to the grassroots? At the grassroots level, do you have a monitoring system to see how the gender relations interact in accepting your views?

This is a difficult question. Two years ago when I tried to conduct gender training, I received a lot of resistance not only from men, but also from women. Over three or four years we have experimented using different approaches. Our target group is women, but for men, you have to use an innovative approach. Men never easily accept that they are the exploiters of others. I approach the issue in terms of human resource development: how many people's potential have been used? Only 23 or 25 percent of people have been used. Somehow this attitude has to be impartial, because if we look at men in biased terms, they feel that we are protecting only women. So we have to extend sympathy to men, too, in order to get cooperation and decrease resistance. It is a new concept for the government to accept NGOs.

It has just changed recently, because the Constitution guarantees the right to association, the right to form groups. And the NGOs have done good work in trying to balance grants made directly to the community level. For example, there have been conflicts over the World Bank-supported Social Investment Fund. It is a very controversial Programme that many NGOs and Thais are against because they feel we have borrowed enough. The cash is important and necessary for the unemployed who are returning to their homes now. What are they going to do when they go back home?

They cannot live in their communities longer than one month because there is nothing that belongs to them-no land, no work. How can their families help them for six months, or even for one month, until they get another job? Immediate assistance at this time is very important, and even if we have to borrow money, I think it is legitimate. I have done research and writing on the Asian values issue and teach about the comparative political economy of Asia. Women constitute the single largest class or group in society that is dissatisfied with the status quo.

In general, women therefore constitute the largest group advocating for human rights or other rights. So, it was a bit of an eye-opener for me to suddenly make the connection those women's rights issues, or NGOs emphasizing women's issues, are really much broader and have a much broader potential impact. And this is particularly true in the Thai example of the impact that women have had on the political process with regard to the new Constitution. Now my particular interest is in Japan and Japanese politics.

In the particular case of citizens advocacy for the NPO law, as I mentioned, about 70 private nonprofit organizations and many individuals initiated a coalition to focus on the creation of an NPO law. That is C's. C's also expanded its national outreach through its own networking and through the establishment of contact with other citizen's networks and groups that had been involved in discussing a review of Article 34. I can say that the citizens' network centered on C's and took effective approaches to the creation of an NPO law.

The citizens' network vigorously lobbied Diet members and briefed many local grassroots organizations and small community-based organizations on the contents of the law and received feedback from them. The citizens network approached Keidanren and Rengo to involve them in the discussion. Since the long-ruling Liberal Democratic Party lost in the election and a coalition government was established in 1993, the Japanese political scene was somewhat unstable, as many of you know. Many new parties were created and some abolished. The framework of the coalition government has changed from time to time.

When an NPO law was discussed, the ruling parties consisted of the Liberal Democratic Party, the Social Democratic Party of Japan, and the Sakigake. The differences among the three parties in terms of policies actually allowed different ideas to come into play. These provided citizens' groups room for their opinions to be positively reflected. Involvement of the Keidanren and Rengo, especially Keidanren, sharply expanded the discussion of social change in Japan first initiated among citizens' organizations. Now we tend to look at the civil sector as an emerging sector for the nation. Positive coverage of NGOs and NPOs by the media also helped the movement. Some business leaders argued that the expansion of the civil sector might create new fields for employment and business opportunities.

Keidanren decided to support the passage of the law not only because they believed in a strong civil society but, also, because they hoped that growth of NPOs would open up new fields in society which would benefit the business sector and Japanese economy. The legislative process was not easy. For example, differences among political parties at one time resulted in divisions over the legislation among various citizens' networks. Finally, however, all the political parties involved unanimously supported the law. Different citizens' networks also got together because they concluded that the passage of the law should be prioritized. They continue to discuss future amendments to the law, particularly the issue of tax deductibility.

Immediately after the passage, some citizens' groups increased their briefings to local governments on the content of the law and began discussions on implementation procedures once it takes effect. Diet members of different parties also are said to have started discussion on the issues. According to the NPO law, implementation of the law will be at prefectural government level. Is the women's NGO movement in Mongolia having an impact at the decision making level-on the real changes in the government and at the other decision making levels in your country for the future of women?

Women's organizations were established from political parties, because the primary reason for the emergence of those groups was political. After they realized their nonpartisan nature they broke with the political parties, but they never gave up their work in politics. The common approach for women's organizations is to target politics and decision making, and they are promoting women's issues a lot. For example, they did an awareness campaign on the labor law, which prohibits women from working in certain jobs. Thanks to that campaign, women now know that their rights are restricted in terms of employment and that some are suffering from those restrictions. However, there has not been the usual big campaign regarding this law and changes are not going to be adopted soon.

As another example, the coalition of women working to increase women's representation in the government was extremely successful, in my mind. Because of that coalition, political parties had women's issues on their agenda during the 1996 election and developed a quota for the candidate nomination list. At that time, there were not very many empowered, bold, and committed women to run for Parliament, but they managed it and indeed women's representation doubled, although there has been a degree of backlashes in the executive branch of the government.

When we have conducted surveys across Asia, women often listed this as the number one problem they face. It deters their economic participation and their political participation and it certainly affects their family life, status, etc. We are addressing it through the Women's Political Participation Programme because it is such a priority issue. But the Beijing conference put domestic violence as a term and a concept on the map. Many countries, including Mongolia and China, did not have any term for domestic violence. In China, the translation was 'bothering your wife.' The Beijing conference changed that-it is not 'bothering your wife,' it is now, 'a crime against women.' There are various movements to find ways of addressing this through law, through culture, and government accountability on these issues.

Worldwide, it is an enormous issue that is moving from the private into the public domain in many of these societies for the first time. When we commissioned a survey in Cambodia, it emerged as a tremendous problem. The question is, how do you deal with it? For instance, there was no legislation in Cambodia although now there is a new draft law, but the problem probably is not really the law, it is cultural attitudes. As in Cambodia, many women said they would never admit to being beaten, just as women in most societies would not because if a woman spoke out she would not be a perfect wife, so she conceals it from her family and friends.

We support efforts to bring the issue from the private into the public domain, raise awareness, and try to encourage legislation that protects women-working on it in a number of dimensions. Maybe B. Oyunbileg will talk a little bit about Mongolia and its work on violence. In 1994, when we had our first meeting in the region and women were talking about domestic violence, our Mongolian participant was unaware of this term. When we explained that it is when a man beats his wife, she said it is a big problem but there is no term for it.

It was something that was not mentioned or addressed. But then when the term was introduced, all the women's organizations joined this movement in a flash and spread this concept. We are now talking about violence against women, which is an increasing problem and about how to address domestic violence. The women's movement is being engaged very intensively nowadays. Every woman's organization is addressing violence against women, and some NGOs have a specific focus on domestic violence. With the initiative of women's organizations, the Center Against Violence was established, which now has its own shelter.

This is a specialized women's organization that is leading all the efforts to provide services and educate people about violence against women, as well as conducting research on the status and dynamics of domestic violence in Mongolia. The Center Against Violence's 1995 survey and the 1998 update show that although half of police arrests are cases of domestic violence, they are not labeled as domestic violence cases, but rather as "administrative" cases, like misbehaving in a public place. Violent men are not punished; they are brought in and then let go. The police do not even try to hold them responsible for wife beating.

The women's movement is campaigning for a new domestic violence law. The Women's Lawyers Association and the Center Against Violence participated in the Singapore World Conference on Family Violence and they will participate in a study tour in Thailand and Malaysia to learn from these countries' experiences on how to advance this law, how to mobilize the community, and how to use it afterwards for better protection of women's rights. It is also an issue on which women mobilize and perhaps are much more active, even women who have never been politically active in the sense of voting or being supportive. It draws women in, because it is such a huge issue once it gets out into the public domain and is recognized.

When you are training women in the political system in Thailand, is it even an issue that women are pushed into the social services ministries or that they are encouraged to run for office because they are morally different, as opposed to because they are people who have expertise and should be in the department of defense, etc. Has this come up as a concern among women parliamentarians in Thailand and also just in your training courses for training women in politics and women as politicians?

There is an emergence of women role models in Thai politics, but it is still not enough. At the local level, women are caring and concerned about health and social issues. But at the provincial and national levels, many women politicians do not want to be labeled as just someone who is good on social issues, although there must be some women who volunteer to be labeled as someone who cares about social issues. At this time we still have to use some kind of reinforcement to increase the number of women in the political domain.

We often say within the organization that our field offices and our field staff are the jewels in the crown of The Asia Foundation. I am glad that you have had this opportunity to get to know some of our key staff who are working on important issues in their societies and actually having some impact-not only on the empowerment of women, but on developing civil society, good governance, and other democracy issues. Ms. Ketphol was appointed this year as an advisor to the Standing Committee on Justice and Human Rights for the Thai House of Representatives.

She has also advised the House Subcommittee on Women's Issues, the Ministry of Justice Subcommittee on the preparation on the International Convention on Civil and Political Rights report, and the Subcommittee on Women's Political Participation for the National Commission of Women's Affairs of the Office of the Prime Minister.

From December 1996 to October 1997, Ms. Ketphol was a Member of the Nalehon Ratsima Provincial Hearing Committee appointed by the Constitution Drafting Assembly. Ms. Ketphol joined the Foundation in 1992 as Programme Officer in the Foundation's Cambodia office, where she managed Foundation assistance to nongovernmental organizations working in the areas of women's participation, human rights, and media.

Prior to joining the Foundation, she conducted training of Trainors on human rights in the Cambodian refugee camps on the Thai border for the United Nations Border Relief Operation. She was also a Joint Voluntary Agency Field Worker and Interpreter in the Indochinese Refugee section of the U.S. Embassy in Bangkok. Ms. Ketphol received a B.A. in political science and has a certificate in gender training of Trainers from Australian National University.

Ms. Kuroda has designed a capacity-building Programme for future NGO leaders and is working to develop local and regional networks for women in politics. She is also engaged in the Foundation's efforts to advance the U.S.-Japan Common Agenda, an agreement between the U.S. and Japanese governments to cooperatively address global development challenges through public-private partnerships.

3

The Diasporic Hybridity of Southeast Asian and Female Images

Looking from the sea towards the land, Southeast Asia is seen as a continuum of physical and cultural environments. Sustainable cosmopolitan settlements in Southeast Asia have been developing around the "Mediterranean of Asia", referring to the coastal regions around the South China Sea, Java Sea, and Malacca Strait, since the establishment of the inter-insular and inter-continental maritime trading activities from the first century until today. The cosmopolitan culture has been formed through complex layering processes of various cultures, ideologies, economies, and ecosystems sustained over a long extended historical period and clearly manifested in the complexity and hybridity of the production of its settlements' morphology and architectural typologies.

Southeast Asian societies and cities are characterized by rich and complex collage and interweaving of cultural diversity, hybridity in the built-forms and variety in material culture. In Southeast Asia the cultural and geographical boundaries are always blurring, overlapping, or intersecting, and cannot clearly be defined. People in different places, islands or continents have kept moving, communicating, and intermingling from past till present, influencing each other and producing hybrid, fused, diverse architecture and material culture.

In the 1980s, Sutan Takdir Alisyahbana - an Indonesian esteemed scholar - proposed a geographical term for this dynamic region "Bumantara", literally means "region in between", located at the centre of international maritime and commerce, and in-between corridors for trades, migrations, and exchanges, between Asia and Australia continents, and between the Pacific the Indian oceans. For centuries, this region was politically unified under Funan.

It was continuously shaped and enriched by various cultural layers, constantly nurtured and developed along its long and intermingling historical timeline. Rivers and fresh water springs are the lifeline of the human settlements, and its origin can be traced back to these primary water elements. Early settlements that bore the seeds of urbanity appeared on the waterfront at the connection point between the outside worlds with the interior hinterland. This waterfront settlement in many areas in Southeast Asia is known as *Kampung,* The vernacular building tradition in Southeast Asia is the results of adaptation to local climate, innovation in building materials and techniques, and creative integration of belief system.

Steep pitch roof, wide eaves, raised floor, breathing roof, and porous walls are the responses against the equatorial tropical warm-humid climate, affected by monsoon with plenty of rain, and to ensure comfort for people who lives within it. The timber construction system using flexible joints are reactions against earthquakes, especially in the Indonesian. The forested hills and mountains provided steady supply of fresh water through the rivers to the community living in these settlements for their daily life and cultivations.

Therefore to ensure the continuous flow of this lifeline, the forests were protected against violations and destructions, through rituals and social rules. The choice of location for the built-up area of the settlement is carefully considered against natural and supra-natural factors, in order to ensure the harmonious relationships between human, nature, and the spirits. In rational sense, it is also to ensure the survivability of the community's existence and its livelihood for perpetuity,

Archipelago, which are continuously rocked by active volcanoes and the movement of continental plates. On the land based farming settlement in Southeast Asia, there is a strong indication that the vernacular stilt-house was developed out of the rice growing culture in the warm-humid tropical region, originated from granary architectural typology, which was then further developed into dwelling places.

The attic under the roof works as a storage for rice, goods and valuables, while the middle space is meant for living. It is a direct respond to the forces of nature, creative innovation in using available resources, and manifestation of belief in supra-natural powers by special ornamentations placed on the roof. From the earliest vernacular traditions of Southeast Asia, we learned that local architecture and native urbanism are able to offer the best and integrated solution towards human needs in their relation with nature, social, and supra-natural environments. It is the medium for human survival in both mortal and spiritual worlds, for reconciling the power of nature and the desires of human being.

HARMONIOUS COEXISTENCE

People of Southeast Asia had been learning from Indian philosophy and cosmology since the first century, and applying the formal and spatial ordering principles - known as *Mandala* to their architectural typology and settlements morphology. This is understood as the tri-partite divisions of the cosmos in macro-, meso-, and micro- levels. This tri-partite cosmological divisions or hierarchy corresponds to the metaphor of the human body (the head, the torso, and the feet), and to the metaphor of the universe: the sky where the divine spirits reign, the ground where the human lives, and the underworld where the evil spirits dwell. It may be seen in two-dimensional plane, or applied to three-dimensional space and form.

Traditional planning of the settlements in many local contexts in Southeast Asia follows this ordering principle, by situating the village in between the mountain and the water body (sea, lake, or river). The most important building or function (like temple of origin, chieftains' house, or ancestral graves) is placed on the vantage point of the village or towards of the mountain. Functions associated with death or impurities (like temple of death, or waste disposal) are placed down towards the opposite direction. In many cases the rice barns – the most important function for the rice growing community – are situated on the eastern side of the village facing the sunrise, symbolizing life. Islam entered and spread throughout Southeast Asia through two different main trading routes: through the Asian mainland ("Silk Road") and through the Indian Ocean ("Ceramic Road").

The Arab, Yemeni, Gujarati, and Tamil traders from West- and South- Asia were the earliest catalysts for "Islamisation" in Southeast Asia, followed by the Chinese Muslims particularly during the voyages of Admiral Zheng He to Southeast Asia and the Indian Ocean during the Ming dynasty in the 15th century. Islamisation processes in Bumantara started from the urban centers along the northern coast of Java (Gresik, Tuban, Demak, Semarang, etc.) and the northern tip of Sumatra (Samudra Pasai in Aceh), then spread to other coastal port cities in the peninsular Malay and Indonesian Archipelago including the Philippines. The fusion process of the new Islamic design principles with the existing buildings and urban spatial typology was evident.

The transition and transformation processes took place peacefully and naturally through absorption of the old craftsmanship and building traditions and integration with the new architectural and structural vocabularies. The artists and builders from different racial and cultural groups worked together and blended their artistry and skill into new and unique building tradition and architectural totality. Community groups of different religions and origins lived together side by side in close-knitted settlement fabric. The Chinese Diaspora had been passing through and many had settled down in Southeast Asia since the establishment of the maritime trading route between China, India, Arabia and Africa.

During the cyclone periods of the changing monsoon seasons, the traders stayed in Southeast Asian ports, while waiting for their trading partners from other parts of the world to come. During their stay here the crew and passengers of the ships populated the city and mingled with the local population. Many of them settled down and formed early waterfront towns and coastal cities with a cosmopolitan character. Trade came together with the promulgation of Islam in this region. Therefore it was a common phenomenon in coastal Southeast Asia that an old Chinese temple was situated adjacent to an ancient mosque within the historical urban core, in close proximity to the waterfront in the middle of a multi-racial community.

The voyages of Ming dynasty's Admiral Zheng He (1405-33) to Southeast Asia and the Indian Ocean had left tangible traces along the coastal regions of Southeast Asia in the form of Chinese trading posts and colonies, and strengthening the cosmopolitan characters of the coastal settlements here. Some of these early settlements then grew into flourishing entrepots, and some of them grew into bigger emporiums. One example of the transplantation and indigenization of coastal Diaspora's morphological construct is the Mazu.

The generic urban core morphology was a double nucleus of the native's and the foreigner's settlement areas. Both settlements were interconnected by the main market close to the harbor or the shipyard. The market was the meeting place for different people and functioned as the heart or the common space of the town. Locals and foreigners mingled in the marketplace and within the urban neighborhoods. Unique identity and belief of each group would be preserved and nurtured, and at the same time a new communal hybrid identity was created. The layering process of vernacular, Hindu, Buddhist, Chinese and Islamic cultures and its materialization had been going on peacefully since the creation of these cosmopolitan settlements and communities around the Mediterranean of Asia.

As an expression of respect to the local or indigenous spirits who guarded the place, the newly arrived Chinese immigrants paid their tribute to local objects such as a sacred stone, an old tomb, an ants' mound, or an old tree. Later these kind of objects were manifested as a person by a statue of a local "deity", known as Datuk-Kong – a peculiar combination of the Malay honorific title "Datuk" and the Chinese holy-man "Kong" worship. In every southern Chinese immigrant's boat a special shrine for Mazu was installed to guard the compass or the steering wheel, the sailing direction, and all passengers aboard. Once the ship reached a good place and they decided to settle down, the ship would be dismantled. The memory embedded in the spatial-cosmological concept remained and transplanted into the new adopted land to form a new urban nucleus.

The settlement's new spatial structure was in fact a reconstruction of the cosmological geometric pattern of the immigrant boat, as the Mazu temple was placed at the end of the axis facing the harbor and two masts were placed in front of the temple. A small community of Chinese fishermen and traders was then formed around the harbor, living together side by side with the local population and other foreign communities with a hybrid urban culture and architecture. The Datuk's shrine is located next to the thresholds or entrances to the town, neighborhoods, temples, and houses, even until today.

In later periods other popular vernacular deities from Southern China would also appear in the expanding diaspora's settlements. They were followed by the Taoists and Buddhists who converted (or "colonized") the pre-existing temples or built new temples and monasteries. These, again, were followed by the Confucians and other cults and sects, in a continuous hybridization and layering process within the multi-racial settlements and assortment of religious temples. All developments resulted in a mix of various elements from different belief systems and production of a richer blend of cultural artifacts.

On the building typology level, one good example of this cultural blending process is the typical trader's house in Palembang. The house plan and some of its construction method are of the southern Chinese courthouse, but the saddle roofs, open veranda, timber material, and its raised floor were definitely local. From different cases of the same locality, visible and easily recognizable elements of Arab, Indian, and even European origins were blended into the Chinese and local-vernacular fusion typology. In many instances, the Chinese simply used and adopted the local architectural typology for specific functions, such as temples, association halls, or dwelling. The new building typology has an eclectic nature especially in details and ornamental levels.

MODERNITY: CONTEXTUALIZATION, MODERNIZATION AND INNOVATION

The Europeans began to spread out their hegemonic ambition since late 15th century, initiated by the Portuguese (to India, Malaka, Jawa, eastern Indonesia, Philippines, Taiwan, Japan), followed by the Dutch (to India, Malaka, Indonesia, Taiwan, Japan), British (to India, Malaya peninsula, Bengkulu, Jawa, China), Spanish (Philippines), French (to Indochina, China), and German (to China). Numerous new typologies and functions were introduced into the urban infrastructures, urban design, and architecture, such as boulevards, streetscapes, façade, building techniques, and new functions (military establishments, public buildings, churches, urban squares and plazas, markets, railroads, stations, plantation houses, and many more).

At the very beginning, the European design was directly applied into tropical Southeast Asia with minor modifications, resulted in a not so comfortable living condition within the building. Responding to this, then a more responsive design solutions were invented, by adapting building and urban design into local climatic, aesthetic, and social-cultural conditions. European style buildings with deep verandah and ventilation holes, mixed with Chinese, Indian, Malay, Arab, and others design features, evolving into unique and rich regional styles. Similar to the previous process, the European influences were naturally and openly accepted and absorbed into the vocabulary of Southeast Asian architecture and urbanism.

On the later period of European colonization, the segregation policy of dwelling areas according to different races was implemented almost in all colonial cities in Southeast

Asia. The urban population was racially segregated, generally divided into three classes: the European, the 'oriental' (Chinese, Arabs, and other Asians), and the native population groups. Usually there was no clear physical boundary which separated the different racial zones, although in some cases there were rivers, walls, or roads which functioned as the physical boundaries. Nonetheless the non-physical legal boundaries had caused an internal densification process within each restricted zone especially in the non-European quarters. The over-densification would later push the colonial cities into environmental disasters and worsening of public health conditions. In early twentieth century the colonial governments' policies shifted to a more ethical approach towards their colonies, parallel to the rise of ethics and socialist movements in Europe.

New housing areas were planned and developed inside and around the city, to accommodate the rapid increase of urban population. Infrastructure and housing improvement Programmes were implemented to improve the well being of all segments of the urban population. Garden cities and hygienic housing typologies were developed in the capital cities, municipalities and smaller towns. Modern building codes and regulation were introduced in order to improve sanitation condition and public safety in the inner city. New building types were invented and old building typologies were improved following the new regulations to provide pedestrian arcades, open backyard with utility functions, fire escape, etc.

The harbors were enlarged or rebuilt, industrial estates were developed, and the central business districts in the city centers were rejuvenated. Trade fairs were organized to accommodate the rapid growth in local and international commerce and trade. The port cities in Southeast Asia had grown up to the level similar to other modern port cities in the world of that period. Some cities across Southeast Asia such as Penang, Singapore, Medan, Batavia, Semarang, Surabaya, Makassar, and Manila were linked to the modern international maritime trade networks and developed into the major regional growth and distribution centers. With the opening of new architecture and planning schools in Southeast Asia by the colonial governments, new tropical-regionalism discourses were actively debated and practiced by young architects and urban planners in the region. Fresh ideas from modern urban planners and architects were manifested into city plans, urban designs, and architectural styles - blended with the elements from the local, natural and cultural contexts.

A large dose of idealism and hopes were put into the transformation and the future of the coastal cities in Southeast Asia in early twentieth century. However the global economic recession and the two World Wars which raged on the first half of twentieth century had terminated these dreams. Political movements for national independence, urban riots against the colonial rulers, and social unrest against inequalities and oppressions, were proliferated all over the region. The economic recession and social-political instability had terminated some urban development projects and had left many parts of the city dilapidated and deteriorated.

POST-WAR LAYER - INTERNATIONALIZATION & FRAGMENTATION

The Second World War and the invasion of Japanese Imperial army to East Asia and Southeast Asia gave the final blow to end the colonialism history in Southeast Asia, and changed the course of urban history and morphology of this region. Almost 300 years of European colonization history had to come to an end. A new chapter of the Southeast Asian urban history began to emerge, riding the waves of decolonization and the spirit of national independence. Soon after the War newly independent countries were appearing in a very fast rate across Southeast Asia. For around two to three decades since 1945, the countries in Southeast Asia were struggling to overcome the past legacies of colonialism - such as divisions and poverty - and at the same time trying very hard to re-build the nation politically, socially, economically, and physically.

The International Style and the ideas of Modernism were used to express the breakaway from the colonial past and the emergence of the new spirit of Nationalism by the leader of the newly independent countries of Southeast Asia, such as Soekarno's Indonesia, Sihanouk's Cambodia, Tunku Abdul Rahman's Malaysia, and Ho Chi Minh's Vietnam. Modernist urban plans and locally developed modern architectural styles were produced and implemented in the cities across the region. Very often the implementation of this modernist city plans was partial and haphazard due to limited economic capacity and technical capability of these newly born nations, causing fragmentation and disintegration of the city. The layers of urban history and heritages which kept the shared memory of the whole community for many generations have been forgotten and even erased systematically, to be replaced with a totally new forms alien to the existing contexts, following a certain political agenda or economic market forces, ignoring the past and speculating for the future.

POST-SCRIPT

Coastal cities with its long history of networks and cosmopolitan entrepreneurial spirit have been always playing vital roles in the economic growth and cultural sustainability of Southeast Asian nations. Fifty years after War, the wave of globalization and free trade agreement sweep across Asia and the rest of the world. Many of the national and regional capital cities in Southeast Asia have risen into metropolis, megalopolis, and world city, which play indispensable roles in the interconnected global market and economy. Unfortunately this rapid growth has accelerated the cultural and physical transformation process, which often speeding up the fragmentation and destruction of old urban fabrics and creating serious problems of cultural identity of its citizens.

We have learned that cosmopolitan Southeast Asia is a dynamic source of identities, a place where great civilizations met, collided, and blended. Since the very beginning, our cosmopolitan city is always been a collage of different cultures and styles, physically manifested in the patterns of neighborhoods, streets and waterways, marketplaces, buildings, communal spaces, and hybrid architectural typologies. Multiculturalism is not considered as threat or liability, but as asset and opportunity. Southeast Asian sustainable settlements and cosmopolitan urban communities are similar to webs of different elements and colors, and yet integrated as a continuous fabric. Adaptation, formalization, hybridization, rationalization, and contextual-modernization, are some of the processes that we can learn from cosmopolitan Southeast Asia context.

It may provide the keys to common understanding of the sustainable nature of architecture, urbanism, and environment, which may serve as the starting point to change our paradigms towards a more sensible, sensitive, and contextual actions. For more than two millenniums of its urban history, many cities in Southeast Asia have been demonstrating their ability in preserving its primary elements and basic morphological patterns, tangible fragments and intangible traces, linkages, and connections, while continuing to be transformed and reborn. All of these can be learned, understood, adapted and appropriated, decoded and reconstructed, to enrich our inventory and vocabulary to educate future generation of scholars and professionals.

It is a well-known story that Chinese travellers were amazed when in what is now Southern Vietnam to see Cham women riding horses and taking part in market vending. Those same travellers - most notably the diplomat Zhou Daguan, whose memoir tells us so much about life in the Khmer Empire - were also surprised to see the high status which women enjoyed in Southeast Asia. In nearly all of the states of that region, women have had more freedom to organise and control their own lives more than in many other parts of the world.

That does not mean that they had equality with men, of course or that they were not oppressed in certain circumstances. However, sexual freedom and the opportunity to work outside the house were much more likely to be found in this area than in most others. The many legends of female warriors support this idea, as also do the various myths and folk tales of strong women taking the lead which are to be found. Even in Chinese literature, when women have this kind of power and ability, they are generally considered to be 'Southern' or in some other way removed from the Chinese heartland.

The Yueh sword maidens, for example, combined the concept of a fighting woman of great beauty who hailed from the area of Northern Vietnam and its neighbouring Chinese regions. Within the Khmer Empire in particular, it was possible for women to ascend to high office and to administer government facilities and departments. In the time of Jayavarman VI, for example, the northern princess Tilaka was especially well-favoured: "Adolescent, she acquired not only the superior beauty associated with perfect conduct, but also a high position worthy of her race, with the esteem of the greatest families".

The nature of rice-paddy agriculture in the region promotes the independence of women as well, to some extent. While men work in the fields, women tend to stay at home and are occupied with domestic and childcare labour, as well as some craft activities which might in due course bring some additional income. Sharing childcare responsibilities enables some women to gather together in villages and, in addition to reinforcing social networks, they may also participate in some production activities. Village based factories provide status, income and purpose and they are important means of promoting rural regional development.

In the post World War II period only fifty women have been elected heads of state of their respective countries. Of these fifty women, eleven have come from South and Southeast Asia, including the first female head of state, Sirimavo Bandaranaike of Sri Lanka. These eleven women represent the second highest number of elected women presidents and prime ministers in a world region, behind Western Europe. Unlike Western Europe, however, the South and Southeast Asian societies from which these women have emerged as elected leaders continue to be associated with patriarchy and the subordination of women.

From agrarian economies like Indonesia to relatively liberal polities like the Philippines, men still cling to traditional gender-biased attitudes and perceptions whereby the home and the care of the young and aged are considered the responsibility of women. In Bangladesh, women are often secluded to the domestic sphere as a result of poverty and *purdah*, the veiling and segregation of women. The case of Burma shows that, Buddhism, the dominant religion in the country, is a major influence in creating subservience of women before men.

While tradition and religion circumscribe certain freedoms of the female population in this region, some governments have taken an official stance on promoting this situation. The former government of Zia Ul-Haq of Pakistan pursued an Islamization Programme that idealized the image of women faithful to *chador aur char diwari* (remaining veiled and within the confines of the four walls of one's home).

This manner of gender discrimination in Pakistan has resulted in one of the lowest female literacy levels in the world; barely one sixth of the female population has attended a minimum of three years' schooling. Thus, it is clear that social forces in this region of the world relegate women to the private sphere. Given the relatively low status of women in this region, one question why these societies voted for women to lead their respective countries; how so many women have occupied the highest echelons of power while their countrywomen suffered from discrimination, poverty, illiteracy and other societal woes.

Many studies have addressed this intriguing paradox. The extant literature on the subject demonstrates that the election of women into these positions of power is a result of the confluence of institutional, structural, and cultural factors. Linda Richter's study (1991) on the political prominence of South and Southeast Asian women demonstrates the interaction between these categories.

Her study offers "ideology of patriarchy, familial ties, martyrdom, social class, female lifestyles, the historical context, prison experiences and electoral arrangements" as the most significant explanatory variables to the phenomenon in question. Mark Thompson (2003) presents a similar set of explanatory variables in his study on female leadership of democratic transitions in Asia. In contrast to the analyses of Richter and Thompson, the scope of this study is narrower.

This study identifies the factors that are important to the respective national electorates of this region when making the electoral decisions that result in the elections of female heads of states. It seeks to address the paradox of why individual voters decide to elect women when the patriarchal norms of their societies dictate that women should not be public figures. The voters' general mindsets that lead to these electoral decisions can be represented in the region's political cultures. Thus, this study focuses on the role that political culture plays in the election of women heads of state in the South and Southeast Asian region.

While this approach does not negate the importance of structural factors (e.g. electoral arrangements) or institutional factors (e.g. the candidate's social class), factors which Richter and Thompson's studies have shown to be significant, it provides a closer perspective on the cultural aspect of this political phenomenon. Indeed, the most complete explanation for the phenomenon in question is offered by the combined effect of the different institutional, structural and political cultural variables.

This study, which focuses on political culture, is intended to be a complement to the greater body of extant literature on the subject. This chapter contends that the political cultural variables that influence voters in the South and Southeast Asian region in electing female heads of state include the following: patriarchal perceptions of women, affinity for charismatic leaders, public regard of elite dynasties and public experience of the effects of colonialism. The substantial number of elected female heads of state in this region, shown in the table, affirms that the elections of these women cannot be easily dismissed as a collection of anomalies.

The examples of countries like Bangladesh and the Philippines where more than one female head of state have been elected and the cases of Sri Lanka, Pakistan, and India where individual candidates have been elected on multiple occasions, illustrate that the election of women in this region is a recurrent phenomenon that constitutes a discernible electoral pattern. The variables considered in this study are not independent of each other.

For example, the effects of the variable "charisma" are also present in some aspects in the discussion on "public regard of elite dynasties." Another characteristic of this set of variables is that, in most cases, a variable and its influence to the phenomenon will be shared across the polities of the different South and Southeast Asian countries considered. A discussion of the effect of political culture in the emergence of female heads of state in this region gives rise to the question of what are the characteristics of the political cultures of the countries of the South and Southeast Asian region that have not elected women into the office of chief executive.

The case of Vietnam may provide an answer to this query. The political cultures of the countries that did elect women are highly hierarchical and are marked by great class inequality where women with high social status are able to use this identity to legitimize their authority as political figures. However, in post-revolutionary societies like that of Vietnam, social class is less of an issue and thus, women do not have the advantage that high social status confers upon them.

Also, according to Neher (1994), unlike the countries considered in this study, Vietnam has a smaller degree of personalist politics, "as the nations' leadership kept their dignity by staying aloof from the people." However, these explanations do not account for the other South and Southeast Asian cases like Thailand, Laos, and Malaysia that also have no record of elected women leaders.

Indeed, the cultural contexts of these cases and their influence upon the phenomenon in question deserve scrutiny, but lie beyond the scope of this particular study. In contrast, this study concentrates on the countries that have actually elected women into power and the political cultural determinants in those countries that affected those elections.

EXTANT DISCOURSE ON THE EXPLANATORY VARIABLES

The political cultural approach taken by this study to the phenomenon in question modifies and expands certain variables used in the extant literature. In their respective studies, Richter and Thompson show that a variable is important but stop short of explaining how the variable affects the voters' electoral decisions. For example, while Richter states that familial ties to prominent male politicians are important, she does not elaborate on how the polity perceives these family connections and how this translates into voting behavior those results in the election of women heads of state.

This chapter, on the other hand, shows how the polities of this region synthesize and internalize a variable such as "familial ties to political elites" through the lenses of their respective political cultures and how these cultural perspectives affect the electoral decisions and voting behaviors that create this phenomenon. In terms of this particular variable, this connection will be explained by showing that the female candidates' familial ties to political elites are important to the larger citizenry because patron-client structures bind the South and Southeast Asian "commoner" to the political causes of elites.

The study also argues that the non-elite suffers from an inferiority complex in his or her relations with the elites and will, therefore, choose to be governed by them. The election of these patrician female heads of state is presented as a manifestation of the divide between the elite and non-elite in this region. These are examples of socio-political factors that Richter and Thompson do not elaborate in their studies and seem to take for granted. For instance, the very label that Richter uses for the discussion of this particular factor, which is simply "familial ties" or "social class," reflects this inadequate methodological approach.

In contrast, this study considers this factor as "public regard for political elites," in order to capture its political cultural dimensions. Thus, by analyzing the national political mindsets of this region and how it affects electoral decisions, this study makes a logical extension to the variables discussed in previous studies. Both Richter and Thompson address the effect of patriarchal norms on the emergence of female heads of state in this region. This study refines this particular variable by contending that patriarchal beliefs significantly affect the phenomenon in question if they manifest themselves within the context of a period of crisis.

It shows that the "cult of motherhood," a patriarchal notion that mothers are caring and incorruptible, which manifests itself in varying forms in the political cultures across this region, is particularly contributory in the election of women in times of crisis. The extant literature indicates that the colonial experiences of their respective countries affected the personal situations of the women who eventually came into power. Both Richter's discussion of "prison experiences" and Fernando's description (2004) of how daughters of political figures were politicized by their fathers' involvements in independence struggles explain some of the effects of these experiences.

This chapter, in order to emphasize the political culture of the region's electorates, shifts the focus from the effects of colonialism on the individual female candidates to the manner in which the effects of colonialism prepared the larger citizenry to accept these women as their countries' leaders. Therefore, the variable, "public experience of the effects of colonialism" explains how the spread of Western values of gender equality through colonial educational systems, influential colonial individuals and the imposition of laws by the colonial government affected the polities of this region.

The variable of "affinity for charismatic leaders" has not been previously considered in the extant literature. Using Max Weber's analysis of charisma, this study asserts that these female leaders' personal situations and the political atmosphere within which they rose to power placed them in a charismatic light. Since personalist politics is an integral component of the region's political cultures, there is a high affinity for charismatic leaders. Thus, this public perception of the candidate as charismatic is demonstrated as instrumental in the election of these women into political office.

PATRIARCHAL PERCEPTIONS OF WOMEN

The perceptions of South and Southeast Asian women by their societies arise from a highly patriarchal cultural milieu. Deniz Kandiyoti (1988) terms the system of male dominance in South and Southeast Asia as the "classic patriarchy." Here, a patrilocal-patrilineal complex centers on the operations of the extended household where the senior man has authority over all. The implications of this complex affecting the women of this region are remarkably uniform; they entail forms of control and subordination that cut across cultural and religious boundaries, such as those of Hinduism, Confucianism and Islam.

This system extols a public realm of manly virtue and citizenship as independence, generality, and dispassionate reason, thus creating the private sphere of the family as the place to which emotion, sentiment and bodily needs must be confined. The generality of the public then depends on excluding women. The few women from this region who managed to break out of the "politically irrelevant" private sphere and into the public recognize these deep-rooted gender biases, which as Judith Squires (2000) explains, are "systematic social constructions of masculinity and femininity that are little if at all constrained by biology."

Benazir Bhutto of Pakistan summarized her difficult ascent to power in the face of male dominance thus: It was a Muslim country with very strong patriarchal tendencies...I found that a whole series of people opposed me simply on the grounds that I was a woman...The clerics took to the mosque saying that Pakistan had thrown itself outside the

Muslim world and the Muslim Omar by voting for a woman, that a woman had usurped a man's place in the Islamic society...I can deal with political differences, but how do you deal with it when someone says I don't like you because you're a woman and you've taken a man's place?

It is clear that Bhutto felt indignant at the subservient position of women in the Pakistani patriarchy. Her policy pledges articulated in the Pakistan People's Party 1988 Manifesto, such as repealing all discriminatory laws against women and signing the United Nations Convention on the Elimination of all forms of Discrimination against Women reflect her resentment towards the social position of the Pakistani woman. All of these attempts met with stiff resistance from the Islamic political forces of Pakistan and proved to be an insurmountable barrier to realize much of Bhutto's agenda on gender equality.

However, some female heads of state, though enjoying power and a higher status than the vast majority of their countrywomen, did very little to change the status quo, thus implicating themselves in the prevalent patriarchy. The Sri Lankan president, Chandrika Kumaratunga, stated: "I think women must participate in the political processes but, as nature has decided that it is a woman who will have the children...it is a difficult thing."

Hardly a clarion call for female representation, the above statement shows that gender biased mindsets are embedded in the political culture to such an extent that women like Kumaratunga, who were capable of rising above the shackles of patriarchy, still perform and acknowledge hegemonic scripts. Similarly, Bhutto's decision to enter into an arranged marriage with Asif Ali Zadari in 1987 also shows a capitulation to the pressures of patriarchy.

She describes how the influence of her patriarchal environment deeply affected her person- al life: "I couldn't rent a home because a woman living on her own can be suspected of all kinds of scandalous associations...I decided to make a personal sacrifice in what I thought would be a loveless marriage, a marriage of convenience." Thus, patriarchy emerges as a pervasive and prominent facet of the political cultures of this region.

With patriarchal worldviews serving as the lens with which womanhood is evaluated, it is clear that these perceptions dictate that women should be confined to private spaces. However, paradoxically, these very attitudes that relegate women to the confines of the home and a lower status served those few women who came to power as a political advantage. One such patriarchal attitude is the sanctity of motherhood, a highly symbolic feminine attribute that was projected upon and sometimes exploited by these female heads of states during their ascendance to power.

A Cult of Motherhood Catherine Reissman's study on childless women in India (2000) demonstrates the cultural importance of women to bear children: "Motherhood is [a woman's] sacred duty - a value enshrined in religious laws for Hindus, Muslims, Sikhs, and Christians alike." Indeed, the married woman who is childless in India exists at the margins, in a liminal space that is socially betwixt and between. Remaining childless after marriage challenges strong cultural beliefs about the "ordinary and natural" life course for Indian women. The occurrence of this particular gender construct is quite uniform in the South and Southeast Asian region and Asia in general. Patriarchy dictates that women are of great value when they grow into mothers and into a particular type of mother.

A recent study covering 1200 mothers in 12 Asian countries shows that a typical Asian mother is expected to be "a good mother, maid, manager, mediator, and mate." In these societies motherhood increases female status and leverage, albeit within their own homes. The mother simile or matru upamawa in Sri Lankan Theravada Buddhism illustrates the elevated status of the mother in the home.

The simile states that the Buddha is the mother of the world, connected to all beings, consoling and compassionate. In the Sri Lankan imaginary, the Buddha is the mother of the world, while it is the mother - and not the father - who is the

Buddha of the home. Other social constructs in this region intensify the public regard of motherhood to the point of adulation and worship. This worship of the mother goddess is deeply rooted in the belief in Shakti or feminine power, a widespread cultural construct in Hindu, Buddhist and Islamic societies. Thus, religion, tradition and myth consecrate and celebrate motherhood in South and Southeast Asia.

It is clear then that in this region, the woman as a mother is a highly legitimate and respected figure. Thus, when women with families run for political office they are "reassuring" candidates. Although they enter a traditionally male domain in seeking political office, they do so within a traditional gender role. These women can hardly be perceived as the stereotypical "threatening, man-hating feminists, bent upon upturning the patriarchal status quo." Dom Moraes's biography of Indira Gandhi (1980) illustrates this point well.

The biographer notes that the acceptance of Gandhi by the Indian male public was "uncomplicated" because "she was a widow, the mother of sons, and she was powerful, like the mother of a household to which a young man returned." Thus, the sanctity that Gandhi's identity as a mother gave her made her palatable to a polity unaccustomed to female leadership. Some female candidates actively portrayed themselves as mothers.

For example, Chandrika Kumaratunga of Sri Lanka, during her campaign for the 1994 election that swept her into power by a landslide, often incorporated her identity as a widowed mother of two into her political rhetoric. Thus, she invoked the popular Sri Lankan literary theme of the "sacrificing mother" to legitimize her candidacy. The perceptions of Kumaratunga and Indira Gandhi by their respective polities illustrate how South and Southeast Asian cultures recognized and embraced the trope of motherhood as a legitimizing influence on the candidates' identities.

However, this raises the question of whether this identity alone was enough for these polities to vote for a woman. Upon analyzing these women's paths to power, a significant pattern emerges that indicates that another factor aided their elections:

almost all of the women rose to power in the midst of a period when their countries were experiencing a significant crisis in governance.

This largely consistent pattern of South and Southeast Asian women's elections during times of crisis is rooted in the electorate's perception of these women as mothers, and the adulation and respect that the candidates accrue from this maternal identity. Perceptions of female candidates as "maternal" or "caring" become more potent and relevant when the polity is weary and resentful of instability or illegitimacy. Indeed, many of these candidates actively portrayed themselves as the redemptive alternative to the presiding government.

For example, when Megawati Sukarnoputri ran against the Suharto regime, she referred to herself as "Mother Mega" and won the public's acceptance as a figure that would "genuinely care for and soothe an Indonesian public that felt abandoned by the state." Indira Gandhi, upon her accession to power, was also expected to have a similar cleansing influence on the government; the Indian populace idealized her and looked to her to clean up the game of dirty, corrupt politics. Thus, by invoking the maternal metaphor, the candidates both posited themselves and gained acceptance as the anti-thesis of and solution to the illegitimacy and instability that characterized the presiding regimes.

This redemptive attribute of motherhood and its applications to the elections of female candidates is a common theme in the political cultures of this region. The public evaluates the identities of these female candidates in the context of these ancient mythologies and traditions that speak of the "savior mother." For example, the Filipino mythological character, Inang Bayan (mother of the land), who represents aspirations of justice and independence during times of turmoil was frequently compared by the popular media to the role that Corazon Aquino played in ousting Ferdinand Marcos.

A Sri Lankan cook's testimony during the run-up to Kumaratunga's election victory also indicates that the general populace made this connection between the candidate's identity as a mother and the palliative that motherhood bestows: "As a mother she is well-equipped to understand the problems of the island, because she sees them in the light of paticca - samuppada (the Buddhist concept of regarding relations through compassion, a motherly virtue)". Thus, the female candidates' identities as mothers emerge as a political advantage in their elections to heads of state. Even though they were acting in the predominantly male realm of politics, they were doing so in the highly legitimate, symbolic role of the mother.

The patriarchies of the region, influenced by mythology and tradition, had created a concept of motherhood that represented incorruptibility and loving care, characteristics that became more potent and relevant during times of crisis. The circumstances in which women won elections as chief executives in these countries have been overwhelmingly those that were marked by high crises in governance.

This shows that the trope of mother hood as articulated by the political cultures of the South and Southeast Asian region have aided these women in their elections. Other Patriarchal Perceptions of Women Along with the prevalent notion of perceiving female candidates in the light of motherhood, other patriarchal cultural constructs have also aided these women in their ascendance to the office of chief executive. Many South and Southeast Asian women were elected to office upon the death of a related male political figure, such as a husband in the case of Sirimavo Bandaranaike, or a father in the case of Aung San Suu Kyi.

The bereavement these candidates experienced as women elicited sympathy from a patriarchal populace that views them as fragile and weak. These attitudes towards these women have garnered them "the sympathy vote." That political parties of these countries are cognizant of this effect recently widowed candidates have on voting behavior is well illustrated by the 1994 presidential election in Sri Lanka, in which the widowed Chandrika Kumaratunga ran against Srima Dissanayaka, who lost her husband (who was a minister and frontrunner in the opposition party at the time of death) to murder several weeks before the election.

Corazon Aquino, whose husband was murdered by her rival's regime, observes the South and Southeast Asian electorates' tendency to grant sympathy votes to widows thus: "It's very simple. I just tell my sad story, and people weep...(her party) had to present somebody who has been a victim... and I am the best-known victim." Another political cultural aspect that underscores the patriarchy that pervades these countries is the tendency of political parties to nominate women (who will potentially garner votes by virtue of their identities as widows or mothers), as candidates for the chief executive because the male party "veterans" believe that as women they will be easily malleable and could be influenced to carry out these party members' agendas.

For instance, the "Old Guard" of the Congress Party who considered Indira Gandhi to be a "chit of a girl" pushed for her candidacy because they thought that she could be easily manipulated than the usual pool of ambitious and ruthless male politicians. Indeed, certain female heads of state, such as Sirimavo Bandaranaike, were clearly influenced by the powerful males in their respective parties.

While this aspect of political culture that views women as "malleable" does not directly speak to the larger polities' electoral decisions (because the motives of these "party uncles" are mostly kept to themselves), it is important in that it increases a woman's chances of nomination as a candidate. For example, in the case of Bangladesh's Begum Khalida Zia, she admits that she would not have considered running for office had the party not requested her to do so.

Since, in many of these cases of female candidacies, party veterans thrust power upon them or the public requested them to take up the mantle of leadership, the electorates perceive these women as "self-effacing" and "modest," as opposed to the stereotypical male politicians who follow a self-initiated and ambitious path to power. Indeed, this quality of modesty is an essential cultural element of the women of this region.

A Burmese shopkeeper articulated his appreciation of this quality in Aung San Suu Kyi thus: "She speaks with modesty. When we listen to government leaders and then to her, I think every Burmese can agree about who is the better person." Another illustration of the public approval of this characteristic is the instance when Sonia Gandhi, following her convincing election victory in 2004, renounced power as India's prime minister, the public media hailed her action as "a noble vedantic renunciation" and even honored her by referring to her as "Saint Sonia" and "Gandhi the Mahatma."

Indeed, many of these women, upon being approached by various quarters to take up power, have made it known that they initially declined the offer, but later reversed their decision by making statements such as that made by Sheikh Hasina Wajed: "When one of the MPs called me to inform me that I was appointed (as candidate) I was very angry. But they needed me. I felt it was my duty."

The facts that these women were offered the reins of the state (as opposed to them seeking it for themselves), that they initially refused it, and that they later took up the offer for "higher purposes" indicate to the electorates that these women are modest and do not pursue politics for personal gain. Thus, they stand in stark relief, as the more trustworthy alternative, to the corrupt male politicians to whom the polities of this region are accustomed. Affinity for Charismatic Leaders Max Weber defines charisma as "a certain quality or qualities of an individual personality by virtue of which he (or she) is set apart from ordinary men (and women) and treated as endowed with supernatural, superhuman, or at least specifically exceptional powers or qualifications."

Weber also argues that individuals may claim legitimate authority based on charismatic grounds. Loewenstein (1965), commenting upon Weber's notions of charisma, observes that charismatic leadership is most likely to be found "in those areas of the world in which a popular belief in supernatural powers is still widespread, as in some parts of Asia and Africa." Indeed, in South and Southeast Asia the appeal of "personality" is part of a general emphasis on person-centered politics. (This contrasts with the emphasis on the politics of "issues," for which North Americans pronounce a preference.)

The polities of this region often worship charismatic leaders as heroes. The social forces of religion and tradition sanction this idolatry of leaders. For instance, in Buddhist Southeast Asia, religious belief dictates that those in authority deserve their high status because of their good karma. Also, in the Hindu tradition, the concept of the *deva-raja* (god-king) maintains that the magical powers inherent in rulers provide the basis for their political authority. In these ancient worldviews, the political order is a microcosm of the cosmic order.

Therefore, the ruler is to his or her kingdom as God is to the cosmos. Today the leaders of this region continue to wrap themselves in these traditional metaphors that establish and affirm their charismatic authority. Close analysis of this concept of charisma reveals that the identities of the female chief executives in the South and Southeast Asian region and the circumstances in which they arose to power conform to many elements that bestow charismatic authority upon them. Weber qualifies charismatic authority as a force that is "sharply opposed to bureaucratic and to traditional authority, whether in its patriarchal, patrimonial or any other form... it repudiates the past and is a specifically revolutionary force."

Even though the female heads of state of this region benefited from patriarchal norms (such as the trope of motherhood) in legitimizing and enhancing their ascensions to power, their very presence in the highest echelon of governance, poses a challenge to the status quo of this male dominated realm. This is especially true when these women, now in power, deviate (with varying degrees of success) from the patriarchal scripts that were written for them during their elections. This became evident when leaders like Benazir Bhutto actively tried to change the greater patriarchal social structure through legislation and when Indira Gandhi gave little heed to the recommendations of the male Old Guard of the Congress Party.

Since these women offered their candidacies as the alternative to the corrupt and authoritarian regimes that they were running against, they conform to Weber's definition of "prophets":" individual bearers of charisma, who by virtue of their missions proclaim commandment. "As symbols of "feminine, maternal attributes" they heralded a fundamental change in governance and have thus taken on the role of the prophet, and indeed, as Weber notes, follow the "fluid transition from prophet to legislator."

Also, since Weber's concept of charisma is born out of "suffering and conflict," and as mentioned before, these women have endured bereavement and persecution in the midst of a general atmosphere of national crisis, these adverse circumstances further enhance their appeal as hallowed individuals worthy of charismatic authority. Thus, in respect of their presence in the traditional male sphere of politics, the reformist orientations that they bring to office, and the adverse personal conditions within which they arose to power, these women leaders have repudiated the patriarchal scripts that define traditional authority in this region, and thus acquire charismatic authority.

Another factor that gives these women charismatic authority in the eyes of the public are their biological relationships to former male leaders, most of whom were slain and subsequently considered martyrs. Weber explains this as charisma that is "routinized through heredity," which refers to a public recognition that is no longer necessarily connected to the charismatic qualities of the individual, but to the legitimacy of the position that he or she has acquired by hereditary succession. This was especially true of Sirimavo Bandaranaike who was largely considered to lack in charisma but was able to invoke her husband's name and political agenda to bolster her legitimacy as a candidate.

An Indian newspaper comments on the manifestation of this aspect of Indian politics: "In India the easiest way for a woman to enter politics is to marry a politician." While Bandaranaike, Corazon Aquino and Indira Gandhi invoked the name of their deceased spouses, in the cases of Aung San Suu Kyi, Benazir Bhutto and Megawati Sukarnoputri, the personas of their fathers, which were firmly connected to the respective independence struggles of their countries, were often invoked during these women's election campaigns. The charisma of these women is essentially a function of the public's perception of them. Indeed, a leader is charismatic insofar as the followers recognize his or her charisma.

Public attitudes towards these female leaders during their election campaigns and the initial period of their governance show that, their charisma was well recognized. The following account of Corazon Aquino's election well illustrates this point: "Filipino culture invited the reassuring intervention of a charismatic leader...This helps explain the meteoric rise of Corazon Aquino from "simple housewife" to beloved leader in a very few months." Thus, the political cultures of this region show warm acceptance of political figures who, through attributes of their own or through attributes routinized through heredity, are perceived as charismatic.

PUBLIC REGARD OF ELITE DYNASTIES

As discussed, female heads of state in this region acquire a high public regard, that partly stems from charisma that is routinized through their relationships with prominent male political figures. Since all of these women followed their male relatives to power, their respective polities regard them as elements of political elite dynasties. However, with regard to the women's connections to these dynasties, routinized charisma is not the only factor that contributes to their high level of public support. These women leaders hail from long-established elite families that command recognition and respect in their respective societies.

Historically, traditional indigenous hierarchies like caste systems, prevalent in many of the countries in this region, have created and nurtured their elite status. In Sri Lanka, where the vast majority of members of parliament and heads of state (including the two women heads of state), have been of the higher govigama caste, a candidate's caste affiliation emerges as an extremely important factor for general voters in making their electoral decision. The common experience of colonialism in these countries further strengthened the elites' hold on political power. For example, the Spanish colonizers of the Philippines controlled land through the elites, thus increasing the rest of the polity's dependence on these local "middlemen."

The elites and the masses in these countries interact in the context of patron-client relations. This serves as a tangible mode of creating authority. Wurfel (1988) illustrates this relationship with regard to the Philippines: "Peasants and their urban cousins have a deferential style towards elite authority figures. This deference is in part habitual, demanded by generations of patrons. It is also calculating, both because of the favors it helps earn and because of the trouble it avoids." Thus, the deference to elites by the masses is also based on material relations as well as the more intangible effects of routinized charisma.

During colonial times, the elites of this region had the opportunity to acquire an education in the colonial tradition. Thus, the elite's ability to communicate in colonial tongues widened the divide between the elite and the "commoner." Also, as colonial education acculturated the elite in the colonial ways, they became more separate from the masses on both a cultural and economical level. Ironically, the masses still looked to these elites to represent their interests in government. This paradox is partly explained by the great value that is attributed by the cultures of this region to education, coupled with the fact that the elites were those who were equipped with the best education.

Today, the educational systems in these countries mirror the inequalities in opportunity between the elite and non-elite. Another modern manifestation of this situation is reflected in the elite's ability to use their wealth to educate their children in Western countries. Thus, the non-elites of these countries have been denied opportunities that were enjoyed by the elites, and continue to be misrepresented by these elites who are culturally and economically separated and have little empathy towards the "commoners" situation. However, these masses profess relatively high satisfaction towards the system that maintains their dependence on the elite.

Generations of social inequality created by indigenous caste systems, nurtured by colonialism, and manifested today in lop-sided educational opportunities have created an inferiority complex on the part of the masses towards elite dynasties to which the female heads of state of the region belong to. Patron-client relations provide the material underpinning of these inequities. Indeed, this public attitude of deference towards the traditional elite is a significant characteristic of the political culture of this region.

This attribute has contributed to the public perception of these patrician women as legitimate figures of authority. It is an extension of the deference that the masses have been showing to the elite dynasties upon which they have dependent for generations. Thus, public regard of elite dynasties emerges as a significant explanatory factor of the election of these women to power.

PUBLIC EXPERIENCE OF THE EFFECTS OF COLONIALISM

All of the countries that these female leaders come from have a history of colonization by Western powers. As these colonial powers established themselves in these South and Southeast Asian countries, they socialized the local polities in their own political values. With regard to gender issues, the colonial values often clashed with the patriarchal norms that relegated women to a subservient social role. However, these values implemented through the policies of the colonial government and the actions of other influential colonial individuals forced these patriarchal societies to confront their treatment of women.

These early inroads to the emancipation of women made the polities of these countries more familiar with the public presence of women and their political participation, and have thus contributed to the rise of the female heads of state of the region. The educational institutions established by the colonials in these countries encouraged discussion of gender issues and taught upper class locals to question the subjection of women.

Although the elite following of these liberal attitudes could be interpreted as their desire to emulate Victorian moral codes (a practice that labeled these elites as "Brown Sahibs"), rather than a result of genuine concern for the situation of their countrywomen, this Western education introduced the debate of gender issues to these societies. Prior to this, gender relations remained frozen in sacred laws and customs. Although this education was largely limited to the upper classes of the colonies, as these elites assumed power post-independence, they instituted policies that would reflect their liberal attitudes.

Policies such as the introduction of formal schooling for women ensured that the effects of this colonial education trickled down to the larger polity as well. Policies followed by the colonizers themselves also helped to familiarize the local polities in the gradual process of granting social and political rights to women. These policies were especially evident in India where the British colonial government banned the deep-rooted Hindu traditions of child marriage and the self-immolation of widows called sati. Additionally, widow remarriage, previously castigated by pious Hindus as an "illegitimate desire," was made legal. The British also initiated the movement for women's education in both Sri Lanka and India (and therefore, the states that are now known as Pakistan and Bangladesh, but were part of India at the time), a right denied to these women by the system of *purdah*, or concealment of women from the public eye. Furthermore, against the wishes of Indian nationalists, the colonial government imposed a quota system for female legislators in the Indian legislature, a policy that has endured throughout the post-Independence period. The modern form of this policy reserves 30% of the seats in the legislature for women.

Along with the above effects of the colonial experience, the polities of these countries were also influenced by prominent figures in the colonial society. One such figure was Annie Besant, an Englishwoman who went to India to lobby for the rights of Indian women during British rule. Her efforts were instrumental to the realization of equal suffrage for Indian women in 1921, seven years before British women were given this same right. The effect Besant had on the local polity was evident in the tribute she received in the widely circulated daily Hindu: "Annie Besant has proved that women can indeed be noble and great."

Thus, the experience of colonialism exposed the polities of these countries to liberal attitudes towards gender issues. While these attitudes, implemented through policy by both the colonial and post-independence governments, were unpopular among the large conservative, patriarchal segments of society, they did acclimatize the polity to the notion of female political participation and leadership. While the public experience of the effects of colonialism certainly did not make the respective political cultures approve the emergence of women into the public sphere, it did make the political culture more tolerant of female political participation.

Whereas previously, gender relations were not the subject of public debate, Western colonial influence provided the catalyst for addressing the situation of women. Thus, the post-independence political culture of these countries has embraced the tension between patriarchy and the movement for female political efficacy, and is now represented by strong local advocates for both sides of the debate. These progressive changes that have come about in the political cultures of this region made the electorates more conducive to accept the women leaders discussed in this chapter as the heads of their respective states.

This chapter has demonstrated the interaction between political culture and the emergence of female heads of state in the South and Southeast Asian region. Patriarchal notions such as the cult of motherhood, warm acceptance of charismatic leadership, public regard of elite dynasties and public experience of the liberal agendas of colonial rulers are all aspects of the political cultures of this region that have aided in paving the electoral paths to power followed by these exceptional women. While political cultural attributes may influence political decisions, they do not necessarily determine them.

Therefore, the evaluations of the political cultural variables presented in this study must be regarded as complementary explanations to other institutional and structural variables. Indeed, the aggregate effect of these disparate factors must be considered in order to fully explain complex phenomena such as the election of female chief executives in patriarchal societies. This chapter has dealt with these female leaders' respective ascensions to the highest echelon of power. However, there is much evidence that suggests that the political cultural aspects that enabled these women to win elections have also contributed to the women's difficulties in consolidating their authority while in power.

Indeed, as Thompson observes, "the ideology of patriarchy dictates that to topple a corrupt regime (as many of these women leaders have done) is one thing, to run a country another." These women's inability to establish their authority as heads of state is evident in the prevalence of both military uprisings against and political infighting within their respective regimes. This particular relationship between South and Southeast Asian political culture and female leadership at the stage when these women assumed office as heads of state provides a potential logical extension to this study.

4

Reproductive Health in Southeast Asia

In the last decade, the life expectancy of the population has shown a remarkable improvement. The world has witnessed the development of revolutionary medical breakthroughs. Yet, despite the significant progress that has been made to prevent and control communicable diseases, 585,000 women continue to die around the world every year from pregnancy and childbirth-related complications. Of these, the WHO South-East Asia Region accounts for nearly 40% or 235,000 maternal deaths - an unacceptably high percentage of the total.

A large number of maternal deaths can be prevented. The means to prevent these deaths are known, the skills and the technology to address the problems are simple and available locally. What is missing are the matching infrastructure, resources and the will to act resolutely. WHO believes that partnerships employing the public health approach can work most effectively in promoting and protecting the reproductive health of populations, particularly women and adolescents who are the more vulnerable sections of society.

Linkages between different health Programmes and services must be created. Quality heath care must be ensured to women throughout their lifespan, and not just the reproductive years. For, good reproductive health-begins with the birth of a baby, and that, in turn, is dependent on the health and general well-being of its mother and her worth in society. Moreover, every delivery must be attended by trained personnel who can recognize complications and provide timely interventions to save lives.

Women are the very foundation of society, and the fulcrum around which the family's welfare revolves. We owe it to them and to the well-being of our future generations to protect and promote their, reproductive health rights. WHO is committed to helping Member Countries with strengthening reproductive health-care services. We hope that this information booklet will enable those concerned about reproductive healthy, including individuals, families and communities, to address this issue effectively.

REPRODUCTIVE HEALTH

WHO defines 'Reproductive Health' as "a state of complete physical, mental and social well-being and not merely the absence of disease or infirmity in all matters relating to the reproductive system and its functions and processes. Reproductive health, therefore, implies that people are able to have a satisfying and safe sex life and that they have the freedom to decide if, when and how often to do so. Implicit in this last condition is the right of men and women to be informed of and to have access to safe, effective, affordable and acceptable methods of family planning as well as other methods of their choice for regulation of fertility which are not against the law, and the right of access to appropriate health- care services that will enable women to go safely through pregnancy and childbirth and provide couples with the best chance of having a healthy infant."

REPRODUCTIVE ILL-HEALTH

Although the last decade has seen a marked improvement in survival and a significant reduction in infant mortality in the countries of the South-East Asia Region (SEAR), similar achievements have not been made in the fields of maternal health. Maternal mortality remains high in all countries of the Region except in DPR Korea, Sri Lanka and Thailand.

Pregnancy is not a disease, yet over 585,000 women continue to the each year from pregnancy-related complications, and the majority of them are in developing countries. Of the 585,000 deaths each year from maternal causes, nearly 40 per cent of them are from the SEAR countries. The numbers are unacceptably high in Bangladesh- Bhutan. India, Indonesia, Nepal, the Maldives and Myanmar.

FACTORS CONTRIBUTING TO REPRODUCTIVE ILL-HEALTH

There is a complex interplay of socioeconomic, environmental, and cultural factors that contribute to the reproductive ill-health of populations, particularly women, in developing countries. Poverty, ignorance, illiteracy and malnutrition are major determinants of women's health status.

Also significant are the age at marriage and pregnancy, the number an frequency of childbearing, and the numbers of unwanted pregnancies and abortions that contribute to morbidity and mortality among women and their babies. The lower the status and worth of women in society, the higher the maternal mortality. And, not least important, are the health service-related factors such as lack of access to quality reproductive health services.

SITUATION IN SEAR COUNTRIES

The high maternal mortality in the Region is primarily a syndrome of the failure and neglect of women by society. Amongst the health service-related factors, poor coverage and quality of antenatal care, lack of trained assistance during delivery, lack of access to essential emergency obstetric services for high-risk and complicated cases, and lack of referral and transport system, are major reasons.

Reproductive health status:

- Globally, WHO estimates that reproductive ill health accounts for 36.6 per cent of the total disease burden in women as compared to 12.3 per cent for men of the same age.
- The mean age at marriage in most SEAR countries continues

to be low and data shows that maternal mortality is three to four times in the 15-19 year age group compared to the 20-30 year group.

- Antenatal care and trained attendance delivery varies from 18 to 97% and from 6 to 97%, respectively.
- Available age-specific fertility data show that women in Bangladesh, India and Nepal have early peak patterns, with fertility highest for women aged 20-24 years and with more than 50% of women giving birth by the age of 20.
- Prevalence of anaemia in pregnant women varies in the Region and is estimated to be from less than 20% in Thailand to over 60% in Bangladesh, India and Nepal.
- The proportion of infertility caused by reproductive tract infection is estimated at 15 to 40%.
- Contraceptive prevalence for the Region is estimated to be 40%.
- It is estimated that abortions contribute to about 13% of maternal mortality in the Region.
- HIV infection among pregnant women vanes from 1 to 8% in various parts of SEAR countries.

OBJECTIVES OF RH PROGRAMMES

The objectives of Reproductive Health Programmes are to ensure that people benefit from the enabling conditions necessary information and care so that they can:

- Have the capacity for healthy, equitable and responsible relationships and experience healthy sexual development and maturation;
- Achieve their reproductions intentions - the desired number and timing of children - safely and healthfully;
- Avoid illness, disease and disability related to sexuality and reproduction and receive appropriate counseling, care and rehabilitation when needed; and
- Avoid injuries related to sexuality and reproduction and receive appropriate counseling when needed.

Vulnerable points in reproductive health:

- A woman's general health is the outcome and reflection of her own health status as a newborn which, in turn, is determined by her mother's health status during pregnancy, during and just after delivery.
- There are three critical points at which intervention is required in order that the health of women, children and families is not compromised. These critical points are at birth, during adolescence, and during the reproductive years.
- Thus, though at each stage of life, an individual's needs differ, there is a cumulative effect across the lifespan - events at each phase having important implications for future well-being.
- Reproductive health must, therefore, be promoted, protected and restored by social as well as medical interventions across the lifespan of individuals, particularly women, using the "Lifespan Approach".

REGIONAL RH STRATEGY

A Regional reproductive health strategy for South-East Asia was developed through a consultative meeting and consensus involving Member Countries, relevant UN agencies and NGOs in 1996. It was observed that SEAR countries still had very high levels of maternal mortality, low contraceptive prevalence and unsafe abortions contributing to high MMR, high prevalence of STDs and a large number of adolescent pregnancies. Therefore, an essential package of priority interventions focusing on the reproductive age group was identified and recommended by levels of care within the context of primary health care as a short-term Programme.

The essential RH package for SEAR countries defines the minimum services in priority areas for each level of care - community level, health post level, health center level and district level. The essential RH package consists of: safe motherhood, family planning, prevention and management of reproductive tract infections including sexually transmitted diseases, prevention and treatment of complications of abortion, and adolescent health. The meeting suggested a comprehensive RH package involving the lifespan perspective. This package also addresses problems like violence, reproductive, tract cancers and problems of the elderly as a long-term Programme.

NATIONAL RH STRATEGIES

Since all of the reproductive health issues cannot be effectively addressed immediately, the SEAR countries have prioritized interventions which have the highest impact on the reduction of reproductive morbidity and maternal mortality.

COUNTRY PROGRAMMES

SEAR countries have adapted the Regional framework according to their national priorities:

Bangladesh

Bangladesh has identified an essential package of basic services which includes reproductive health:

- The strategy is based on client's needs, especially women's, client-orientation, quality of services and informed choice, investing in women's groups and provision of information and services for young people, including adolescents.
- The goals are to prevent adolescent pregnancies, postpone births, enhance services for safe pregnancy and delivery, including fertility regulation, treatment of abortion patients and managing reproductive morbidity and mortality, including STD/RTIs.

Bhutan

Bhutan has identified priority RH interventions for the community, basic health units and outreach services, and for regional and national referral hospitals:

- The government is committed to the safe motherhood Programme and expanded choices for FP methods and ensuring appropriate actions at intersectional and interministerial levels.

India

India has reoriented it's existing Family Planning and Child Survival and Safe Motherhood Programmes and integrated them in the Reproductive and Child Health (RCH) package:

- The RCH package has been defined by the four levels of care. The states are using the target-free approach to family planning and propose a decentralized planning exercise for, RH Programmes.
- Efforts are under way to develop training materials including RTI into FP/MCH services.

Indonesia

In Indonesia, a multi-sectoral national RH Committee has been set up. This committee facilitates implementation of essential reproductive health care through functional integration of various existing Programmes using the incremental approach:

- Highest priority is given for reduction of maternal mortality. Other priority RH Programmes include family planning, STD/RTI/ adolescent health.
- In addition, the Indonesian strategy promotes the involvement of men and family members as effective partners.

Myanmar

The Myanmar RH strategy focuses on expanding family planning services, strengthening maternal care, and training MCH staff on the management of reproductive tract infections:

- The Programme also included enhancing public awareness and community involvement in RH Programmes.

Nepal

In Nepal, the RH strategy, has defined 'reproductive health' as an approach which will strengthen the existing Safe Motherhood and Family Planning Programmes through a multi-sectoral approach and development of necessary linkages with other Programmes:

- Nepal is using the incremental approach through the addition of other components, e.g. STD/RTI/infertility and adolescent health.
- Nepal has added a fifth level - the family level - to the other four levels of rare.

Sri Lanka and Thailand

Sri Lanka and Thailand have brought down MMR, and have achieved a high Contraceptive Prevalence Rate (CPR). Therefore, the RH Programmes are focusing on development of adolescent health services.

ESSENTIAL RH PACKAGE BY LEVELS OF CARE WITHIN PHC

The essential RH package for SEAR countries defines the minimum services in priority areas for each level of care. The levels of care include community level, health post level, health center and district level. The regional strategy also identified areas in training, information, communications and research needed to support the implementation of the strategy.

PRIORITY RH INTERVENTIONS

The priority reproductive health interventions identified in the strategy are:

- Safe motherhood, including care of the new-born;
- Family planning;
- Prevention and management of complications of abortion;
- Adolescent reproductive health; and
- Prevention and management of Reproductive Tract Infections/Sexually Transmitted Diseases (RTI/STD).

SAFE MOTHERHOOD

Though safe motherhood is a high priority Programme in all countries of the Region, many countries are unable to ensure all deliveries are attended by trained personnel and there are still obstacles which cause delays in obtaining emergency obstetric care in case of complications. Midwifery-trained personnel have crucial roles at various levels in PHCs in providing clean/safe delivery services at each level. Midwifery-trained personnel in the SEAR context include various categories of auxiliaries, e.g. ANMs, MCH workers, family welfare visitors, family welfare assistants, etc.

Effective community-based midwifery services and referral system and advocacy and multi-sectoral social action should ensure that all negative socio-cultural barriers are removed and emergency obstetric care is accessible, affordable and available to pregnant women when and where needed.

FAMILY PLANNING

The Contraceptive Prevalence Rate (CPR) has increased impressively in all countries of the Region and fertility is coming down with the small family norm becoming accepted by a majority of the countries. However, the CPR is low when compared to the high awareness levels about family planning. There are unmet needs because of several reasons such as lack of contraceptive choices, and cultural and economic barriers. The challenge is to fulfil these unmet needs at the earliest.

ADOLESCENT/YOUNG PEOPLE'S REPRODUCTIVE HEALTH

WHO defines adolescents as those aged between 10 and 19 and young people of 10 to 24. In many countries of the Region, early marriage and childbearing trends pose reproductive health problems. The use of contraceptives is lowest amongst women where the need is higher. Maternal mortality ratio amongst the 15-19 year age group is higher than those in over 20 years. Even when the age of marriage is higher, unprotect sexual relations amongst unmarried adolescents leads to unwanted pregnancies and abortions, oftentimes hazardous conditions, leading to maternal deaths.

Another major consequence of unprotected sex in adolescence is the risk of infection from a sexually transmitted disease. Thought reliable data are not available, it is known that adolescents are specially vulnerable to STD/HIV because of their high-risk behavior.

Reproductive health of young people (10-24 yrs.)					
Country	10-24 yrs as % total population	Average age at first marriage (females)	% currently married (females)	% giving birth by age 20 (15-19 yrs)	% using contraceptive (15-19 yrs)
BAN	34	18	48	66	25
IND	30	20	38	49	07
NEP	32	17.9	50	50	01
SRL	29	24.4	07	60	20
INO	31	21.1	17	33	36
MMR	30	22.4	16	--	--
THA	30	22.7	16	24	43

(Source: The World's Youth, Population Reference Bureau)

With the recent recognition of the special vulnerability of adolescents, adolescent health Programmes are currently operational in Bangladesh, India, Indonesia, Myanmar, Sri Lanka and Thailand.

PREVENTION AND MANAGEMENT OF COMPLICATIONS OF ABORTION

It is estimated that abort-ions contribute to about 13% of maternal mortality in the Region. Most abortions are induced when there is an unwanted pregnancy. This is attributed to the clandestine abortion practices prevalent in many countries where abortion is not legal or where safe abortion services are not accessible.

Therefore, prevention of unwanted pregnancy through counseling, emergency contraception and greater use of FP services is the key to the prevention of abortion. Where this is not possible, safe abortion services should be made accessible and affordable within the cultural context of the country.

RTI/STD/PREVENTION OF INFERTILITY

Nearly 50 million sexually-transmitted infections occur annually in SEAR countries. Incidence of curable STDs in SEAR countries varies from 7 to 9 cases per 100 women in the reproductive age. WHO has developed the syndromic approach for the treatment of STDs.

However, in many countries STD services are run in clinics which cater mostly to men. To address the issue of RTI/STD among women, RTI/STD services should be integrated with FP/MCH services in the context of PHC. Orientation and training of MCH/PHC workers in STD/RTI needs to be provided.

IMPLEMENTATION OF RH STRATEGY

A public health approach to reproductive health within the context of primary health care, is recommended. Such an approach responds to people's needs and involves them in Programme formulation, implementations monitoring and evaluation so that a strong feeling of ownership is established. It seeks sustainable strategies and actions that have the greatest impact for the most people at an affordable price. It includes women's empowerment and gender perspective as an integral component.

The public health approach recognizes that:

- An individual's reproductive health affects, and is affected by, factors other than health-care interventions - such as the economic circumstances, family and social environment, cultural and religious beliefs, traditional and legal structure within which they live, and their access to education and employment.
- Gender relationships and sexual exploitation play a critical role in determining the reproductive health status of women.

The reproductive health strategy, therefore, advocates the integrated approach- stressing the importance of free, informed decision-making in reproductive health issues. It stipulates that people themselves must be involved in the development of services as partners.

GENDER PERSPECTIVE AND WHD

In applying a gender approach to health, WHO moves beyond describing women and women's health in isolation to bring into the analysis how different social roles, decision-making powers and access to resources between women and men affect their health and access to health care. In a gender approach leads to a consideration of all factors that affect women's health, not only biological factors; more attention to all of women's roles and relationships across their lifespan; more attention to the roles and responsibilities of men and the inequalities between men and women; and more involvement of men in bringing about change. The WHO Programme on Women, Health and Development (WHD) aims to address the critical issues of women's health within this broader context and their vital role in development and to integrate a gender perspective in national health Programmes. Key activities focus on advocacy - especially for emerging or previously neglected WHD issues - information dissemination, gender training and compilation of WHD country profiles in collaboration with all countries in the Region, to address the need for reliable and gender disaggregated information.

ROLE OF WHO

WHO collaborates with Member Countries in the following broad areas:

- Advocacy and technical cooperation with countries for strengthening RH Programmes at various levels.
- Promotions and support for operational research aimed at Programme improvement.
- Development of training Programmes at regional and country levels.
- Development of prototypes and training materials to be adapted by countries.

THE ROLE OF GOVERNMENT

Governments should adopt healthy public policies that:

- Advocate intensively for health, especially for family and reproductive health.

- Ensure quality health services for women, children and families.
- Create conditions to promote health, particularly those of women and children.
- Ensure quality and relevance of training for health personnel in reproductive health.
- Strengthen epidemiological surveillance and health information.
- Strengthen existing partnerships and forge new ones for health development at all levels.
- Ensure adequate access to food and proper nutritional status.

THE ROLE OF INDIVIDUALS AND COMMUNITIES

WHO emphasizes partnerships to promote reproductive health. Key interventions for better reproductive health that can be promoted by individuals families, communities, health-care workers, policy makers and the media:

Role of individuals:

- Individuals, both men and women, should practice and promote family planning - too many, too early, too frequent, or too late or unplanned pregnancies can affect a woman's health. To avoid unwanted pregnancies and STDs, they should practice safe sex, and women should adopt hygienic practices during menstruation.
- Pregnant women should eat adequate quantities of nutritious foods with pulses, legumes and green, leafy vegetables along with meat and milk products when available.
- They should recognize the danger signals during pregnancy and seek help when needed.

Role of families and communities:

- Communities should discourage discrimination against the girl child. They should ensure equitable access to heath care, educational and recreational opportunities to boys and girls.
- Community leaders should advocate and promote delaying the age at marriage and first pregnancy and childbirth to

save lives. Early marriage educational and future employment opportunities.

- Communities should ensure that women are accorded equity and respect - a woman's worth determines her health status.

Role of health workers:

- They must provide appropriate education and counseling to enable people to promote RH and prevent RH problems.
- They must provide reproductive health care and arrange appropriate referrals when needed.
- They should involve communities in the planning and implementation of RH services.
- They must adopt a client-oriented approach in providing health services.

Role of NGOs:

- NGOs should try to influence social attitudes towards women.
- They should advocate the rights of the girl child and the special reproductive health needs of women.
- NGOs should also provide RH services which are complementary to government efforts.

Role of media:

- Media should strive to generate social action to end discrimination against the girl child. They should plan advocacy role to abhor violence and social injustice against women, and provide adequate health services to women.
- They can highlight the need for improved reproductive health practices through articles, features and advocacy.
- They can document success stories in the Region.

Reproductive health is a crucial part of general health and is central to development. It affects everybody and involves intimate and highly valued aspects of life. Not only is it a reflection of health in infancy, childhood and adolescence, it also sets the stage for both women and men to achieve healthy reproduction, and has pronounced effects from one generation to another.

International agreements affirm that adolescents have a right to age-appropriate sexual and reproductive health information, education, and services that enable them to deal in a positive and responsible way with their sexuality. Programmes and policies are typically designed for older adolescents, however. This brief-part of the International Women's Health Coalition's series on young adolescents-uses evidence on their sexual and reproductive knowledge and behaviors to argue for more responsive policies and Programmes in South and Southeast Asia as well as globally.

We define all boys and girls between the ages of 10 and 14 as young adolescents. The countries of South and Southeast Asia encompass a richly layered mix of cultures, religions, languages, racial and ethnic groups, and economic and political systems. Although South and Southeast Asia are very different settings with regard to many aspects of adolescent sexual and reproductive health, there are also important commonalities.

Most young adolescents throughout the region have little if any accurate information about their bodies and their sexual and reproductive health. Known or suspected sexual contact of any kind by unmarried girls and women in some parts of South and Southeast Asia may result in personal censure, loss of family honor, or forced marriage.

SEXUAL INITIATION

Premarital sexual intercourse remains generally taboo, meaning that timing of first intercourse is often assumed to correspond with marriage and that direct evidence on premarital sexual relations is scarce. In South Asia, 26% of all Bangladeshi girls ages 15 - 19 were married at age 14 or younger compared with 14% in India, 9% in Nepal and 7% in Pakistan. Arranged marriages of girls before age 15 do appear to be declining in these countries. In Bangladesh and India, 6% and 2% of all girls ages 15 - 19 became mothers at age 14 or younger, most without the help of a skilled birth assistant. Maternal and newborn deaths and complications for these girls are common. In Nepal, 20% of all 15 – 19-year-old boys say they had heterosexual intercourse before age 15, often with sex workers, compared with very low proportions elsewhere.

Although evidence is scarce, ethnographic studies suggest that some boys in India, Bangladesh, and other South Asian countries engage in same-sex intercourse during adolescence. In Southeast Asia, very few girls ages 15 – 19 were married or say they had intercourse before age 15- from 3% in Indonesia to virtually none in Vietnam-and almost no girls had babies this young. In a survey of unmarried adolescents ages 15 – 19 throughout Vietnam, only 14% of boys and 19% of girls report ever having a girlfriend or boyfriend. Norms of sexual purity remain strong, resulting in very low reported levels of premarital sex before age 18 and virtually none before age 15. In a metropolitan region of the Philippines, adolescents begin dating in groups at ages 13 – 16.

Romantic relationships and physical intimacy are postponed to later adolescence: at ages 17 – 19, 30% of boys and 20% of girls report having intercourse, and higher proportions engaging in kissing, petting, and other intimacies. Among vocational students ages 15 – 21 in northern Thailand, approximately 2% of girls and 15% of boys report having sexual intercourse before age 15 and about 30% and 40%, respectively, by age 18. Early sexual initiation is associated with other risk-taking behaviors among both male and female students. In India, more than one-quarter of women in one sample who had been sexually abused were exposed to the abuse between the ages of 9 and 12.

Half were abused by more than one person and almost all were abused repeatedly. Similar patterns of incest and sexual abuse are reported throughout the literature, but it is challenging to provide representative data because of the hidden nature of the practice. Throughout South and Southeast Asia, girls from poor families are susceptible to being recruited or sold into prostitution by their families, which places them at high risk of HIV and other sexually transmitted infections (STIs). Boys are also vulnerable: in Sri Lanka, for example, a majority of child prostitutes are boys.

Sexual and reproductive health information, education, and services for adolescents are viewed as unnecessary or even morally dangerous throughout much of South and Southeast Asia. Widespread sexual taboos and the high value on premarital virginity, especially for girls and young women, means that little if any information is passed on from mothers to daughters until "needed." Boys may also be uninformed. Young brides in India are often shocked and frightened by their (sometimes forced) sexual initiation on their wedding night because they lack even the most basic knowledge of sexual relations. A sample of young adults ages 18 – 25 in Pakistan reported that the information they received about puberty and sexual development when they were younger often led to confusion and stress.

Young women learned most from female family members; young men from friends, family members, religious sources, magazines and films. Some young women said they had no information about sexual relations prior to their marriage. In Bangladesh, adolescents ages 12 and over enrolled in a non-governmental reproductive health Programme were eager for information about their bodies, romantic relationships, sex, pregnancy, family planning, and STIs. Much of what the boys already knew came from pornographic videos which they secretly watched with friends. In Bangladesh, India, and Indonesia, only 5% of married girls ages 15 – 19 know without prompting that condoms prevent HIV, and only 9% in the Philippines. In contrast, 24% of married girls ages 15 – 19 in Nepal and 65% of married boys know this. Far higher proportions of all 15 – 19-year-olds in Cambodia and Vietnam know that condoms prevent HIV, although many need prompting.

POLICY AND PROGRAMME RESPONSES

Evidence shows that withholding information and services from young people only increases the likelihood that if and when sexual initiation occurs, it will be unprotected. Young people require not only basic information about their bodies, preventing HIV/STIs, and pregnancy, but also Programmes that address gender equality, empowerment, rights and responsibilities, and sexual and reproductive negotiation and decision making. The meaningful participation of adolescents in the design of Programmes, laws, and policies that affect their sexual and reproductive lives should be guaranteed. Policies and Programmes to eliminate the marriages of girls 14 and younger and to promote delayed marriage and informed consent among older adolescents are urgently needed.

Sexuality education

High proportions of 10 - 14-year-olds are currently attending school in most countries in the region. Providing sex education in schools will require overcoming entrenched cultural conservatism and securing parental and community support at state and local levels. In India, in 2007, several states banned sex education, in spite of a national HIV/AIDS policy that supports such Programmes for young people.

Sexual and reproductive health services

Awareness-raising is required among public health providers and non-governmental organizations (NGOs) of the need for special clinics or Programmes for adolescents, especially where premarital sex is increasing. Laws prohibiting the provision of family planning services to unmarried adolescents should be eliminated in Indonesia, Vietnam, and wherever else they exist. Health care providers need to be trained to work with young adolescents and to be sensitive to the possibilities of incest and sexual abuse of both boys and girls. In countries where a substantial number of girls marry and give birth at 14 or younger, special efforts are needed to ensure that secluded, newly married girls obtain contraception for birth spacing and good prenatal care, and that their deliveries are assisted by trained birth attendants prepared to deal with emergencies such as hemorrhage and obstructed labor.

Other approaches

Some NGO Programmes and special government projects across the region (especially UNFPA-supported) are developing innovative methods of reaching young adolescents with accurate and nonjudgmental sexual and reproductive health information-such as media sources, out-of-school Programmes and the Internet. These and other approaches need to be evaluated with respect to their impact on the sexual and reproductive health and rights of young adolescents and their potential for adaptation in other settings.

Culture refers to beliefs, attitudes, values, behaviours and traditions that are learned and shared by virtue of membership and socialization in groups. Since these constituents of culture are not ascribed or sacrosanct, they are dynamic and are therefore prone to changes at the individual or group level as a result of exposure to new information and contexts, or acquisition of new needs or goals. Among the most determinative groups are the family, religions, ethnic and national groups. In addition to culture being learned and dynamic, an important element that is often contested is the extent of homogeneity of culture. Societies are comprised of groups varying on a range of socio-economic factors such as geographic location, religion, occupation, age and class categories, attesting to cultural diversity. So, for example, there are youth cultures, sports cultures and women's cultures.

The determinative factors are membership, or even aspiration to membership in a group, and sharing the group's values and behaviours. The reality of the contemporary world is that most societies are not only heterogeneous and multi-cultural but even individuals themselves embrace and exhibit multiple cultural identities through membership in different groups. Among other influences, globalization and information technology have contributed to this trend of multi-culturalism. Culture is complex and all-encompassing. It needs to be taken into consideration in all areas of social development, particularly when looking at education, economics, health and gender.

As a subject matter, culture has been and remains a topic of extensive theoretical, applied and policy research in many fields. To this end all development practitioners, including UN agencies, highlight cultural issues in their work and address it in their Programming. Recent examples of this include the UNDP 2004 Human Development Report, UNESCO's development of a comprehensive toolkit to address the issue of building cultural competence in health research and health delivery in varied Programming contexts, UNFPA 2004 document on Culture Matters , and the UNIFEM ESEA 2004-2007 Programme, which will facilitate the implementation of the Convention on the Elimination of All Forms of Discrimination Against Women (CEDAW) through varied approaches including 'cultural channels'. Additionally, the UNDP/UNFPA/WHO/World Bank Special Programme of Research has recently launched a new cross-cutting activity to promote optimal sexual health and an affirmative view of sexuality for women, men and young people. One of its two specific objectives is "to increase knowledge and understanding of the social and cultural factors related to harmful sexual practices in order to develop strategies to abolish these practices."

UNFPA FOCUS

Since the International Conference on Population and Development (ICPD) in 1994, UNFPA focus on culture has intensified and broadened, especially its linkage to issues of gender and reproductive health. Culture, along with gender and human rights, has increasingly become an important analytical and Programming tool. These three elements are closely interlinked and constitute an end as well as a powerful means to address the respective issues of gender inequality and inequity, human and reproductive rights, and cultural values and practices that are inimical to attainment of sustainable human development.

"Cultural and religious beliefs are the very essence of our individual and collective identities. They manifest themselves in different ways in the countries in which we work and in the lives and behaviour of the people who are the real stakeholders in development. We therefore need to better understand the parameters of cross-cultural encounters in the context of our development and humanitarian Programmes. And we must understand the opportunities and constraints that the differences in cultural values bring and how this understanding can inform our Programmes. UNFPA must therefore respond to increasing cultural challenges by helping countries, communities and individuals to link universal principles with their cultural values and by designing culturally-sensitive Programmes in systematic and well conceptualized ways that fit into different religious and cultural identities and understandings."

UNFPA views culture as a window of opportunity for the implementation of ICPD through partnerships with local power structures and institutions, to address issues of gender, human rights and reproductive health that are rooted in religion, traditions, customs and social practices. UNFPA 2004-2007 Multi-Year Funding Framework specifies, "Institutional mechanisms and socio-cultural practices promote and protect the rights of women and girls and advance gender equity" as one of its six outcomes towards achievement of ICPD and the MDGs.

SCOPE AND OBJECTIVES

This review is narrowly focused on illustrating the interface between culture, gender and reproductive health issues addressed by UNFPA. It draws attention to challenges and opportunities in terms of both issues and strategies that have implications for Programming interventions. There is need to understand that operationally, religion is just but one dimension of culture which may sometimes be so intertwined with other cultural traditions that it is not easy or possible to discern their respective influences. This is especially true in theocratic states while in others, which are secular, the distinction is clearer. Another important clarification is that reference to "cultural factors" for Programming, focuses on two elements:

1. Marginalization, discrimination, or stigmatization of groups on the basis of their unique cultural attributes and
2. The cultural beliefs and practices of those groups which make them vulnerable to poor reproductive health status. In this regard, the paper contains references to a selected

number of published and unpublished materials on those cultural factors of gender inequality and cultural vulnerability as they impact on RH in East and South-East Asia (ESEA).

Some of the materials are from UNFPA – supported projects whilst others come from academia, government, NGOs and development agencies. Broadening the scope of resources beyond UNFPA provides the opportunity to consult studies and materials containing information and observations of relevance to project design and implementation, which are usually not always readily accessible to UNFPA Programme managers. In the main, the review is intended to increase understanding of the challenges of applying cultural lens to addressing gender and RH issues in ESEA, especially among marginalized groups, and to share examples of good or innovative practice.

5

Assumptions about Culture and Cultural Approaches

Culture is a set of values and norms that constrain and permit action by establishing ideological parameters, offering reference points of rational decision-making... Many RH and gender issues are "sensitive" or controversial because they are subject to different interpretations, some of which are considered divine or sacrosanct and hence cannot be subject to change. They thus attract many vocal allies and adversaries. Culturally sensitive issues are best addressed in the context of health: technical or scientific perspective can make discussion and acceptance of such issues easier. Cultural norms are not fixed, but can be contested and adapted, shaped by changes in political, economical systems and even technological and scientific developments. In modern times, almost all societies are heterogeneous and hence there is a diversity of cultures or "sub-cultures" articulating positions congruent with or opposed to the official dogma or mainstream norm on any particular issue. The sensitive nature of the issues that UNFPA deals with such as reproductive and sexual health (RSH) and reproductive rights (RR) and gender equality impinge on people's private space and their cultural norms, beliefs and practices. Some cultural issues require more political than cultural sensitivity because politicians may not wish them to be addressed for fear of antagonizing a political constituency or losing votes.

The paper covers four broad topics namely: gender inequality and cultural vulnerability as key challenges; harmful beliefs and practices; cultural barriers in provision of reproductive health services and strategies in cultural Programming. The choice of these topics has been guided by UNFPA mandate on reproductive and sexual health and the recognition that these issues are linked to, among others, broad issues of economic, political, technological, and medical developments. The paper sets out to demonstrate that it is imperative to recognize and address cultural dimensions in gender inequalities on one hand and cultural vulnerability on the other, in order to attain the global development targets and goals. UNFPA Programmes are directed at addressing the constraints and obstacles that lead, for example, to poor reproductive health outcomes such as maternal mortality, STDs/HIV/AIDS, abortion, unwanted pregnancies, and sexual pain and dysfunctions.

At the cultural level, the entry point is on identification, prevention and mitigation of factors such as harmful beliefs and practices, as well as promoting positive health seeking behaviour and providing high quality reproductive health information and services in culturally sensitive and equitable manner. In this regard, the paper seeks to demonstrate how incorporation of certain cultural factors, such as partnerships with key stakeholders in different cultural settings, can facilitate delivery of desired reproductive health and sexual health outcomes. The shared vision of a much-improved world by 2015 is articulated in the Millennium Development Goals, which are based on various global consensuses of the 1990s including the International Conference on Population and Development (ICPD), Fourth World Conference on Women (FWCW) and the human rights framework and CEDAW. Cultural dimensions are at the heart of these agreements and need to be fully addressed if their goals are to be achieved.

Whatever issue or goal is examined – whether it be access to reproductive health services, elimination of gender disparities in education, employment, and political participation, or eradication of poverty – cultural factors can either act as constraints, or can be harnessed to bring about change for the better. Gender inequality and cultural vulnerability are two issues that constitute particular challenges to achieving the eight MDGs all of which are inextricably linked to reproductive health. Until gender equality and women's rights are realized, progress is going to be severely constrained. The existence of a goal to promote gender equality and empower women is evidence of international commitment to the issue, although the key MDG target for this goal specifies only elimination of gender disparities in primary and secondary education. However, the status of women also affects realization of the other goals, including those that fit most closely with the UNFPA mandate: to eradicate extreme poverty and hunger, improve maternal health, combat HIV/AIDS and reduce child mortality.

Significantly, several of the MDGs goals and targets are inextricably linked to components of reproductive health. Cultural issues are behind the observed differentials between men and women in terms of participation in the different spheres of development. Gender factors such as stereotyping, socialization practices, and lack of power at the household, community and national levels account for these differences. A combination of cultural and institutional barriers is implicated in the root causes of poverty, reproductive ill-health and indicators of the poor socio-economic status of women. The association between women's empowerment and improved reproductive health and child health - through education, employment, decision-making, access to social services and credit facilities, for example - is strong testimony to the dividends that accrue from investing in gender equality. Regarding cultural vulnerability, reference is made to:

1. Ethnic and religious minorities, two of the key groups that are often outside of the mainstream socio-cultural setting in a country and
2. Groups which practice or are exposed to risky reproductive and sexual beliefs and practices.

These two sets of groups are often subject to discrimination of some form or another. In this regard, it is significant to note that despite progress already made towards achieving the MDG targets in a number of ESEA countries, regional disparities exist within most countries. This is demonstrated in every country by health indicators that are worse for such marginalized groups than the national averages. Often living outside the mainstream population, such groups tend to constitute the poorest in society and more often than not, they also have least access to reproductive health services and information. For example, despite the differing overall HIV prevalence rates in Thailand, China, Indonesia, Vietnam and Malaysia, intravenous drug users in all of these countries have been identified as under-served population groups with high rates of infection, comprising 'concentrated epidemics'. The same is the case with sex workers, and men who have sex with men.

All these groups require focused interventions if the epidemic is to be prevented from spreading further or into the general population. Likewise, ethnic minority groups in many ESEA countries, the majority of whom live in geographically remote and difficult environments, have higher maternal mortality, and less access to education and health services, than the majority populations. Among indigenous Papuans in Indonesia, MMR is 1,025 per 100,00 live births, compared to 307 for those living in Central Java. In China the overall MMR is 43 but amongst Tibetans it is 399. In southern Lao PDR, inhabited mainly by ethnic minorities, MMR is 700 per 100,000 live births, compared with the national average of 540. The national MMR in Thailand is 24, whilst MMR in the southern provinces of Satun and Pattani, inhabited primarily by Muslims, are 90 and 49 respectively per 100,000 live births. These indicators point to some of the differentials that are likely to hinder achievement of the MDGs, unless cultural factors, including gender issues, are taken into consideration in development planning and implementation.

There is no doubt that cultural factors combined with non-availability and inadequacy of services, are issues at the heart of socio-economic stagnation of these groups. Undoubtedly, this situation requires building alliances with under-served people so as to ensure that their needs are prioritized. The section below examines more closely how gender inequality and cultural vulnerability are central issues to the social development agenda generally and with particular reference to the ICPD and its close links to the MDGs.

GENDER INEQUALITY

Gender is a socio-cultural construct par excellence. Gender is defined as society's traditional expectations, explanations, justifications and prescriptions of what men and women are, what they can and should be, and how they should act, in different spheres of life. These prescriptions and proscriptions are characterized by inequality and inequity in the division of labour, power relations and allocation of status and privileges. Gender is thus structured hierarchically with men dominating the public domain, senior positions and reaping most benefits, while women predominate in the domestic domain and lower ranks at the same time as carrying a disproportionate share of burden and responsibility in social reproduction. These unequal and inequitable gender norms are internalized by both men and women, often accepted as 'natural' and therefore sacrosanct, and are manifested in all spheres of life. Sexual and reproductive health is strongly affected by these hierarchical norms.

For example, son preference and women's economic dependence on men contribute to high rates of fertility in many settings. Inability to negotiate sex on equal terms, or to use contraception leaves the majority of women and girls at risk of unwanted pregnancy, illness and death from pregnancy-related causes and STDs. Some of the negative practices impacting on women's physical and psychological well-being are described below. Among the prominent cultural barriers preventing men, women and the youth from accessing RH services are those, which are gender-related. Many of the barriers are rooted in gender inequalities that restrict women's access to income, mobility, decision-making power, that together culminate in a general lack of empowerment. At the same time, the 'culture of silence' and restrictions in social interaction between the sexes, pose additional constraints to health seeking by women.

In some societies, women do not feel comfortable to be examined by a male doctor or health worker and, within certain groups, it is also against religious or cultural norms. In an Indonesian study, the main suggestion for improvement of reproductive health services was to hire more female doctors as a significant number of women said they would refuse a variety of services from male providers. In China too, village women became dissatisfied when men replaced women as birth planning cadres. The policy was said to have adversely affected women's access to support, as they were reluctant to talk to men about physical and contraceptive problems.

This shift translated into reduced follow-up care after sterilization because of the perceived impropriety of a man visiting another man's wife. In Indonesia, where use of the IUD was being promoted as part of the family planning Programme, male service providers expressed concern regarding the insertion of IUDs. Negotiations resulted in the recommendation that preference should be given to the use of female providers or, in those cases where only male service providers were available, another woman or the husband of the client should be in the room.

Sexual double standards

As in many other societies around the world, countries in ESEA subscribe to a number of chauvinist cultural views on sexuality, including the perception of female sexuality as being passive, devoid of desire and subordinate to male needs; prescription of virginity and sexual monogamy for women while condoning multiple sexual partners for men before and during marriage; and to the norm of conjugal sexuality as being mainly oriented towards reproduction. Confucian tenets such as "respect the male, disregard the female," Buddhist advice regarding the restraint of personal passion for women, and the practice of couples living in extended families and sleeping separately after having children, are some of the additional factors contributing to notions of sexual passivity in several of the countries in the region.

A consequence of cultural perceptions regarding the norms of male and female sexual behaviour is that legal systems are usually more punitive to women who are adulterous than to men. In the Philippines for example, definitions on what constitutes adultery are different for men and women. A married woman commits adultery simply by having sexual relations with a man who is not her husband, whilst a man does not commit adultery unless he keeps a mistress within the conjugal dwelling, cohabits with another woman, or has intercourse with another woman under scandalous circumstances. The Penal Code on extra-marital sexual relations provides that women should have a maximum penalty of six years imprisonment, and men four years - thereby reinforcing the double standards regarding sexual infidelity.

Sexual double standards are part of the masculinity norm, resulting in negative reproductive health consequences for women, which are manifested in many forms. For example, in cultures where virginity is highly valued, unmarried young women may be persuaded to engage in anal sex or other practices that preserve their virginity, but place them at higher risk of infection. Virginity norms may also make young women reluctant or ashamed to seek treatment for reproductive tract infections (RTIs). On the other hand, masculinity norms as expressed in macho complexes lead men to engage in reckless behaviours such as having multiple sex partners, patronizing sex workers and perpetrating violence. In Thailand, it is reported that young men's infidelity is generally accepted such that if a young man does not patronize prostitutes he would be thought to be homosexual.

Lack of decision-making power

Inter-spousal communication on reproductive health is hampered by women's subordination and other hierarchical gender relations. The absence of open, equitable discussion between men and women impacts on a wide range of RH issues including sexual relations between young people; STD/

HIV/AIDS and condom use inside and outside of marital/ partner relationships; preferred number of children, and whether or not to avail of temporary or permanent family planning methods; and gender violence. In a survey in Indonesia, for example, most women reported that communication with their husbands was good, and that they could talk freely about almost anything. However, in-depth interviews 4 revealed that this communication was characterized by wives' needing to get their husbands' opinions on most matters, as well as their permission to participate in social activities. About one in seven of the respondents said that their reason for not using contraception was because of opposition from husbands.

Additionally, the decision to stop childbearing was not one that a woman could usually make independently as her husband's opinion had much influence on the issue. The main reason cited for stopping childbearing, given by both women and men, was for economic reasons, whilst in fact women tended to also have other, more personal motives, such as concern for their health. On the other hand, it has been shown that there is ready husband's approval on family planning methods which their own comfort. For example, a Programme in Sulawesi, Indonesia, which aimed to increase spousal communication in relation to family planning, had the unforeseen consequence that male participants stopped relying on their wives to decide which method to use and began to take the decision themselves - often in terms of their own pleasure and convenience. In the same vein, it was shown that in Vietnam where until recently the IUD was the only contraceptive method offered through the health services, husbands' approval was high for the IUD because of their perception that this method does not interfere with male sexual pleasure and poses no threat to their health, whilst also being reversible and more effective than traditional methods.

CULTURAL VULNERABILITY

Vulnerabilities refer to dangers, risks, disabilities or insecurities. Many forms and levels of vulnerability are experienced by groups of people on the basis of factors such as age, sex, religion, race, ethnicity, geographic location, physical and/or mental disability, sexual orientation and occupation. These characteristics can form the basis for discrimination, marginalization, stigma and inequitable and unequal access to social services, or participation in the development process and its benefits. In the context of UNFPA cultural Programming, the focus is on sub-cultural groups that are underserved in terms of reproductive health. The second type of group consists of people with beliefs and practices that expose them or their partners to risky sexual and reproductive health.

Ethnic minorities

Most countries in the ESEA region have minority population groups with different languages, religions, and other belief systems from the mainstream ethnic population. The term minority is here used in the sociological sense that is of lacking power and status rather than in the numerical sense. In this regard, there are instances of numerical minority groups which oppress the majority and many numerical majorities which are the oppressed or marginalized. There is a variety of nomenclature applied to minority ethnic group: indigenous peoples, native people, tribal people, people in remote areas, isolated people, rotational forest farmers, nomadic people, cultural communities etc. These terms refer to their places of habitation and/or occupational lifestyle.

A common factor is that ethnic minorities tend to have minimal access to health and other social services and are characterized by considerable gender gaps. Some governments are less inclusive towards ethnic minorities than others, which subsequently impacts negatively on ethnic peoples' rights, including rights to access education and health services. Some ethnic groups that are constrained by language, limited economic resources and geographic isolation, do face more overt and covert forms of discrimination. In Viet Nam, there are 54 ethnic groups in the country of which the largest is the Kinh (Viet) comprising 86 percent of the population. The remaining 53 ethnic groups exhibit a high degree of diversity with regard to language, agricultural practices, kinship system and gender relations. It is notable that whilst these ethnic minorities constitute only 14 percent of the population, they account for 29 percent of the country's poor.

In north and north-east Thailand, of the estimated one million highlanders, nearly half are classified as resident aliens and do not have citizenship. This restricts their access to government services and to employment, and makes them easy prey for traffickers and unscrupulous employers. Lao PDR, as with neighbouring countries in the Mekong River Sub-Region, also has a diverse ethnic population. The Lao Loum (lowland settlers) comprise 68 groups which constituting 65 percent of the population. They are the dominant ethnic group politically, culturally and socio-economically. The Lao Theung live in the foothills and comprise 22 percent of the population, whilst the remainder are Lao Sung who are highland settlers. The Lao ethnic minority populations are national citizens, but geographical isolation and different cultural practices and languages mean that they face immense difficulties in accessing services.

Their reproductive health challenges include high fertility rates, poor uptake of health services including ante-natal care, attended deliveries, and contraception. The remote areas throughout the country where minority groups live have been designated as 'focal sites' by the Lao government to receive a wide range of development attention. Recent economic developments have resulted in the 'opening up' of the country, through the building of roads linking countries in the region. Such infrastructural projects bring disadvantages as well as development.

There is evidence of increasing involvement of young girls in the sex industry - either for the economic opportunities afforded, or because ethnic girls are easy prey for traffickers, as in northern Thailand. Ethnic girls in the north are reputed to be preferred as sexual partners by the Chinese as they are perceived to be free of HIV infection. As the country becomes land-linked, so HIV is likely to spread to areas of the country which were previously inaccessible. Similarly, in the Chinese city of Jinghong in Yunnan Province, China the Dai-Lue minority girls are exoticized and eroticized in entertainment venues and are exploited in the booming sex industry.

Another aspect of ethnic minorities is that they also feature prominently among migrant workers, a large proportion of whom tend to be illegal or unregistered and as a result of which they are often excluded from social services including health, education and pensions. Migrant workers returning to Lao PDR from Thailand, for example, have been found to have higher rates of HIV infection than among the general population, even though the overall prevalence in Lao PDR is low. In China, according to UNFPA Country Office, two-thirds of maternal deaths in urban areas appear to be of migrant women, who account for only 10 percent of total pregnancies. Migrant workers often face specific reproductive health risks. Within the Burmese migrant community in Thailand, many young Burmese women are involved as informal commercial sex workers, servicing men from within their own communities.

Access to condoms and other contraceptive methods is difficult, not least because of language and financial constraints. Pregnant women are unable to access antenatal care or skilled assistance during labour, and their babies do not usually receive the full complement of vaccinations, if any. Burmese migrant workers involved in the fishing industry are at risk of contacting HIV/AIDS, which has a high prevalence among fishermen. They are also involved in self-harming practices such as penile implants. It is difficult even for NGOs to access them through prevention and IEC Programmes due to their 'invisibility' and reluctance to be identified by the authorities. In the aftermath of the tsunami in Thailand the needs of Burmese illegal migrant women, often wives of fishermen, were neglected by the host government due to their illegal status. Their already perilous reproductive health status was further threatened by their reluctance to come forward for help, because of fear of being prosecuted.

With respect to reproductive health, there is a host of beliefs, myths and practices implicated in maternal morbidity, mortality and child survival among certain ethnic minority groups. For example, yu kham, wherein a recently delivered woman lies on a bed over a hot fire for a period of up to one month, is a post-partum practice found among most ethnic groups in South-East Asia. Various explanations are given as to why this practice is followed include a rite of passage, to protect against evil spirits, to 'dry up' the womb and to delay the next pregnancy. Among many ethnic minority groups there also exist beliefs about the power of animal sacrifice to cure various ailments and fevers by appeasing the spirits. Failure to follow prescribed practice can lead to further ill health or death, affecting not just an individual or a family, but sometimes even a whole community.

For those whose belief-systems constitute such a reality, there is a natural reluctance to give up these practices and beliefs. The case of Katang forest people in Lao PDR, further illustrates risky birthing practices. Infanticide is also occasionally practiced in accordance with strict criteria defined by spiritual leaders among the Akha people who live in the mountainous regions of China, Thailand, Lao PDR and Myanmar. Specifically, there exists a tradition of infanticide of twins or infants born with disabilities, in the belief that they are not truly human and are born as a sign of the spirits' displeasure.

Ritual purification for the parents of such infants, and indeed for the whole community, has to take place to appease the offended spirits. Increased contact with majority population groups has resulted in these practices taking place less frequently however, and infants who would previously have been killed are now sometimes given up for adoption instead. Due to the highly sensitive nature of even using the taboo words to describe such practices, anthropologists have cautioned against outside intervention by those with limited or no understanding of the cultural context.

Youth

Contemporary socio-economic and technological developments have tremendous potential to impact on the youth sexual and reproductive health culture. Formal education, globalization and information technology have created a "global village" syndrome in which the youth culture is one of the most pronounced. Among the potential cultural changes for the youth is the increased heterosexual interaction in school, entertainment and occupational settings, increased age of marriage, increased availability and diversity of information on matters of love, sex, music, dress and entertainment due to exposure on the internet and in the popular culture media.

The rate and magnitude of these changes vary across countries, rural and urban residence and religious and socio-economic groupings. The cultural vulnerability of the youth is manifested in the sense that traditionally they are not expected to engage in pre-marital sexual activities and as such parents and other socializing agents often restrict their access to sexual and reproductive health information, education and services. Some of the barriers are backed up by conservative interpretations of religious texts and in some instances are also embodied in legislation. Yet, according to WHO review of literature and projects on sexual and reproductive health of adolescents and youth between 1992 and 2005 for at least five countries in ESEA, there is notable evidence of premarital sex activities, unwanted pregnancies, abortion and STI/HIV/AIDS.

Lack of access to proper reproductive health information and services is a factor affecting young people's knowledge and attitudes in relation to many sexual and reproductive health issues. In China, Indonesia and Malaysia, providing contraceptives to unmarried adolescents is illegal. In other countries it may, technically speaking, be legal although the access of young people to contraceptive services may be hindered by a number of external factors. One is a belief that adolescents and youth are not sexually active and that knowledge of contraception and access to commodities would promote immoral behaviour. This belief manifests itself in a lack of services targeted to young people and in negative attitudes on the part of service providers. Hence, at best, most interventions have been 'knowledge-based' and without the option of services for those who are sexually active.

A study on correct knowledge of HIV transmission conducted in China found that young unmarried adolescents were the group least likely to know that condom use prevents HIV transmission. Information about contraceptives in China has until recently been mainly targeted at married couples. In Indonesia, a Programme experimented with a 'family-centred' approach of providing sexuality and RH information to young people through their parents. However, given the strict rules of propriety and filial respect that place the discussion of sexuality out of bounds of the nuclear family, parents felt embarrassed and reluctant to talk about sexual health matters such as masturbation and menstruation with their children. Another important finding was that age-group peers of the 15-19 year-olds generally lacked self-confidence to carry out effective ARSH counselling and education to their peers.

Instead, the Programme resorted to training the 22-35 year group as mentors or youth advocates who then successfully played the role of peer educators. A study conducted in Vietnam among single, sexually active women showed that they associated contraception with married life, especially when the desired family size had already been reached. Secondly, keeping sexual relationships secret was extremely important. Respondents disclosed that their reputation and future chances would be destroyed should anyone find out that they were already sexually active. Buying contraceptives was considered very risky because if someone they knew saw them, their reputation would be ruined.

Close living quarters in cities is another practical barrier to use of contraception among the unmarried: hiding contraceptives in the family home is practically impossible, and the risk of parents or other family members finding out about them is considered worse than the risk of pregnancy. Most of the interviewees considered it important that their new partners should believe that they were virgins and sexually inexperienced. They were reluctant to mention contraceptives or other information that would reveal that they knew more about sex and reproductive health than is common among virgins. Thus, at the beginning of a relationship, the power in negotiating safe sex seems to lie solely with the man. On the other hand, when the girls became pregnant, all reported that they made the choice of terminating the pregnancy on their own, and seemed quite confident about their decisions.

Sex workers (SW)

The ESEA region has become a target for sex tourism and trafficking of women, men, and children for many reasons, but chiefly for sexual purposes. These activities constitute thriving cross-border businesses especially in the Mekong River basin. The nature of and attitudes towards sex work in the region are varied. In Thailand, despite a large and visible sex work industry, sex work is nevertheless illegal. In Cambodia, prostitution itself is not illegal, although it is illegal to facilitate or profit by it and sex workers have no legal rights. In Viet Nam, Indonesia, Philippines, Myanmar and China, sex work is illegal, socially condemned and hidden, making it particularly difficult to address the RSH needs of such women and men. Due to unequal gender relations, sex work tends to be a highly stigmatized profession, with female sex workers at risk of prosecution, whilst male clients are free to buy sexual services with impunity, and are often regarded as being quite 'normal' for doing so. Because of cultural definition of men's perceived physical needs, in most of the ESEA countries it is quite acceptable for men to visit prostitutes, or even to have second, 'minor' wives.

Whilst virginity is highly rated in a bride and monogamy within marital relationships, men are nevertheless perceived as needing an outlet for their sexual urges. Hence there is tacit approval for prostitution in most countries in the region. Sex workers themselves however are generally looked down on and are regarded as a necessary social evil, whilst the legal status of commercial sex work varies between countries. Although illegal, in the Philippines sex work is divided into two categories, registered and freelance, as the authorities make some attempt to regulate prostitution. Registered sex workers are employed in various entertainment establishments and carry a 'health card' whilst they are working. They are supposed to undergo medical examinations at government-sponsored Social Hygiene Clinics on a monthly basis which, in theory, is a positive initiative ensuring sex workers have access to essential services.

Freelance sex workers are more vulnerable though and do not necessarily have the same access to health care. In reality however, corrupt systems and limited law enforcement means that the health of women is rarely protected. Sex workers can request their clients to wear condoms but cannot insist on safe sexual practices. Of increasing concern is the number of child sex workers in the region. In Thailand, girl children from the hill tribe areas, from Myanmar, China, Lao PDR, and Cambodia are sold into the sex industry. Although sex with children is illegal, the law has rarely been enforced and increased internal and external efforts to do so have resulted in the trade going 'underground'. In Cambodia girls from rural areas and from Vietnam are coerced or sold into prostitution.

In China, prostitution is seen as immoral, a symbol of corruption, and one of the so-called 'six evils', labelled as a crime against the state. It is therefore an illegal and unregulated business. However, despite the presence of public security officers in urban China, brothels thrive and are a profitable business in the emerging market economy. Due to its illegality however, there is no established system for providing sex workers with the necessary information and services to protect themselves and their clients from increasingly prevalent STDs and HIV/AIDS. In Vietnam also, the selling of sex is considered to be a social evil - a practice strongly condemned by the state, which can result in severe punishments for those found to be involved. In the small border town of Jinghong, known for sex tourism in China, a study found that whilst condoms were in plentiful supply in local shops in boxes promoting 'pregnancy prevention', sex workers used them only when clients did not object.

The sex workers emphasized that all they needed to do to avoid AIDS was to keep themselves clean by bathing after having sex with customers. They also said that they would never have sex with foreign men, particularly men from Thailand, who were perceived to be AIDS carriers. In the absence of RH information and services - despite the ready availability of condoms - sex workers health was frequently at risk. Such insights into the beliefs and practices of sex workers, as well as those of their clients, can provide useful information that can enable agencies involved in the provision of RH services to identify entry points for service delivery and strategies for addressing specific RH issues.

The perception of SW by clients is another issue, which is implicated in the perpetuation of risky sexual behaviours. A study carried out among 50 male clients of commercial sex workers in Bali found that the most common protection used by clients against HIV infection was careful selection of 'clean-looking' sex workers, followed by the practice of taking prophylactic antibiotics, vitamins or herbal potions *jamu* before or after having sex. Only one client mentioned using condoms. When clients were asked about symptoms of sexually transmitted diseases, their responses included a wide variety of non-specific symptoms including lethargy, a pale face, bad breath, body odour or sunken eyes. Nearly all respondents considered STDs to be prevalent among prostitutes in Bali and considered infection in a sex worker to be readily identifiable by 'screening' for the above-mentioned 'signs'.

Men who have sex with men (MSM)

Men who have sex with men constitute another group outside of mainstream society, which finds it particularly difficult to access reproductive health services because they are often looked down on or discriminated against by society at large. Interventions focusing on providing access to information and services rarely target MSM however, leaving them highly vulnerable to HIV/AIDS. The cultural context, as well as the legal situation regarding MSM varies greatly between the ESEA countries. In most of the countries, homosexuality has been hidden within society for a long time and the HIV/AIDS epidemic and the gay movement from the West has influenced the need for its recognition as an existing sexual behaviour, as well as a legitimate lifestyle choice. Some MSM also have sexual relations with women, thereby creating a 'bridge' between homosexuals and heterosexuals.

In Cambodia there is not a homogenous group of MSM. The distinction locally is often made between MSM short hair and MSM long hair, with the understanding that the former are men who present and identify as men with normative masculine gender characteristics, and the latter are men who present with more feminine characteristics and whose identity may sometimes correspond to the 'transgender' category. Some MSM also have sex with women, indicating that they may constitute a 'bridge' in terms of HIV transmission. In Thailand, the homosexuality scene consists of *kathoey* (transgender and transsexual males called 'lady boys', lesbians or tomboys and male sex workers. So far homosexual sexual minorities face no legal sanctions or religious interdictions but they operate in a legal vacuum with respect to their rights. In none of the ESEA countries is there a gay movement carrying on a discourse about their rights. They instead face a lot of negative stereotypes as being of being social misfits and emotionally deviant and culturally violent.

The stigma and discrimination faced by MSM pose obstacles to effective sexual health promotion, especially in relation to prevention of HIV. MSM long hair, in particular, face discrimination because they are more easily identifiable as MSM. MSM short hair, on the other hand may conceal from health workers that they have sex with other men, therefore making it unlikely that they will receive appropriate clinical services. Access to information on HIV prevention specifically addressing the needs of MSM is limited and confusion exists as to whether prevention messages targeting heterosexual partners also apply to men. Discrimination against MSM long hair by the police is prevalent, with police forcing physical examinations to 'prove' sexual identity, and demanding money and, occasionally, sexual favours. Studies among MSM in Vietnam have found that many men believe that sex with men is safer than sex with women – largely as a result of public education campaigns stressing the risks of drug use and female prostitution as HIV transmission routes, as well as non-recognition of homosexuality.

Lack of attention to MSM in campaigns has also resulted in misconceptions about risky sexual practices, in that several respondents considered oral sex to be riskier than anal sex. Accordingly, it was found that among MSM, condom use with female partners was consistently higher than with male partners, whether regular, non-regular or commercial sex workers. A study of MSM in China found many misconceptions regarding what constitutes safe sexual practice. Over a quarter of respondents believed that they would not get HIV if they withdrew before ejaculation, or if they did not ejaculate inside their partner. Almost a quarter of them believed that they could only get HIV from foreigners, whilst 18 percent believed it was not possible to get HIV if they only have sex with someone they trust. Almost two thirds of the respondents reported having sex with women in their lifetime, and almost a third within the last six months. MSM are therefore a potential bridge of HIV transmission to heterosexual women, and vice versa.

Trafficked women

The UN Protocol to Prevent, Suppress and Punish Trafficking in Persons defines trafficking as: "the recruitment, transportation, transfer, harbouring or receipt of persons, by means of the threat or use of force or other form of coercion, of abduction, of fraud, of deception, of the abuse of power or of a position of vulnerability or of the giving or receiving of payment or benefits to achieve the consent of a person having control over another person, for the purpose of exploitation". Trafficked women are likely to be amongst those with least access to reproductive health information and services. Many of them are highly vulnerable to sexual abuse and physical violence, unwanted pregnancy, STDs and HIV/AIDS due to the nature of the work they end up doing at their destination points. Due to their social and legal 'invisibility' they often have no way of accessing health care.

According to the United Nations Inter-Agency Project on Human Trafficking in the Greater Mekong Sub-region (UNIAP) and other sources, in the Greater Mekong Sub-Region alone - comprising Cambodia, China, Lao PDR, Myanmar, Thailand and Vietnam - hundreds of thousands of women, children and even men are estimated to be trafficked between countries and, in some instances, further afield. Trafficking takes place amid high levels of internal and cross-border migration, much of which has been going on for generations, and occurs in a wide range of settings and for a variety of purposes. In Vietnam, Lao PDR and Myanmar, girls are trafficked to China where there is high demand for brides as a result of the sex imbalance. Girls are also trafficked from Vietnam to Cambodia, and within Cambodia from rural to urban areas to cater for the vast domestic and international sex trade.

Within China, trafficking of babies extra to the permitted quota per family takes place to cities by poor families. In villages in Yunnan Province, for example, where a variety of factors, including extreme poverty, contribute to the powerlessness of women, trafficking of babies 'additional to the national quota' is not unusual, and is seen by village women as being 'a better option than leaving such babies to die'. The average price for male children is considerably higher than that for females – $250 as opposed to $60 per infant. The distinction between economic migrants and those who are trafficked for the purposes of employment or sexual exploitation is difficult to draw, and it is argued that increased promotion and protection of migrant workers' rights could reduce trafficking. Within the region there are a number of traditional and emerging cultural beliefs and practices, some religiously-based, which impact negatively on the sexual and reproductive health of women and men.

The harm may be physical or psychological, and immediate and/or long-term. Commonly, the physical damage manifests in medical symptoms, whereas the psychological impact may be reflected in ways such as negative self-image and lack of coping skills in social interaction. Four broad categories of issues deemed to be of particular relevance to UNFPA Programmes are presented here: son preference, gender-based violence, harmful sexual practices, family instigation of sex work and myths and misconceptions.

Son Preference

Son preference is a prevailing cultural norm in a number of countries around the world. It is most pronounced in China, India, Republic of Korea and Japan where for many years, it manifested in sex ratio imbalance approaching or even exceeding 120 baby boys born for every 100 girls, which is far beyond the natural ratio of 105 male infants born to every 100 female infants. In ESEA, the countries that exceeded the normal sex ratio at birth according to a 2005 source are: China 112, Myanmar 106, Republic of Korea 108, and Vietnam 108.

Characteristics of Son Preference Societies

Patrilineal and patrilocal kinship relations including residence and inheritance Reliance on sons to carry on the family name through religious ceremonies for the spiritual nourishment of ancestors. Confucian cultural traditions on the duty of children in providing security for aged parents, descent groups, repairing ancestral shrines and compiling genealogies. Sons bestow strength and prestige on their families and descent groups by helping them to compete for economic and political resources Sons provide labour, economic security and continue the male line by performing ancestral worship, whereas after marriage daughters leave to become members of their in-laws' families. Labour intensity of male dominant tasks in some animal and cash crop production and trade which gives the impression that males are more skilled and able than women who are responsible for domestic chores, subsistence vegetable cultivation and raising pigs.

Coercive population policies such as China's one-child policy

The sex imbalance in these countries is attributed to preference of sons over daughters, such that female babies are abandoned, under-reported, aborted or killed. Republic of Korea is reputed to have the strongest son preference in the world while in DPR Korea this does not appear to exist, due to legal, urbanization, and surveillance factors. Despite the criminalization of the use of ultrasound for pre-natal sex determination in China and India, the practice prevails with subsequent abortion of female foetuses.

GENDER-BASED VIOLENCE (GBV)

Gender-based violence is defined as physical, sexual, psychological or economic mistreatment of men, women or children, for whatever reason. It takes many forms including domestic violence, sexual violence, sexual abuse, sexual harassment, sexual assault, and trafficking and culture-driven gender violence. These forms of violence may include threats of such acts, coercion or arbitrary deprivation of liberty, and may occur in public or private contexts including the home, schools, places of employment and in entertainment, conflict and disaster situations. While all these forms occur in various degrees in ESEA, the most prevalent is domestic violence. Additionally, trafficking has become an issue of immense proportion both in supply and demand and it has been estimated that approximately one-third of the global trafficking trade in women and children takes place in this region.

While acknowledging that there is a strong culture of stigma and silence around GBV and that it is rarely brought to the attention of family members, or other gate-keepers and law enforcers, the reported number of cases (mostly in metropolitan areas) is still high in those countries in the region which have such data available. In Thailand for example, a number of surveys referred to in the 2004 Thailand MDG report testify to the magnitude of the problem. In 2003, the police department reported 4,037 rape cases. The number of women approaching crisis centres for help was also relatively high. Within the first six months of 2000, the Hotline Foundation provided counselling services to 891 women on domestic violence and 131 on rape. The following year, the Friends of Women Foundation provided services to 869 women on domestic and sexual violence.

At the same time as reports of physical abuse and rape have been rising alarmingly over the past decade, it has also been reported that the victims are younger than previously, ranging from 4-15 years of age. The involvement of young male youth in acts of violence is reported also in Cambodia. Some research revealed a disturbing picture of an increasing number of young men gang raping sex workers, garment workers or other *srey kalip* (modern women). Interviews revealed that a phenomenon known as bank – gang rape – was common among male university students. Bank involves taking a woman, often a commercial sex worker, sometimes by force, to a hotel where several men are waiting and proceed to rape her.

The men justified bank by saying that the victim was "sexually available" – in other words, because she was not a virgin, she was "fallen" and therefore the rape was acceptable. Gang rape of commercial sex workers is also widely recognized and even accepted among young people. Only 13 percent of men and women interviewed recognized bank as rape if the woman did not give permission to have sex with many men. The most common concern was that the perpetrators might contract a sexually transmitted disease – but there was no expressed concern for the victim. Cultural perceptions of what constitutes acceptable or unacceptable behaviour, especially within marital relations, make it difficult to address gender-based violence.

For example, a study in Vietnam found that law enforcement officers in Vietnam regarded a certain level of domestic violence as being quite acceptable. "A couple quarrel, then several slaps... these are all normal, not violence," commented a district judiciary officer. Many district and commune level officers believed that unless serious physical harm was incurred, physical or verbal abuse from a man towards his wife was normal. "I thought, being a wife, women should accept many things and please her husband's feelings. This is the most important factor

Child prostitution

The Ministry of Labour, Invalids and Social Affairs reported that in 1995, there were about 70,000 prostitutes of whom 13 percent were children. In big cities, such as Hanoi and Ho Chi Minh, children constituted an estimated 16 percent of prostitutes. Organizers of prostitutes entice poor rural girls to leave their homes by painting a bright future with city employment as maids, sales girls etc. The Vietnamese police estimated that 5,607 women were sold to China in 1996. In Cambodia, the Human Right Commission in 1996-97 counted 14,725 young women in brothels, bars, and massage parlours, private accommodations and hotels and of these 18 percent came from Viet Nam.

Child abuse

In 1998-99 lowest level courts in provinces and cities sentenced 1,337 defendants for raping children. Of the offenders, 7 were put to death and 175 were given life imprisonment.

Marital disharmony and abuse

During the 2002 9th National Congress of the Vietnamese Women, the Vietnamese Women's Union (VWU) reported on the number of GBV cases they had supported during the period 1997 - 2002: 3,078 cases at central level, 5,533 at provincial level, 21,558 at district level and 105,738 at grassroots level. Various issues were addressed including marriage and family problems, adult sexual abuse, child sexual abuse and other forms of violence. They also gave a figure of 2,488 trafficked women assisted by the Union in 5 years. Despite these high figures, the rate of intervention and assistance provided by the authorities in cases of family violence was low.

According to research conducted by the WU in 2000, 62.7 percent of cases were resolved by neighbours; 36.3 percent by the Women's Union; 2.9 percent by the local authorities, and 4 percent by police. The main reason for limited support from the authorities was that victims had little trust in law and authority, whom they considered to be ineffective, slow and untimely. Additionally, women regarded violence as being a family issue unless they were physically injured. The majority of divorce cases was filed by women and was mainly due to family conflict, gender violence and maltreatment. Such cases accounted for 52 percent in 1998, 56 percent in 1999 and 62.62

percent in 2000. The Law on Marriage and Family 2000 stipulates that all divorce cases must pass through reconciliation procedures. There is concern that such 'reconciliation' might be more concerned with 'honour and dignity' of the family, rather than the human rights and health of the victims of violence.

Female genital cutting/female circumcision

In the literature, the various forms of cutting of the female genitalia is variously referred to as Female Genital Cutting (FGC), Female Circumcision (FC) or Female Genital Mutilation (FGM). Studies have documented this practice in Indonesia although there is no official endorsement of the practice in the mainstream Islamic teaching in the country or for that matter in any other parts of the world. According to these sources, FC, as it is known in Indonesia, is a practice, which has traditionally entailed either removal of part of the clitoral hood, or merely symbolic gestures such as "sticking" the clitoris with turmeric and then cutting the turmeric rather than the clitoris. The procedure of actually cutting the clitoris is sometimes practiced because of pressure from the family who feel guilty if this is not done, whereas traditionally the symbolic gesture usually sufficed.

For those who practice FC, it is performed under their understanding that it is a part of Islamic teaching and therefore a form of devotion to Islam or rites of passage. FC service providers comprise modern health practitioners such as midwives, nurses, and physicians and dukun, traditional healers recognized particularly by those living in rural areas, who are deemed to have a supernatural ability to drive out evil spirits or to cure diseases. It is reported that short-tem side effects of FC, such as infection or bleeding, can occur as a result of scratching the labia very deeply. Girls are circumcised at 7-40 days. In Indonesia, the practices of both FC and male circumcision have increasingly become commercialized and promoted with the advent of modern medical facilities and equipment. The availability of medical equipment and medication means that pain can be reduced and the risk of complications eradicated. Health staff are in a strong position to promote the service and are themselves gaining financial benefits due to the costs involved. It is ironic however

Female circumcision (FC) household survey findings among 1694 mothers of female children under nineteen years of age in Indonesia: 92 percent of families in Muslim communities support continuation of FC because they perceive it as both a societal custom or tradition and a religious duty. Many maternity clinic midwives have begun to market FC part of a birth delivery package. The danger of medicalization of FC lies in the fact that midwives tend to use scissors which result in cutting of the clitoris (incision accounting for 28 percent and excision accounting for 22 percent of all the cases in the study area), whereas traditional providers usually use penknives for a more symbolic act of scraping, rubbing, pricking or piercing the outer part of clitoris, accounting for 28 percent of cases in the study area. FC involves pain and is potentially harmful. FC violates the rights of the child as guaranteed under the Convention on the Rights of the Child, ratified by the Indonesia government in 1990. that a practice which, in Indonesia, has traditionally tended to be more of a symbolic gesture, has now been adopted in a more radical form due to advances in medical practice, which complement an increased adherence to orthodox Islamic practice in that country.

Dry sex

In parts of Indonesia, Malaysia and Thailand, research has shown that women consume a variety of herbal medications and also insert herbs, astringents, and alum to dry and tighten the vagina so as to increase friction, which is deemed to be more pleasurable for men during intercourse. In an evaluation of a peer education project in Indonesia, two types of herbal preparations were widely used by young women: one to bring on menstruation in cases of unwanted pregnancy, and another to cause vaginal drying or tightening for having sex. This practice is potentially harmful to young women in particular, exposing them to increased risk of infection from STDs/HIV. Since the sensitive lining of the vagina is not fully developed, it is highly vulnerable to tears and scratches, which can become easily infected.

Family Instigation of Sex Work

In at least two countries in the region - and possibly more - it has been observed that cultural perceptions of sex work as a prospective employment opportunity are changing, particularly amongst the very poor. Whereas traditionally a girl's 'virtue' was seen as being of ultimate importance - both in terms of her future marriage prospects and also in terms of the family's 'honour' - in some places daughter's are increasingly being seen as a potential source of income and material possessions through their involvement in sex work, without the associated stigma. Thailand has long been known for its sex industry, but the pattern of those becoming involved in sex work has changed over the past fifteen years. Some families, particularly poorer families in the north, actually encourage their daughters to become sex workers in order to be able to access more income and material benefits. As daughters are usually responsible for caring for their parents in old age, it is difficult for girls from such families to refuse to enter the sex trade.

In some areas prostitution has come to be seen as an acceptable occupation, with families who do not sell their daughters being regarded as foolish, especially as the income to be earned from commercial sex is considerably higher than that earned through unskilled labour. Although pre-marital sex is frowned upon, the 'sin' of being involved in commercial sex is offset by the merit gained by being able to provide financially for the family. While many children and young women in Thailand have been 'sold' into the sex trade, most available data suggest that the process is not always involuntary or forced. For many young women involvement in commercial sex is seen as an economic opportunity and men are seen as targets, a source of income. In one study, when asked how they entered commercial sex, 58 percent of women said it was their own decision, 37 percent said a friend or relative had advised them and only 3 percent said they were either sold by their parents or recruited by an agent. In Indonesia, a field survey was conducted among 300 households in the places of origin of sex workers (West, Central and East Java), and of 400 sex workers operating in the same localities. Interviews were conducted with sex workers' parents, youth and community/religious leaders.

Key findings from the survey are highlighted in the box. For parents with limited employment opportunities and unable to afford keeping their daughters in school, access to the sex work industry is relatively easy. The financial contribution such daughters bring to the household income was reportedly considered to be an expression of daughters' love for their parents. Attitudes towards entering the sex industry vary; in some areas it is viewed as being quite acceptable. Other socio-cultural factors also contribute to the likelihood of young women becoming sex workers. These include the perceived value of children, especially daughters, in relation to future family life, early marriage of women leading to divorce, perceptions about sex workers, and perceived life success and role model of sex workers.

Perceived value of children especially young daughters access to sex work is relatively easy and less demanding than education and formal sector jobs sex work is seen as a promising route to support the family and is seen as an expression of love to parents.

Marriage at early ages leads to a high divorce rate poor parents who could not keep children in school tended to marry off their daughters at age 16 or 17 to stop community gossip early marriage tends to end in divorce usually with delivery of a child such young daughters, with no job and in difficult living conditions, view sex work in major cities as being the most viable option for a better life.

Perceived life success and role model of sex worker no social or other sanctions from the family and/or community against sex worker possession by sex workers or their contributions of jewelry, family conveniences and properties looked upon as symbols of life success within the larger community This section presents cultural issues that pose constraints in delivery of reproductive health services. The constraints may be due to the cultural or religious values of the service providers themselves or determined by political and administrative decisions. Service providers may also be constrained by the mainstream culture, which may be opposed to delivery of certain messages and services on reproductive health issues. These issues are presented in some details below.

HEALTH PROVIDERS AS 'MORAL POLICE'

Service providers sometimes reflect their own cultural or religious values, particularly when dealing with sensitive issues such as unwanted pregnancies and contraceptives. Whilst in most countries in the region there are widespread family planning campaigns encouraging small family size and promoting increased use of modern contraceptives, access to services remains poor for some client groups, and many women continue to resort to abortion in an effort to deal with unexpected or unwanted pregnancies. Abortion remains illegal in countries including Myanmar, Indonesia, Thailand and the Philippines. Thus abortion remains politically sensitive in most countries and attracts widespread negative public opinion. Yet, even where family planning is available through regular service provision, there continues to be a demand for abortion among married women who experience contraceptive failure and among adolescents wishing to terminate unwanted pregnancies. In this case, service provider attitudes do not make it any easier for such women.

In Indonesia a study found that due to their own religious beliefs or for fear of reprisals, some health providers were unwilling even to treat complications of illegal abortions. Others adopted a more pragmatic approach, some expressing a wish that abortions could be performed in safe medical facilities, hoping that this would lead to fewer severe complications from unsafe abortions. Service providers seemed to be more tolerant towards clients wishing to terminate unwanted pregnancies due to contraceptive failure, rather than for other reasons. In all cases, however, continuation of the pregnancy was usually recommended. In Myanmar many health providers felt they should scold the clients who came in for post-abortion complications, and that this scolding was in the interest of the clients in order to keep them from seeking abortions in the future.

Many village women delayed seeking help for even severe complications due to fear of being reprimanded, as well as fear of neighbours finding out about the abortion. In a survey carried out among formal and informal sector health providers in Lao PDR, 18 percent of the providers considered it their duty to inform the parents of their children's sexual activity. They hoped that the parents could exert influence on their children to refrain from sexual relationships. In some cases, health service providers subscribe to myths, which inadvertently contribute to people's reluctance to seek treatment. In Viet Nam, for example, service providers perpetuate several myths about STDs. Rather than raise the possibility that the patient's husband or partner might be having extramarital sex, service providers have been known to accuse women presenting with STD symptoms of having poor personal hygiene. Such an attitude has resulted in women being reluctant to discuss the situation with their partners, or to seek health care. Another commonly held misconception in Vietnam is that reproductive tract infections are 'women's diseases,' caused by working in dirty water in rice fields.

POLITICAL SENSITIVITIES

Political contexts shape the institutions which impact on individual and community level responses to health interventions. The political agenda may be geared to achievements of certain family planning targets or projection of a harmonious or equalitarian society or an environment devoid of violence or certain diseases. In those countries where policies have been centrally-controlled for many years, the role of some state institutions and mass organizations is to implement at community level health interventions determined at national level, even when such a stance may be counter-productive to developing positive relations with clients. Thus some countries, including Thailand, first hesitated in responding to the HIV/AIDS epidemic for fear of slowing their tourist industry. Altogether, these political considerations can compromise quality of reproductive health services or the rights of individuals or couples to choose methods they want or access other reproductive health services.

For example, in rural China, where male dominated village committees are commonplace, research has shown those family planning institutions and Women's Federation-run community education activities promote and reinforce local gender and family norms which uphold women's subservient status and character: virtue, submission to authority, industriousness and aptitude for meticulous work. Although these officially sanctioned pedagogic activities may well have empowered women by providing them with knowledge and resources, researchers found that the over-riding objective was to moderate women's behaviour in ways compatible with their role as mothers of the next generation of Chinese citizens. A study in China revealed that management staff and health workers in hospitals and medical centres denied coming across cases of domestic violence such as wife-beating in their practices, with some even denying its existence over the past 10-15 or even 30 years.

Staff even went so far as to prevent researchers from accessing medical records. A review conducted in 2000 of Viet Nam's laws on family violence showed that within the local authorities, including the Women's Union, the preferred solution for addressing family violence was reconciliation - even where elements of crime were involved and the cases should have been directed to properly constituted legal authorities. Similarly, Women's Unions and mediation teams in many places believe that an important part of their role was to ensure that couples remain together, irrespective of circumstances. They considered that they had failed in their work if they had been unsuccessful in preventing a couple from going to court to seek divorce. Through the one-child policy in China, control over contraceptive use is obligatory for concerned officials. Women's Leaders are expected to know which women in their areas are using contraceptives, which methods they use, and who has become pregnant. IUDs, pills and sterilization are methods currently sanctioned by the state, with IUDs and sterilization being the most popular methods of birth control.

For a long time, condoms have been viewed as both sexually improper and a medically inferior method of birth control. Sterilization is mandatory for all couples with two children and monitoring is done by birth planning cadres who, in most cases, are women although they have been increasingly replaced by men who it was believed would be more effective in achieving quotas for sterilization. One of the areas most affected by political decisions in Vietnam is reproductive rights with respect to choice of timing pregnancy, determining the number of children and whether or not to have children. There are cultural values attached to these decisions, which in the long run are affected by, among other things, political decisions.

Vietnam formally introduced its one-to-two child policy in late 1988 and, though not enforced, it was widely promoted by family planning cadres, mass media campaigns and outreach work. There were penalties in the form of higher fees for health services or the payment of a certain amount of rice or money to the commune for giving birth to more than two children. In the Philippines, where abortion is illegal and public attitudes are very negative, abortion complications constitute a significant public health problem and are a major cause of maternal morbidity and mortality, accounting for 400,000 cases annually, among whom one-quarter is hospitalized.

One of the causes of opposition among some health providers to shifting from using dilation and curettage to manual vacuum extraction is the perceived risk of its being used for induced abortion. According to the Philippines MDG report, following the process of decentralization local government units are now entirely responsible for decision-making on contraception purchase. This is likely to impact negatively on women's access to family planning in more conservative regions and to be further exacerbated by current retrogressive attitudes of the Philippines' government towards funding of modern methods, combined with aggressive promotion of natural family planning.

CULTURAL SENSITIVITY AND ACCURACY IN MESSAGES

One of the main means of empowerment is knowledge. Many UNFPA projects focus on provision of RH information and education and, in this regard, the challenge has been delivering scientifically accurate information on culturally sensitive issues of sexuality, gender violence and reproductive rights. A number of studies have highlighted this issue. For instance, it has been found that the need to have older generations to approve materials targeted at young people can result in materials that, while being culturally sensitive, are not explicit enough in delivering accurate information to enable youth to judge risks involved in different sexual activities. Thus, emphasis on prevention of unwanted pregnancy, can lead young people into modifying their behaviour in ways they think will help to avoid pregnancy, but can result in high risks of STIs.

A focus group discussion conducted among young people in Indonesia found that the chief means used by young boys to avoid pregnancy included coitus interruptus and anal sex. In the same study, comparison of IEC materials on youth sexuality with popular magazines targeted at young people in Indonesia showed that the two sources gave a markedly different portrayal of sexuality. While the image of sexuality conveyed in the IEC materials was very negative and destructive, with emphasis on the terrible consequences of sexuality, the popular magazines and discussions among the young people gave a more balanced and positive image of sexuality.

One article notes that the huge amount of different RH manuals published in Indonesia can consist a problem in itself. Often the manuals have small print runs, and occasionally there is contradictory information. For instance, several of the manuals claim that masturbation is harmful, and can have serious implications for the future of young people's health. Again in Indonesia, a survey on family planning revealed that most women interviewed expressed a very strong desire for more information, especially practical explanations of contraceptive methods. The writers of the article suggest that this might be due to the fact that the Indonesian family planning Programmes have concentrated more on 'motivational' rather than 'educational' messages. In some instances, the "culture of silence" or tabooed discussion on issues identified as culturally sensitive, has turned into misinformation even by service providers including doctors.

For example, in a recent television Talk Show in Viet Nam, in response to a question about whether or not masturbation was harmful, a doctor replied that masturbation causes infertility, is dangerous for young people's health and is a social evil. He also said that pills are only for use by married couples. In other circumstances influential pressure groups or authorities perpetuate myths that support their own particular ethical stance, such as the notion that provision of sexual health information to young people encourages them to experiment with sex. In fact, research has shown that the opposite is correct: informed young people are more likely to delay their sexual debut and to use protection at first intercourse, than those who have not had access to sexual health education.

Certainly, there is a lot of myths and misconceptions held by people themselves and which influence their sexual behaviour and related choices: inaccurate information about ways in which STDs/HIV is transmitted can result in people engaging in risky behaviour; misconceptions about contraceptive methods can limit women's choice; male myths about sterilisation has resulted in this being an under-utilized method of fertility control in many countries in the region. Hence, without having prior knowledge or understanding of existing myths and linked risk behaviour, project interventions can be ineffective. By understanding the context and source of the myth it is easier to develop strategies that bring about behaviour change.

This is particularly successful when IEC materials that counter the myths and alternative narratives are presented. The experiences presented in this section illustrate interventions that have addressed both the needs of health service providers and other gatekeepers in coming to terms with their own beliefs or perspectives as well as that of target groups such as clients or other culturally vulnerable groups like ethnic minorities and sexual workers. At the same time, there is coverage of a variety of approaches and partnerships that have proved successful in addressing culturally sensitive issues in reproductive and sexual health.

ENGAGING IN VALUE CLARIFICATION

Service providers need to be trained to explore and change their own values and attitudes in order to become competent in delivery of required services. A Programme developing mental health services in Cambodia trained health service providers to respect cultural beliefs and explanations in order to enhance patient compliance and satisfaction with the treatment. The Programme found that some of the people trained initially resisted this approach, even though they were quite familiar with the traditional beliefs and approaches. Those from an urban background who had had a western style education tended to view traditional processes in a negative way, at least whilst working in the context of a 'western' Programme. In the Philippines, service providers were encouraged to be self-reflective as part of a strategy to improve post-abortion care.

In 2001-2002, Engender Health adopted an innovative strategy to spearhead a Programme called Prevention and Management of Abortion Complications (PMAC), with the ultimate intention of upgrading health provider skills in post-abortion care. The strategy was two-pronged, consisting on the one hand of a forum of service providers who were encouraged to examine their own values and attitudes towards post-abortion clients and, on the other hand, a technical working group consisting of representatives from Departments of Health, academia, physicians, nursing and midwifery associations, NGOs and tertiary hospitals who were responsible for developing a country-level work-plan for post-abortion care.

A pre-training situation analysis identified that post-abortion care clients did not receive routine counselling or referrals to family planning and other reproductive health services. In addition, providers showed bias in their attitude towards clients, and punitive treatment was the rule rather than the exception. Health staff were then provided with training in post-abortion care (PAC) counselling and family planning counselling, as well as in infection prevention and clinical post-abortion skills.

Subsequently a significant change in service provider attitudes was observed, as providers sought to improve their behaviour and practice. Staff became more aware and supportive of the need to treat clients with dignity and compassion, and was highly sensitized to preserving confidentiality and privacy during procedures and counselling. The intervention proved the value of using participatory, self-reflective approaches to encourage providers to examine their own attitudes and values towards clients and this resulted in improved attitudes and service provision.

INCORPORATING CULTURAL FACTORS IN HEALTH SERVICES

In Lao PDR an intervention was initiated within a local community, in an attempt to encourage women with high risk birthing practice to modify their customs. Among the Katang forest dwelling ethnic group it is taboo to allow blood in the house because of the perceived belief that evil spirits may eat the blood and subsequently cause the death of mother and baby during childbirth. Traditionally childbirth therefore takes place in the forest, with a woman either alone or accompanied by older women and/or her husband. The mother and baby then stay in a small shelter or hut for three days until the bleeding stops. This practice, compounded by endemic malnutrition and high fertility rates, contributes to a high level of maternal mortality. An innovative approach was developed to alleviate women's fear of delivery in the forest, whilst at the same time accommodating cultural prohibitions regarding blood.

Village men decided that, when the time came, a husband would construct a birthing hut for his wife just outside the village, close to the forest or rice fields. In the hut, the woman would have access to skilled attendance in the form of a traditional birth attendant trained by an NGO, and the availability of referral in cases of complications to a district level clinic. The men also decided that, provided the mother and baby were clean, they could return to the home after one day, rather than waiting for three days in the forest. A combination of factors contributed to the successful outcome of this intervention. Participatory rural appraisal (PRA) conducted by the NGO Concern Worldwide brought discussion to the fore about the traditional birthing practice and women's fears of delivery in the forest.

Village men decided to make the necessary cultural adaptations to address the situation, and enabled significant moderations to take place regarding traditional practice. They also took on the responsibility of building birthing huts for their wives. Technical inputs from Concern helped develop local health service capacity through the training of TBAs and by building a small clinic in the locality, thereby enabling referral networks to be established. Women were subsequently more confident than previously and, at the same time, awareness was raised within the community about the importance of being able to access referral services and the link with the possibility of reducing maternal deaths. Another example describes health service providers in southern Thailand adapting their approach to accommodate a cultural practice specific to local Muslim communities.

The number of hospital deliveries, or deliveries assisted by trained health staff, is significantly lower in three provinces in the south than elsewhere in the country, and maternal mortality rates slightly higher. In general, Muslim women living in this region prefer to deliver their babies at home with the support of untrained female assistants. A rapid base-line assessment, conducted with UNFPA support, found that one of the reasons given for preferring home births was because of the ease of conducting traditional rituals associated with the naming ceremony for the baby, which it was not possible to do in hospital.

Subsequently, health service staff were willing to accommodate this post-delivery practice in hospitals, in an attempt to encourage hospital deliveries. Another expressed reason for non-attendance at hospital was because staff did not speak the local language common to the Muslim community, and women wished to be able to communicate in their own language with health staff. Commitment was also made to provide language training for selected service providers who would be interacting most with the Muslim communities.

BUILDING COLLABORATION AND GROUP SOLIDARITY

As one of the causes of stigma against sex workers (SW) is their role in transmitting STD/HIV/AIDS, some notable strategies have been developed to address the issue. Two of the strategies incorporate cultural factors, namely partnership with government agencies and building a sense of group solidarity among SW.

Government Commitment

The 100 percent condom Programme introduced in Thailand during the 1990s, is credited with lowering HIV/AIDS prevalence rate from 10-15 percent down to 1-2 percent. The Programme was based on a public health model requiring the regulation and registration of sex workers, and based on the premise that a positive impact could be made by engaging local health and police authorities in negotiated relations with brothel owners. The Government played a prominent role in policy and planning, and health authorities demanded a guarantee of 100 percent condom use from brothel managers under the threat of legal sanctions. STD services were linked to the Programme and free condoms made available.

The 100 percent Programming included hourly one-minute messages on TV, a government- led promotion of condom use, distribution of free condoms, and required free STD treatment among brothel workers and increased allocation of funds to NGOs. According to researchers however, the strategy, whilst successful in lowering HIV prevalence, did not empower sex workers, as police and brothel owners played a major role and gained additional power over them, usually through government health service intervention. The 100 percent condom Programme in Thailand is still in operation, but with the advent of more 'indirect' sex work taking place in or from entertainment establishments such as bars, clubs and restaurants, there are doubts whether a Programme focusing on promoting condom use among 'direct' commercial sex workers is adequate any longer.

Reaching 'indirect' sex workers with effective preventive Programmes is a challenge, not least because the owners of the establishments where they work are unwilling to admit that sex is traded on their premises. A study found that 44 percent of such owners denied sex was being sold, 50 percent of them had not introduced any measures for condom promotion, and approximately 30 percent did not facilitate STD check-ups and treatment for the sex workers. Although this approach was apparently very successful in Thailand during the 1990s, with national HIV levels dropping from 11.9 percent in 1991 to 2.4 percent in 1998, there has since been an increase in the prevalence of HIV among sex workers from 10 percent in 2000 to 16.6 percent in 2002.

Another consequence was that Thai sex workers stopped working in brothels and moved to less visible establishments, such as massage parlours and karaoke bars where they tended to be replaced by non-Thai women, illegal migrant workers and hill tribe women, whose health is at greater risk due to language and legal barriers which severely limit their access to services. Altogether, despite the fact that the 100 percent condom Programming was not directly empowering to SW, it illustrates the potential of the government and national level orchestrated Programmes in reversing the level of HIV/AIDS epidemic.

Building a sense of community among sex workers (SW)

An alternative approach has been devised in Cambodia, focusing on health promotion and awareness-raising aimed at generating a sense of community and solidarity among SW. This approach is based on the assumption that improved self-esteem among sex workers enables them to have greater control over their working conditions and hence their practice of safer sex. Sex workers themselves are central to the design, implementation and even monitoring of the interventions. Women are encouraged to determine their own priority needs, and resources are sought to address these needs. Peer education plays an important role in this approach.

Targeting indirect sex workers

In Myanmar, UNFPA supports the NGO Population Services International to conduct outreach work, focusing on the provision of information on HIV/AIDS and safe sex, and promoting male and female condoms, among young girls working in entertainment venues, such as karaoke bars. This is an attempt to target the need of 'indirect' sex workers, who are not willing or able to acknowledge the work they are doing. Similarly, projects supported by the EC/UNFPA RHIYA Programme in Lao PDR and Cambodia target 'beer bar girls' - who engage in casual commercial sex, but do not necessarily identify themselves as sex workers - with prevention strategies and negotiation skills.

Peer education has also been used as a tool to promote messages between the beer girls themselves, as well as with their clients. Building alliances with the owners of entertainment establishments - without necessarily openly discussing the nature of the work that takes place 'behind the scenes' - can have positive outcomes. As with *mamasan* and brothel owners, it is in the interests of the proprietors of such entertainment venues to ensure that the girls who work for them are healthy and free from disease. Once positive relations have been established there is usually willingness for the girls to participate in activities.

WORKING THROUGH NETWORKS

Efforts to include community level actors in the process of designing and monitoring health care provision are essential, although care has to be taken in determining which actors participate in which consultations, so as to ensure that the sensitivities of all parties are taken into consideration. In Indonesia, a project aiming to promote an inter-sectoral problem-solving approach to safe motherhood, and to enhance involvement of local level actors in issues that were not solely the domain of the health sector, incorporated village leaders, religious officials and other policy-makers in the audit discussions on maternal deaths in South Kalimantan. It was found however that this approach limited self-criticism among medical providers, who felt rather threatened when weaknesses in clinical management were discussed in the presence of those with no direct expertise in medical matters.

This finding demonstrated that such medical audits are only of value when the professionals involved are confident that the findings will not be used for legal or other actions. A lack of confidentiality in the existing system might have been a contributory factor resulting in resistance to report cases for audit. The study also found that by using the village midwife as the central conduit for reporting, the audit tended to focus on factors contributing to maternal deaths in the community, rather than on those, which occurred in health facilities. Hence the research concluded that whilst such an 'open' approach to audit among health staff encouraged communication and collaboration between the village midwife and higher levels of the health care system, it did not necessarily foster accountability by doctors and midwives in health facilities.

The following case illustrates a successful attempt in the same region in Indonesia to address nutritional anaemia, one of the most prevalent malnutrition problems, utilizing wider networks than usual. The Ministry of Health and Mother Care project incorporated an anaemia control Programme into an existing intervention offering pre-marriage counselling to engage couples. The objective was to ensure that all participants were immunized against tetanus toxoid before obtaining a marriage certificate. The approach involved asking the parents of the engaged couples to register the forthcoming marriages at the sub-district Ministry of Religion office, instead of the young people themselves. As part of this process they were then responsible for collecting and passing on to the young couples IEC materials on the immunization Programme.

Through enlisting the support of family members with a vested interest in the young women being immunized, it was found that there was a clear link with lowering of anaemia prevalence in the subsequent period. Almost 70 percent of the women in the Programme received IEC materials delivered to them by their parents, and there was a subsequent 40 percent decrease in anaemia prevalence between the baseline and first monitoring (one month after the baseline).

The conclusion of the study was that the positive results were attributable to the use of respected family members for counselling of young women on important health matters before marriage. Information originating from a community itself can have a significant effect on major decisions such as contraceptive choice. A census carried out in Thailand in 1984 found that the 51 villages in Nang Rong, a relatively small geographical area, had very different patterns of contraceptive choice, with one method predominant in each village, but significant differences between the villages. An in-depth study carried out to find out the reasons for these differences stressed the importance of social networks in contraceptive choice, noting that conversational networks helped direct and control the flow of information about contraceptive methods in these villages, and thus influence the contraceptive choices to a great degree.

FORGING PARTNERSHIPS

Religious institutions and leaders

The religious and/or spiritual frameworks within which most communities operate can be an important entry point for reproductive health Programming. Through mutual respect and collaboration, results can be achieved which might otherwise be hindered because of pre-conceived ideas about 'entrenched' beliefs or practices. Religious and animistic beliefs often provide the framework within which individuals operate and, by ignoring the existence of these cultural reference points, opportunities may be lost for advancing reproductive health rights and improving people's reproductive health.

Issues relating to sexual and reproductive health are often highly sensitive or even taboo to discuss openly, but when positively engaged and provided with evidence-based information, religious and spiritual leaders are often willing to collaborate and to interpret their teachings progressively. This happens especially when it can be seen that both parties are working towards a common goal, or when a health intervention is either not contradictory to religious teachings or traditional practice, or can clearly be seen to be complementary. In Indonesia, an early decision was made by the government not to promote sterilization or abortion as part of the family planning Programme.

There was also initial resistance from religious leaders towards use of the IUD, due to fears that it might cause abortion. Negotiations were carried out with Islamic leaders on how IUDs could be introduced in ways acceptable to the Islamic faith. Strong support by key politicians at all levels of the country's administrative structure was instrumental in facilitating the smooth operation of this Programme. Similarly, in the Autonomous Region of Muslim Mindanao in the Philippines, a special project was designed to target a community with higher MMR and IMR rates than the national averages.

A core group of *ulama* (Muslim scholars) were invited to help provincial health officers explain the advantages of family planning to Muslim couples. Subsequently they became involved in advocacy and IEC campaigns as key partners of UNFPA and implementing agency POPCOM. Subsequently the *ulama* went on study tours to Indonesia and Egypt, to discuss issues relating to family planning in the context of the Qur'an with other religious leaders. Their findings were used as the basis on which subsequent advocacy materials were developed. By 1999 increased numbers of Muslims in Mindanao were using contraception.

Later, to ensure the support and involvement of all key Islamic scholars in the Philippines, a Special Committee on RH and Family Management, headed by the House of Islamic

Opinion of Central Mindanao, was established, with technical inputs from Muslim doctors. Following several reviews, a religious edict or *fatwah* was drafted, stating that contraceptive methods were acceptable as long as they were safe, legal, in accordance with the Islamic Sharia, and approved by a credible physician (preferably Muslim) for the benefit of both the mother and the child.

The *fatwah* was endorsed by the Grand Mufti of Egypt and publicly pronounced in the Philippines in March 2004 with two hundred Muslim religious leaders from all over the country in attendance. Buddhist values of moderation, self-discipline and compassion have been tapped into in the fight against HIV/AIDS in a number of South-East Asian countries. The temple has always been the heart of the community – the place where people go to seek spiritual guidance and support.

Aware of the role performed by Buddhist and lay clergy within local communities, many organizations, including UNFPA and their partners, have taken the opportunity to use the revered status of the Buddhist clergy to help promote and demonstrate messages of compassion and care, and to raise awareness on sensitive issues relating to sexual health. In Cambodia, supported by the EC/UNFPA Reproductive Health Initiative for Youth in Asia (RHIYA), monks are trained to promote messages on safe sex to adolescents at risk of STDs/HIV and unwanted pregnancies. In addition, they are contributing to the elimination of the stigma associated with HIV/AIDS by providing accurate information on HIV/AIDS transmission and prevention, and emphasising compassion for those already affected.

Politicians and law-makers

Dialogue and interventions on cultural issues can be greatly facilitated or hampered by political leaders. Political statements and support can give credibility to issues that are otherwise stigmatized and steeped in silence and hidden in the family or domestic fronts. Political leadership may come from a charismatic leader either at the level of the head of state, or at any other level, by visibly supporting or opposing an issue or Programme.

For example, the success of the Indonesia Family Planning Programme during the Suharto era from the 1970s through the 1990s has been attributed not only to the effective technical management of the contraceptive delivery systems, but equally to political management by the officials of the National Family Planning Coordinating Board (BKKBN), which was the national coordinating body. In an autocratic political set up, BKKBN officials were able to ingratiate themselves with the politicians, bureaucrats and fieldworkers across national, provincial, district and village levels.

The political management involved securing alliances with the Islamic leaders to diffuse religious opposition, broadening the role of field workers to include a national network of village-level family planning groups including women NGOs and thereby surmounting human resource deficiencies and, lastly, putting FP on the political agenda. To this end a series of decrees were passed which institutionalized high priority for FP inside the Ministry of Home Affairs including criteria for assessing performance were nine numerical FP targets including the crude birth rate, the number of active users of contraceptive methods and the number of village FP groups created. The strong political orientation of the BKKBN chairman, Haryono Suyono, also played an indispensable role in successfully orchestrating the Programme.

Another example at the political level is partnership with an organized group of lawmakers. In this regard, the Asian Forum of Parliamentarians on Population and Development (AFPPD) constitutes an advocacy group on population matters. In particular the Forum's Standing Committee on Women Parliamentarians has highlighted the plight of women survivors of GBV among educated women and men parliamentarians through national and regional workshops to motivate them to take legislative and monitoring role. As a result of such advocacy, many countries in ESEA have taken steps to address the absence of legislation in this area.

Indonesia, Malaysia, Mongolia, the Philippines have passed Domestic Violence legislation in 2004, whilst Cambodia, China, the Lao PDR, Thailand are in the process of drafting and reviewing proposed bills. It is noteworthy that parliamentarian advocacy together with activism of NGOs and professional groups have led also to passing laws or regulations to control other forms of VAW such as the anti-sexual harassment and an anti-rape law in the Philippines, the Code of Practice on the Prevention of Sexual Harassment at the Workplace, and anti-trafficking law and a national plan of action to control trafficking in Thailand, the Zero Tolerance Policy against VAW and the National Plan of Action on VAW in Indonesia, and the Act to Institute Policies to Eliminate Trafficking in Persons in the Philippines.

Promoting male participation

Empowerment of women and challenging gender biased cultural practices require multi-pronged approaches. Among the effective strategies are those directed to changing traditional masculinities through a number of channels including school curricula, media coverage and male participation in social reproduction and reproductive health. In the area of RH it is acknowledged that men as spouses or partners are normally the ones who take decisions in the home and who therefore need to be more involved in RH interventions.

In this regard, it is imperative for boys and men to be socialized or re-socialized to take responsibility for the effects of their own sexual behaviour on their partners' and children's health and well-being. An example of this is male participation in ending gender-based violence. A number of countries including Cambodia, China, and Malaysia have formed men's networks to play an important role in the elimination of GBV, rather than to relegate it solely to women's groups.

In ESEA, since 2000 UNIFEM has implemented a regional Programme on the elimination of violence against women (EVAW), which operated through men's networks. In Malaysia for example, the Man Action Network against violence (MAN.V) was initiated as the first men's group in the country.

It received a wide spectrum of male support, including radio deejays, sports personalities, film actors and policy makers. MAN.V conducts training, talks and seminars in schools, colleges and holds dialogues with policy makers on GBV. A number of RH Programmes in Indonesia which aimed at empowering women on a personal level, showed that whilst women had gained significantly in knowledge and confidence, they still remained powerless within the social sphere, lacking the confidence to question or challenge their husbands.

Recognizing that existing gender imbalances in sexual and reproductive relationships had not been challenged through the Programme, women participants asked the Programme managers to develop strategies to target men. Subsequently, a more holistic approach was adopted, wherein reproductive health activities were introduced to male and female groups at the same time. As a result of this modification, many cultural taboos were challenged and some significant behaviour changes took place in relationships between men and women.

A first year evaluation, based on interviews with both men and women, showed that men had reduced their violent behaviour against women and no longer compelled their wives to have sexual intercourse against their wishes. The overall conclusion of the study was to encourage exploration of multi-faceted approaches, aimed at empowering women, whilst also challenging established gender norms with men, in order to affect change in both the private and public spheres.

A study in China assessed the effectiveness of a family planning intervention with and without husband's participation in reducing pregnancy and abortion rates in Shanghai. Among non- IUD users, the researchers found that pregnancy and abortion rates among women receiving family planning education with their husbands were significantly lower than rates among those receiving the educational intervention by themselves, or those receiving usual care. The findings confirm the importance of men's participation in prevention of HIV and other STDs, and argue for the principle of equitable allocation of the benefits and burdens of reproductive health decisions.

A final example of male involvement in RH is a Philippines initiative that promotes the role of men as potential partners and staunch advocates, while at the same time addressing their health concerns. The initiative began in 2000 and was implemented in the provinces of Nueva Vizcaya, Sultan Kudarat, North Cotabato and Davao del Norte. It started with seminars and short training courses to different sectors, followed by dissemination of information down to the purok level. The intervention evolved into the formation of a male reproductive health association, with male community health workers on tricycles delivering advocacy and IEC/BCC messages, as well as male clinics being set up in rural health units and at district hospitals.

Overall the Programme focuses on the following: Improving available medical services especially for male adolescents Enhancing communication between spouses on the use of contraceptives Prevention of sexually transmitted diseases Screening for prostatic and testicular cancer Referrals for cases of urological problems Tangible results of the Programme have been an increase in number of men accompanying their wives to the clinics for prenatal check up, bringing their children for immunization, and discussion among themselves on family planning methods and on the ways by which they could protect themselves from STDs.

Interventions for Youth Gatekeepers

Successful strategies for addressing the problem of transmission of misinformation on sexual health matters from adults to young people have been developed through some of the projects funded through the EC/UNFPA Reproductive Health Initiative for Youth in Asia (RHIYA). Although inaccurate information has sometimes been provided for 'political' reasons – in the interests of preserving 'traditional values' and 'cultural mores', it has been found that adult 'gatekeepers' are not always aware that the information they are providing is incorrect. On many occasions they themselves do not have knowledge of, or access to, correct information on sexual and reproductive health matters.

By designing activities that educate and inform 'gatekeepers' about reproductive health issues and adolescent needs, community acceptance of interventions with youth is usually much stronger. Youth Union and Women's Union personnel, community leaders, teachers and parents have welcomed access to information they did not receive when they were young. Parents, in particular, welcome the opportunity to learn about subjects that they themselves would choose to teach their children, if they had accurate information. In Myanmar, peer education activities for young people, supported by UNFPA and the NGO JOICFP, proved so successful that young people took on the role of sharing reproductive health information with their parents and other community members, as well as with their peers.

Health services 'gatekeepers' tend to pose more of a challenge in terms of trying to create different attitudes towards service provision for unmarried youth. This is often because they fear the responses of colleagues, senior staff and parents, as well as the possibility of breaking written or unwritten laws, should they provide services for youth. Within the RHIYA Programme, successful strategies have included advocacy campaigns targeting key decision makers and politicians; support for research which produces 'evidence' of unsafe sexual practices among young people, which can then be used for advocacy purposes; and workshops focusing on youth-friendly service provision.

Role plays and other participatory exercises designed to encourage health service providers to imagine how it feels to be a young person unable to access services when faced with a reproductive health 'problem', such as an unexpected and unwanted pregnancy, a STD, or fear of having contracted HIV/AIDS, tend to become much more sympathetic in their attitudes.

Participants take it in turns to play the role of the young person, an 'unfriendly' service provider, and a 'friendly' service provider, and then explore their feelings through group discussions. By enabling them to explore alternative approaches and design criteria for youth friendly services, attitudes can be changed over time. Health staff are often very familiar with the issues facing young people and, once they are convinced of the importance of providing services for unmarried youth, they themselves can become excellent advocates from within the system.

CULTURAL PROGRAMMING CHALLENGES

The paper has covered a number of issues that pose challenges in cultural Programming, and which are fundamental to achievement of the shared vision of a much-improved world by 2015, as articulated in the Millennium Development Goals. It has stressed that many challenges on the global social development agenda are shaped and influenced by culture and are anchored in gender inequality and cultural vulnerability. Unequal division of labour and subordination of women, including lack of autonomy and restrictions in decision-making in the public and private domains are manifestations of this.

These hierarchical gender norms result in beliefs and practices that are inherently harmful to women's sense of self-worth, as well as to their reproductive health and that of their families. Such practices often violate principles of human rights and gender equality and include GBV, son preference, female circumcision, penile implants, dry sex and gender and cultural constraints to RH health seeking and service delivery.

Another challenging set of issues relates to the specific needs of vulnerable groups whose socio-economic characteristics, behaviour or life-style are often the object of stigma and marginalization within the wider society. Youth, sex workers, men-who-have sex with men, and ethnic minorities are among the vulnerable groups whose reproductive health needs tend to be neglected. It is also often the case that members of these groups hold misconceptions relating to sexual and reproductive health, and engage in risky sexual behaviour, whilst at the same time having less than adequate access to RH services.

The reviewed interventions concerning these groups have reflected a diverse cultural discourse, ranging from moralizing attitudes and victimization, to concern about their human and reproductive health rights needs. The paper has referred to the challenges in RH service delivery that can both emanate from and impact on the socio-cultural context. Among these are deeply held cultural and religious values of the service providers and community development workers which may, for example, impel them to breach confidentiality by revealing youth sexual activities to parents, reproach post-abortion care clients, or fail to report criminal cases of GBV.

At the same time, the ramifications of political decisions, and technological and economic developments brought about by globalization, have brought their own challenges to cultural Programming. In some cases, they have created or exacerbated cultural practices such as son preference and sex work. Sometimes scepticism is expressed regarding the value of paying attention to those cultural practices that may not be prevalent but, rather, are restricted to marginal groups. The justification for this is that the criteria for intervention should not be the prevalence, but rather the gravity or degree of harmfulness the practice has on the health and psychosocial well-being of the practitioners and/or their partners.

It is often among these marginalized cultural groups that harmful and practices such as penile implants, dry sex and son preference occur, and a rights-based approach demands that such practices should be researched and strategies developed to address them. The implications for cultural Programming with respect to all these issues is that a wide range of factors have to be taken into consideration when delivering reproductive health services: the socio-cultural orientation of service providers, local ethno-medical systems, local knowledge and relationship to western medical knowledge, health seeking behaviour, cultural perceptions of disease causality, gender issues, and existing community structures and hierarchies. The cultural diversity of the ESEA countries and the rapid globalization impact on sexuality cultures has pointed to an urgent need for a shift from preoccupation with reproductive and conjugal sexuality or "reposexuality", to a concern with sexuality issues of diverse groups including youth, sex workers, the aged, and MSM.

CULTURAL PROGRAMMING STRATEGIES

In terms of strategies, the paper has described a number of interventions where cultural factors have been successfully incorporated into reproductive health service delivery as, for example, the case where the traditional birthing practice of the Katang in Lao PDR was modified. Another example of cultural sensitivity was the training in value clarification for healthcare workers, resulting in staff that were better able to empathise with and understand the circumstances of their clients, leading to less judgmental attitudes regarding the provision of family planning and counselling for post-abortion clients. Likewise, the example of partnering with Islamic religious leaders to overcome opposition to fears among men that the Indonesian family planning Programme promoted abortion and IUD insertion, which subsequently had a successful outcome.

Another strategy featured is that of promoting collaboration between cultural, professional and civil society groups, which in most instances, has contributed to positive results. However, there have been instances where the strategy has resulted in an unanticipated dilemma, as happened when village leaders and traditional midwives were included in joint maternal audit discussions with hospital medical personnel in Indonesia.

The experience had the undesired effect of discouraging transparency and accountability because medical providers felt threatened, particularly when deficiencies in clinical management were discussed in the presence of those with no expertise in medical matters. The important lesson learned there was that there is need for minimal requirements of understanding on the legal and medical dimensions of issues, in order for a meaningful dialogue to ensue with non-professionals. Forging partnerships with religious leaders, men and law-makers' networks is another strategy that has proved effective in cultural Programming. These categories of people are revered and recognized leaders in their respective communities or constituencies, and wield considerable power and influence on moral issues, and on reproductive health, community development and political matters.

Advocacy efforts on a range of issues were described, including Muslim scholars (*ulama*) support for FP in the Philippines and Indonesia, and Buddhist monks' promotion on safe sex to adolescents and de-stigmatization for HIV/AIDS sufferers in Cambodia. In the same vein, the Asian Forum of Parliamentarians on Population and Development (AFPPD) is actively involved in advocacy for legislation several cultural issues particularly GBV. Some strategies aiming to promote cultural sensitivity have had ambiguous results however. An example from Indonesia is cited where providing sexuality information to unmarried youth through parents failed, due to reluctance to overstep cultural boundaries in communication on such a sensitive topic. Conversely, parents willingly complied with passing on health messages in IEC materials to their engaged children. Likewise, with respect to sexuality education, it has been shown in Indonesia and Philippines that delivering culturally acceptable information is sometimes done at the expense of scientific accuracy, which can lead to adoption of high-risk sexual behaviours.

WAY FORWARD

Culturally-sensitive Programming constitutes a cross-cutting strategy in UNFPA. One of the challenges in this regard, is the lack of data, which are disaggregated by cultural variables such as ethnicity, religion and language. Regrettably, these background variables are sometimes considered politically sensitive in some countries so as not to routinely be specified in various data collection exercises. The fear is that they graphically depict the inequalities in social development which politicians and other entrenched power structures may not be ready or willing to address.

However, the human rights perspective necessitates such levels of disaggregation in order to rectify inequalities and inequities in social development. A related area of emphasis is the need for more quantitative investigation so as to clearly discern the prevalence and patterns of distribution of the cultural issues, both positive and negative so that relevant interventions can be made. Lastly, it should be emphasized that, as noted in the introduction section of this chapter, development workers and institutions are increasingly mainstreaming and focusing on culture in their Programmes. In order to gain and strengthen expertise in cultural Programming, partnerships and experience-sharing need to be fostered within and between agencies. In this way, UNFPA strategic goals linked closely to the ICPD, CEDAW and the MDGs can be realized.

6

Organizing for Domestic Worker Rights in Southeast Asia

Feminist Responses to Globalisation

The forces of globalisation increasingly compel feminist activists to engage internationally, either through their involvement in transnational networks and social movements, or by incorporating understandings of the 'global' into local and national practices. Globalisation collapses both time and space, thus fundamentally altering the types of political and economic relationships that states maintain with both citizens and a range of 'others'. For this reason, Rochelle Ball and Nicola Piper (2002: 1031) assert that non-government organisations (NGOs) "will increasingly play a pivotal role in lobbying nationally and transnationally for greater state and multi-lateral institutional accountability to both national and global citizens".

However, as differently situated actors with diverse agendas and priorities come together to address women's rights within a transnational frame they face a range of challenges and contradictions. Rather than simply transcending the 'national', transnational feminist activists must pay particular attention to the roles played by nation-states and national governments in mediating the relationship between local and transnational groups. It is this embeddedness of the national within transnationalism that is often overlooked in romanticized accounts of global civil society. This chapter examines the limits of transnational feminist activism in Southeast Asia by focusing on NGOs that have developed in Singapore and Malaysia to address the rights of female domestic workers.

Specifically, it addresses the role of The Working Committee 2 (TWC2) in Singapore, and Tenaganita in this chapter was presented to the 15th Biennial Conference of the Asian Studies Association of Australia in Canberra 29 June – 2 July 2004. It has been peer-reviewed and appears on the Conference Proceedings website by permission of the author who retains copyright. The paper may be downloaded for fair use under the Copyright Act (1954), its later amendments and other relevant legislation. Malaysia. The comparison of Singapore and Malaysia is important because it provides an opportunity to consider the ways in which different national contexts impact on the opportunities for domestic worker NGOs and networks to advocate for workers' rights.

The countries share a common heritage that includes British colonial rule and ethnically diverse populations. Both have witnessed strong economic growth in the last two decades. However, while both countries are recognised as having strong authoritarian governments that tightly control access to a small sphere of civil society activity, migrant worker rights organisations in Malaysia are greater in number and have a more visible presence. Comparative analysis is important in order to move away from simple assertions of 'authoritarianism' as both a descriptor and explanation for the shape of civil society in both countries. Comparison also highlights the role that relations between nation-states play in shaping civil society.

Malaysia and Singapore have a history of chequered relations with the two major sending countries of foreign domestic workers – Indonesia and the Philippines. These relations have undergone change over time, and are influenced by the character of other bilateral and multilateral ties (e.g. relations with the United States and other 'western' countries), as well as relations between Singapore and Malaysia. While previous studies of NGO activism in Singapore and Malaysia document state constraints on civil society, none have discussed these processes in the context of the life histories of specific organisations.

As a result, there is a tendency to treat civil society as a homogeneous space characterised by consistent state-NGO interactions. My previous research in Singapore, however, has shown that different groups are able to negotiate their relationship with the state in different ways. Closer attention to these differences is necessary in order to develop a better picture of the complexities of state-civil society relations. For example, in some contexts, local activists may find it politically safer to avoid transnational interactions, or to restrict their involvement to groups with similar goals and objectives.

TRANSNATIONAL FEMINIST ACTIVISM

Transnational activism can be defined as "regular activity crossing national borders that involves at least one nonstate actor", in contrast to 'international' activism which primarily involves state actors. Although women's movements have a long history of engagement in the international arena, it was not until the 1990s that women's rights advocates began to organize on an unprecedented scale transnationally. A number of recent studies have sought to document the diverse activities of such groups. This work forms part of a growing body of research on the role of transnational NGOs, advocacy networks and social movements in the emergence of global civil society.

For Valentine Moghadam, the creation of transnational feminist networks is indicative of the emergence of 'global feminism', defined as "the discourse and movement of women aimed at advancing the status of women ... through transnational forms of organizing and mobilizing". Examples of such networks include Development Alternatives with Women for a New Era (DAWN) and Women Living Under Muslim Laws (WLUML). These groups "engage in information exchange, mutual support and a combination of lobbying, advocacy and direct action toward the realization of their goals of equality and empowerment for women and social justice and societal democratisation". Moghadam sees their emergence as a direct response to the processes of globalisation.

On a cautionary note, however, Vera Mackie (2001: 188) reminds us that the "transnational public sphere, if it can be said to exist, is a gendered, raced, classed and ethnicized public sphere". It is not unsurprising then, that the relationship between 'grassroots' and/or community-based activists and transnational groups is often fraught. A number of studies have begun to document the numerous problems facing transnational feminist activists. Few studies, however, have attempted to identify the particular strategies used by local and transnational activists to build cross- cultural, transnational alliances or coalitions. Opportunities for transnational activist groups to advocate on behalf of women's rights are frequently constrained by states that tightly control access to the politically sensitive arena of civil society.

Local and transnational groups must pay attention to the complexities and contradictions of civil society as they consider what kind of alliances to forge and resources to accept. Despite the important role played by the state, few studies have focused their attention on the limitations posed to feminist transnationalism by local state forces. Instead, there is a tendency for scholars and policy- makers to unproblematically project a romance of 'more' civil society as ballast against coercive state power and its excesses. This partly explains the continuing commitment of international funding agencies towards strengthening civil society and thereby addressing 'women's rights'.

In these approaches, civil society is often treated as a monolithic whole with a unity of purpose rather than as a space occupied by range of actors with divergent agendas. In some contexts, local activists may find it politically safer to avoid transnational interactions, or to restrict their involvement to groups with similar goals and objectives. Many groups have found that it is the language of transnational feminism, whether it is reference to 'gender', 'feminism' or 'rights', which makes such relationships politically fraught at the local or national levels. This chapter seeks to explore these complexities through a comparative study of two groups seeking to address the needs of migrant women working as domestic maids.

FEMINISATION OF TRANSNATIONAL LABOUR MIGRATION

Global demand for female domestic workers continues to grow. Women from the Philippines, Indonesia, Malaysia, Burma, and Thailand have joined the ranks of transnational female migrants working as domestic. There is a large body of literature that deals with the debates over language in relation to global feminism maids across the globe. Although there are no precise figures on the numbers of transnational domestic workers, some estimate that there are between 4.2 to 6.4 million Filipinas working abroad as domestic helpers and entertainers. While these women typically migrate to the Middle East, Japan, Europe and North America in search of work, many find employment in Southeast Asia as increasing numbers of women in the newly industrialising countries of the region enter paid employment outside the home.

For example, in Singapore, where women's labour force participation is 53.9%, there are estimated to be over 140,000 foreign domestic workers. Huang and Yeoh (2003) claim that there are almost equal numbers of women from the Philippines and Indonesia working as maids in Singapore, with a significant minority from Sri Lanka. This equates to approximately one foreign domestic worker to every seven households. In Malaysia, there are more than 161,000 documented domestic workers, the majority of whom hail from Indonesia and the Philippines. In addition, there are estimated to be many thousands of 'illegal' migrant women working as maids in Malaysian homes.

The feminisation of transnational labour migration has attracted considerable scholarly attention. Much of this work focuses on the tenuous position of female domestic workers in relation to labour laws and citizenship rights. Female migrant workers face difficult working conditions, poor remuneration, and constant surveillance by both the state and their employers. Despite their dependency on the labour and remittances of migrant workers, sending and receiving states have been slow to address these issues. For this reason, NGOs have begun to play a significant role in both disseminating information and providing assistance to migrant workers. While some migrant worker NGOs are associated with local or transnational women's movements, others are affiliated with religious groups, unions, civil rights groups, and even government organisations. Some adopt gender-specific responses to the plight of domestic workers, while others organise around religion, class, as well as race/ethnicity or nationality (i.e. advocating on behalf of women with a common country of origin).

Much of the literature on migrant worker NGOs has focused on groups based in Hong Kong and the Philippines. These groups have received the most scholarly attention not only because of the significant proportion of female domestic 'maids' from the Philippines who work in the Hong Kong, but also because in comparison with other national groups, Filipinos have the strongest transnational advocacy networks. Several writers have also examined the role of NGOs advocating for migrant rights, including domestic workers, in Japan.

However, despite the fact that Malaysia and Singapore are major receiving countries for female domestic migrant workers, migrant worker organisations in both countries remain under-unexplored. Data on transnational migration in the region is extremely difficult to verify due to the large numbers of 'illegal' or 'unofficial' migrants. In the case of Malaysia, the work of Tenaganita, Women's Aid Organisation (WAO), SUARAM (Voice of Malaysians) and All Women's Action Society on migrant worker rights issues has been referred to by Gurowitz (2000) and Chin (2003). These studies limit their discussion to a brief description of each NGO, rather than an in-depth analysis of the history of their emergence or the scope of their activities. In Singapore, Lyons (in press) has written.

THE CASE STUDIES

Singapore and Malaysia are both characterised by the presence of a strong, authoritarian state and a weak civil society sphere. The activities of migrant worker groups in both countries are curtailed by strict rules governing the formal registration of NGOs, a strong interventionist stance by the state, restrictions placed on the activities of international NGOs and other agencies, and often-fraught diplomatic relations with many migrant-sending countries. In both countries, the Internal Security Act (ISA) is used to discipline the actions of groups seen to be politically threatening. The Act was introduced during British colonial rule and used against suspected communists.

It allows arrest and detention without trial for up to 60 days, and unlimited extensions beyond the initial detention. Both the Singaporean and Malaysian governments have used the ISA against those individuals or groups that they consider a threat to national security. The Societies Acts of both countries are another significant colonial legacy. In Singapore, while the Constitution guarantees freedom of association (Article 14) in principle, organisations with more than 10 members or committees with more than five members are required to register under the Societies Act or the Companies Act.

Individuals who participate in groups that are not officially registered face the threat of arrest and imprisonment for participating in 'illegal assemblies'. All registered organizations are expressly prohibited from engaging in 'political activity'. This combination of legislation and government policy has restricted the emergence of activists groups. As a consequence, most registered societies tend to be professional associations or welfare oriented groups. Article 10 of the Malaysian Constitution guarantees freedom of speech, expression, peaceful assembly and association. The Societies Act of Malaysia covers all groups of seven or more people except those covered by other legislation such as trade unions and co-operatives. The Act has been amended several times, most recently in 1983 after a campaign by NGOs to address the Act's wide definition of 'political activity' (defined as any society that issues public statements).

Although the narrow definition of 'political society' was subsequently removed, the legislation continues to restrict the activities of NGOs. Although the Societies Act of Malaysia requires all non-profit organisations to formally register, it has a much larger and vibrant NGO sector than Singapore. There are many groups active in the fields of women's rights, the environment, consumer affairs, and civil and political rights. In direct contrast to Singapore, Malaysia also hosts several Asian regional NGO networks, thus contributing to the establishment of transnational links. Despite the wider diversity of NGO groups, Malaysia's entrenched security legislation and wide reach of the ruling party has meant that these groups continue to face difficulties on the ground.

For about the relationship between The Working Committee 2 (TWC2) and the women's movement, and Devasahayam (2004) has examined the role of Catholic organisations working to assist migrant workers. For example, a group called 'People Like Us' representing the interests of gays, lesbians and bisexuals has twice been refused registration on the grounds that homosexuality is not socially acceptable in 'conservative' and 'traditional' Singapore (People Like Us 2000). It is much smaller, however, when compared to Thailand, Indonesia and the Philippines. example, the 1971 Sedition Amendment Act limits their activities by removing from public discussion four issues: Malay rights, citizenship rights for non-Malays, the status of the national language and Islamic religion and the rights and privileges of the King and Sultans.

The Printing Presses and Publications Act 1984 has also been effectively used to reduce public criticism or reportage of issues or events that question the ruling party. While activist groups in other countries mobilise around international support and standards, the anti-West/anti-US position of both the Singaporean and Malaysian governments, as evidenced in the rhetoric surrounding 'Asian values', has made such connections more complex. On migrant rights issues both states have demonstrated "little tolerance for public discourse that casts its practices in a negative light". In Singapore, foreign-based NGOs find it difficult to become formally registered, and without registration cannot operate locally. Locally-based NGOs in both countries are wary of receiving funding from overseas sources for fear that this may result in government suspicion about their activities.

This has resulted in a very small international NGO presence and very few transnational linkages between local, regional and global groups. In Singapore, this may be changing with recent government support for improved regional links between NGOs and the suggestion that Singapore may become a 'hub' for international NGO offices. In Malaysia, local NGOs have found that the state has taken a particular interest in their international connections and any financial support received from overseas. Nonetheless, many groups have been able to develop effective transnational links, particularly on Third World or Islamic issues.

For example, Sisters in Islam has distanced itself from western feminist models of global sisterhood preferring instead to forge strategic alliances with women's organisations in other Muslim countries. In both cases, opportunities for NGOs to advance their causes depend in large part on the extent to which their goals are congruent with the state's own ideology and interests. Moderation, consultation, and consensus are key modes of operation by NGOs as they negotiate the constraints of state-civil society relations. When NGOs threaten the ruling party's political foundations, however, the state uses both legislation and other means to clamp down on activists.

The Working Committee 2 (TWC2) in Singapore

For many years, the plight of foreign women working as domestic maids in Singapore has remained 'off- limits' to civil society groups. Like many taboo topics, the issue of domestic workers has not been publicly identified by the state in its official statements as a topic that is 'out-of-bounds', but its association with the 'Marxist Conspiracy' has meant that few

NGOs have been willing to address it. The Marxist Conspiracy is a The governing elite refers to 'Out-of-bounds markers' (OB markers) as points that delimit acceptable civil engagement. Ho (2000: 186) describes these as "issues that are too sensitive to be discussed in public for fear of destabilising or jeopardising public peace and order".

The ruling PAP government is responsible for determining the limits of the OB markers, a task that it largely performs retrospectively with the result that what actually constitutes 'unacceptable political engagement' is unclear term used to describe the arrest and detention under the ISA of 22 people in May 1987 for threatening the state and national interests. Those arrested included Catholic social workers and lay workers at the Geylang Catholic Center for Foreign Workers. The Geylang Centre's workers lobbied for higher wages, social security benefits, job security and employment conditions for all foreign workers.

At the time of their arrest, the government claimed that Catholic organisations were "a cover for political agitation" to "radicalise student and Christian activists". The Geylang Center was subsequently closed. Of those workers arrested, some were later released, while others were detained for varying periods. Those charged had to admit to being a Marxist as a condition of their release. They were 'rehabilitated' with an agreement not to enter into politics. Some members of Singapore's main feminist organisation, the Association of Women for Action and Research (AWARE), were involved in the so-called Marxist Conspiracy. The organisation was silent on the arrests, and many members still believe that they narrowly escaped arrest and the closure of the organisation.

The arrests were interpreted by the membership as a clear signal that domestic worker rights were 'off-limits' and that for AWARE to address the issue would be extremely risky. This partly explains the reluctance of the local feminist movement to address the needs of foreign women working as domestic maids. AWARE adopts a cautious and conservative approach to its activities. Working within the framework provided by the OB markers, members are never completely sure how the organisation's statements will be received and are forced to respond carefully. Fear of negative perceptions or closure means that AWARE tempers its public statements or limits its activities to avoid criticism.

The labour movement has also been silent on issues surrounding migrant labour in Singapore. Most independent unions were closed down or weakened in the 1960s, and replaced by a state-sponsored National Trades Union Congress (NTUC) that acts as an umbrella group for affiliated organisations that are largely supportive of the government's economic and labour policies. In the absence of a local or international NGO presence in Singapore to deal with the rights of domestic workers, religious groups and foreign embassies stepped in and filled the void. Their actions, however, were largely ad hoc. During the 1990s, concerned about the linkage between Catholicism and the Marxist Conspiracy, Christian churches were extremely careful in their public dealings with domestic workers.

As the numbers of Indonesian foreign workers rose, several mosques began to provide support and training services to Muslim maids through their women's Programmes. Both groups acted informally to assist 'runaway' maids to contact embassy officials when they needed assistance. These ties became stronger in the 1990s as increasing pressure was placed on sending countries by overseas workers and their families to address the needs of their citizens working abroad. In Singapore, these claims were crystallised around the arrest and execution of a Filipina domestic worker, Flor Contemplacion, in 1995. The execution caused a diplomatic rift between the Philippines and Singapore as speculation mounted over her guilt. 8 Such activities include religious instruction as well as English language tuition.

As a result of this, and other cases, migrant worker welfare became a significant issue in for bilateral relations between receiving and sending countries throughout Southeast Asia. The Philippines Government established the Overseas Workers Welfare Administration (OWWA) as part of the Department of Labor and Employment.

The OWWA runs a range of services

In a recent attempt to formalize its involvement in migrant workers issues, the Catholic Archdiocese of Singapore established the Commission for Migrants and Itinerant People (CMI) in 1998. One of its goals is to reach out to 'strangers' (including migrant workers, foreign students, travellers and refugees) "who have experienced injustice, oppression and alienation". In addition to services aimed as assisting domestic workers, the CMI has also worked with the Singapore Ministry of Manpower to run workshops for employers on 'How to establish a Harmonious Working Relationship with your Foreign Domestic Helper'. Both groups operate in partnership with the Singaporean government to address the question of individual treatment of domestic workers by employers, rather than dealing with broader questions of labour law, immigration law, or citizenship rights.

As the numbers of domestic workers entering Singapore has risen, so too have reports of physical and sexual abuse of maids by their employers, maid deaths, as well as incidents of assaults or theft carried out by maids. Despite concerns about overstepping the OB markers in relation to maids, the increasing visibility of these issues has made them difficult to ignore. In December 2001, a 19-year old Indonesian woman, Muawanatul Chasanah, died after months of brutal assault by her employer Ng Hua Chye. Ng's neighbour, Mr Neo, was quoted in the media as saying: "Even if I knew, I wouldn't have called the police, it's not my business. He can do what he wants, that's his problem". These comments prompted a number of Singaporeans to meet informally with the goal of addressing attitudes towards and treatment of domestic workers in Singapore, and The Working Committee 2 (TWC2) emerged in late 2002.

The TWC2 was modelled on the short-lived 'The Working Committee' or TWC that was formed in late 1998 and disbanded a year later. The TWC operated as an informal network of individuals and representatives of NGOs and voluntary welfare organisations (VWOs). Its goal was to build links between differently situated civil society actors, and thereby participate in both re-assessing and re- invigorating the sphere of civil society in Singapore. Unlike other NGOs, the TWC was not formally registered through the Societies Act, but operated as a loose affiliation of individuals and organisations.

By deliberately limiting its life span to one year, and focusing its activities on 'network building' rather than pursuing the interests of a particular client or membership group, the TWC was able to avoid the otherwise restrictive requirements of registration under the Societies Act. The TWC provided an important alternative model of civil society engagement for other groups to consider. Several members of the TWC joined together with other activists to establish TWC2 with the aim to "promote respect for domestic workers through education, and secure better treatment of domestic workers through legislation and other means". Like its predecessor, the TWC2 was formed as an ad-hoc group of individuals and organisations with a one-year limited life-span.

International Day to Eliminate Violence against Women on 25 November 2003 marked the culmination of for overseas Filipino workers, including refuges for maids in a number of countries. In Singapore, the OWWA half-way house for runaway maids through the Philippines Embassy. its year-long efforts. Braema Mathi, a Nominated Member of Parliament and member of AWARE, chaired the committee. AWARE was listed as 'partner' organisation and hosted the TWC2 web-site. The TWC2's activities were organised under the banner 'Dignity Overdue: Respecting the rights of maids', and included workshops, public forums, and exhibitions. The issue of domestic worker 'rights' focused on three interrelated topics - reducing demand for domestic workers; employment contracts (including wages and conditions); and treatment by employers (built around a notion of respect for human dignity).

Consistent with other NGOs in Singapore, rather than adopting a direct lobbying role in relation to legislative change, the TWC2 focused its activities on public education. For this reason, part of the group's activities were focused on drawing attention to the gendered division of labour within the home, and finding alternative solutions to Singapore's reliance on the labour of domestic workers. In relation to employment contracts, the TWC2 encouraged employers to provide a day off per week to their employees. Members organised a 'Sunday Off Campaign' that included a Block Party for workers and their employers, and a photography exhibition of maids on their days off. Members also used the forum pages in the local media to raise the issue of standardized contracts for foreign domestic workers.

These, and other initiatives, were successful in raising public awareness of the issues surrounding conditions of work. The PAP government, however, continues to argue that the matter of working conditions is an issue to be negotiated between individual employers (or agents) and employees because of the individual nature of the duties required in each household. The TWC2's interest in the treatment of domestic workers focused on the issue of violence. The group's activities culminated with a series of events focused on International Day to Eliminate Violence against Women and Singapore's first 'White Ribbon Campaign'.

The campaign was supportive of the state's own interest in developing a gracious and more civic-minded citizen, in contrast to the image of the 'ugly Singaporean' conjured up by images of maid-abuse. The interrelated issues of citizenship, marriage, residence, and family migration, were largely unaddressed. In part, this reflects concerns about overstepping the state's OB markers. But, it also points to an inability to address violence as an issue of power embedded in social relations, rather than as an individual, isolated act. The focus on violence also meant that the rights of the vast majority of workers who do not face violence in the workplace, were also overlooked. At the end of its year-long activities, a new group consisting of former TWC2 members announced that they would establish a Maid Resource Centre to deal with, all issues relating to maids, whether these are raised by workers, employers or recruitment agencies. .. It plans to be a one-stop centre for maids, providing information on the industry, a training centre for skills upgrading, as well as a coordination point to link workers, employers, foreign embassies and employment agencies.

The Nominated Member of Parliament (NMP) scheme was introduced in 1990 to co-opt alternative non-partisan voices into parliament. NMPs are nominated by members of the public, NGOs or Voluntary Welfare Organisations (VWOs), and appointed by the government for a term of 3 years. While NMPs share the same parliamentary privileges and immunities as normal MPs, they have limited voting rights and do not play a role in the running of town councils. Block here refers to a housing apartment block, the main form of housing in Singapore. The White Ribbon Campaign is an international Programme organised by men where ribbon wearers pledge 'never to commit, never to condone and never to remain silent about violence against women'. In signalling its intentions to extend the TWC2's work, this group raises the possibility of a stronger, more formalised NGO presence in the field of domestic worker rights.

The new group, retained the original acronym but changed its name to 'Transient Workers Count Too'. It applied for formal registration under the Societies Act in January 2004, but received in principle approval subject to revisions to its proposed constitution. Braema Mathi recently stated that to address the concerns of the Registrar of Societies would significantly undermine the organisations ability to assist migrant workers but neither party has released details of the constitutional clause of concern, and negotiations are still underway. At this stage, it is too early to tell whether they will be successful, and what implications this will have for both domestic worker rights and the expansion of civil society in Singapore. It may be that the 'maid-economy' is now such a public issue for discussion and debate, that a more formal NGO presence and/or the incorporation of domestic worker rights into pre-existing NGO activities (such as those of AWARE), will not be seen to be overstep the OB markers.

Tenaganita in Malaysia

Workers' rights organisations and trade unions in Malaysia are much greater in number and more diverse than their Singaporean counterparts. Although they were quite militant in the early post-Independence years, most trade unions have had their activities curtailed to suit the economic needs of the government. Enterprise-based unions and agreements have replaced industrial trade unions. Enterprise-based unions lack resources for effective negotiation and are discouraged from forming federations. Unlike Singapore, labour organisations in Malaysia have been active in mobilising migrant labour. The Trade Union Act allows legally resident migrant workers to become union members, although this right is often excluded from workers' individual contracts. Sahabat Wanita, a national organisation of women's workers, does not deal specifically with migrant women workers, but refers them instead to migrant worker organisations.

At the same time, however, Sahabat Wanita sees its role as one of education and changing the mindsets of local workers about the needs and conditions of migrant workers, who are often perceived as taking away local jobs. Tenaganita (or 'Women's Force') was formed in 1991 to "promote and protect the rights of all women and migrant workers within a globalized world". Tenaganita's activities are organised under seven Programmes that seek to "empower, organize and consolidate migrant and women workers not only in Malaysia but regionally".

These Programmes are:

1. National Focal Point – collates and shares information through a website, newsletter and publications on migration, migrant workers and women workers;
2. Migrants Rights and Health Desk – an advocacy and support service;.
3. Community Based Interventions to Promote Health care and reduce HIV/AIDS Vulnerability;
4. Domestic workers Programme;
5. Arrest Detention and Deportation – legal support and campaigns;
6. Women, Chemicals and Cancer; and
7. Trafficking in Women and Children.

Since its creation, Tenaganita has been successful in establishing reform amendments to rape laws, model contracts for overseas domestic helpers, and a domestic violence act. Since its inception, Tenaganita has adopted a focus that deliberately links the local, national, regional, and international. Within this framework, the rights of women workers, both Malaysian nationals and foreigners, and migrant workers more generally, are explicitly linked to processes of globalization. Tenaganita's slogan is "Join us today to humanize globalization and bring dignity to workers and women".

What it striking, is that while both Tenaganita and the TWC2 address the issue of 'dignity', in the case of Tenaganita, dignity is broadened to include the needs of women and workers everywhere, whereas in the case of the TWC2 it is narrowly interpreted to refer to the humane treatment of foreign domestic workers in Singapore only. The transnational frame that informs Tenaganita's activities is apparent in the types of linkages that it has forged regionally and internationally. Unlike the TWC2 in Singapore, Tenaganita has formed links with a number of regional and international organisations. For example, several Tenaganita members have held executive positions in the Asia Pacific Forum on Women, Law and Development (APWLD).

Coordination of Action Research on AIDS and Mobility (CARAM) Asia is an NGO based in Malaysia with partner organisations throughout South and Southeast Asia. CARAM Asia seeks to "empower migrant workers and their communities through the promotion and protection of their rights and the creation of an enabling environment at all stages of migration to reduce HIV/AIDS vulnerability". The idea for the formation of regional network of organisations committed to action-research on Mobility and HIV/AIDS was mooted at a regional workshop organised by Tenaganita in 1994. The network was formed as a Tenaganita initiative in 1997 after a series of workshops on Migration and HIV/AIDS. Free University Amsterdam played a key role in its establishment, and is listed as a 'special partner'.

Dr Irene Fernandez, Director and co-founder of Tenaganita, sees a direct links between national and transnational processes, as evident in the expansion of the global economy, and thus the importance of addressing global issues locally: Decisions on the economy of countries are more and more determined by transnational corporations, with local elite and governments as parts of the process of promoting globalization. It benefits all of them, but contributes to the erosion of democratic rights. This quotation points to the centrality of globalization in understanding the place of women workers, including foreign domestic workers, in Malaysia. In contrast, the TWC2's activities pay little attention to forces of globalization, and few connections are drawn between local workers and migrant workers, except in terms of 'reducing demand'.

Irene Fernandez is the defendant in the longest running trial in Malaysia's history. She was charged in 1996 under Section 8A(2) of the Printing Presses and Publications Act (1984) (PPPA) for 'maliciously publishing false news'. Malice was defined as "whether or not the accused took 'reasonable measures' to verify the truth of the news". She was convicted in November 2003 and is currently free on bail pending an appeal. If the appeal is not upheld, she may face a prison sentence. As a result of the police investigation, Tenganita's bank account has been frozen and its members harassed. Among the issues that Fernandez was questioned about during her arrest and subsequent trial were the connections the organization has with overseas groups, and particularly the source of Tenaganita's funding.

Fernandez was arrested in March 1996 after she passed a copy of a Tenaganita report entitled 'Abuses, Torture and Dehumanized Treatment of Migrant Workers at Detention Camps' to the Malaysian daily, the *New Straits Times*. During 1994 and 1995, researchers from Tenaganita compiled over 300 interviews with undocumented migrant workers released from detention camps in Malaysia. The workers interviewed were mainly from Bangladesh, Indonesia and the Philippines. The report, issued in August 1995, documented cases of widespread ill-treatment of undocumented workers and "alleged patterns of human rights violations in the camps, including beatings, sexual abuse, malnutrition, dehydration, and denial of access to medical treatment".

In some instances, these abuses led to deaths from malnutrition, beri-beri and other treatable illnesses. Tenaganita called on the government to open the detention centres up for inspection and to set up an independent inquiry to investigate allegations of abuse. In September that year, the Deputy Minister of Home Affairs appointed an independent Visitor's Panel to study conditions in the camps, but the Panel's findings have never been released. While Irene Fernandez's trial points to the extreme measures that the Malaysian government uses to silence public debate over the rights of migrant workers and the extreme difficulties facing civil society actors who work in this arena, the trial itself has become a focal point for intensified national and transnational activism.

Fernandez herself recognises the importance of the trial in shaping national activism around women's and worker's rights: The trial has had a consciousness-raising effect educating the people about what is really happening... When I walk down the street, people stop me and say, 'we believe in what you're doing'. Indeed, women's organizations and migrant groups are organizing at the grassroots level more than ever. So, while free speech may be suppressed, free association is taking on new life.

As an indicator of the extent to which the Fernandez case has generated grassroots support, in November 2003, 91 Malaysian NGOs comprising women, consumer, human rights, environmental groups, peoples organisations and trade unions, came together to launch a campaign to support Irene Fernandez. Under the banner "Keep Irene Free, Defend the Defenders", the coalition aims to collect a million signatures nationally and internationally. Their activities support the views of Meredith Weiss and Saliha Hassan (2003) who argue that collective action through broad coalition networks may provide one means for advancing social change in Malaysia. Amnesty International and other international human rights and migrant worker rights organisations have monitored the trial and campaigned for repeal of the PPPA legislation. The outcome of the appeal is still pending and may take several more years.

The feminisation of migrant labour clearly is a transnational issue and many groups are working to improve the status of female migrant workers both globally and regionally. This study, however, points to problems that activists face as they attempt to advocate across national borders. Singapore and Malaysia are major receiving countries of migrant labour in the region, and like women elsewhere, domestic workers in both countries face a range of problems. Transnational actors seeking to advocate on their behalf not only face legal barriers to cross-border activism, but also the constraints of working in a narrowly defined sphere of civil society.

In Singapore, local activists are understandably wary of associating too closely with international groups, and limit their activities in ways that support state-defined 'out-of-bounds markers'. The Working Committee 2 tests the boundaries of these markers through its activities. It marks one of the first attempts by local NGOs and activists in Singapore to address a transnational issue. However, it has done so by focusing specifically on 'national' issues and deliberately avoiding affiliations or alliances with non- Singaporean based networks or organisations. But what becomes defined as the 'national' also takes shape within the OB markers. Members of the TWC2, like other civil society actors in Singapore, must pay attention to the complexities and contradictions of civil society as they consider what kind of activities to engage in. The group's decision to remain 'ad-hoc' rather than go through the lengthy registration process points to an awareness of this. While the TWC2's activities are creative, ultimately they remain non-confrontational and consensual.

The group lacks radical potential because its members fail to address the substantive issues of class, gender and ethnicity that underpin the demand for domestic migrant labour, as well as the factors that constrain the rights of these workers. For example, although its work could have provided an important opportunity to address the intersection between domestic violence against all women, and the 'private' nature of violence against domestic workers (that is, a critique of the public/ private dualism implicit in state policy-making), it remained largely focused on migrant women (thus reinforcing an us/them dualism). The campaign was also supportive of the state's own interest in developing a gracious and more civic-minded citizen, in contrast to the image of the 'ugly Singaporean' conjured up by images of maid-abuse.

The interrelated issues of citizenship, marriage, residence, and family migration, were largely unaddressed. In part, this reflects concerns about overstepping the state's OB markers. But, it also reflects the conservative nature of the organisation's gender activism. Although there was scope in the discussion of housework to discuss gender inequality it remained focused on gender difference; that is, it focused on getting more men to do housework, rather than addressing the questions of women's role as mothers in the process of nation- building. In Malaysia, women's and worker's movements are much more diverse and active than they are in Singapore. In part, this may be explained by the different historical trajectories of the two governments and the differential size, geographical spread and ethnic and religious make up of their populations.

Unlike the TWC2, Tenaganita is a formally registered NGO with over 10 years of grassroots experience working with migrant and local workers. Rather than focusing on consciousness-raising activities, it addresses the needs of migrant workers through policy, research and advocacy work. It explicitly employs a transnational frame into its activities by focusing on two issues: 1) the intersecting interests of national governments and multinational corporations in the exploitation of workers; and 2) the common experiences of workers, regardless of nationality. By focusing on structural issues rather than the abusive behaviours of individual employers, Tenaganita's activities transcend the implicit individualism of the TWC2's campaigns. The focus on globalisation is enhanced through Tenaganita's national, regional and international linkages.

This does not mean, however, that the ruling government plays a less significant role in shaping the nature of state-civil society relations in Malaysia. The Irene Fernandez case clearly shows that the Malaysian government is willing to use repressive legislation to crush alternative or critical voices. Rather than limiting the opportunities for transnational engagement, however, Irene Fernandez's trial has become another focal point for re-asserting a global focus to Tenganita's activities. At the grassroots level, it is a rallying point for coalition building among diverse NGOs. At an international level, the campaigning of human rights organisations has not only focused attention on the conditions of migrant workers and worker's rights activists, but also enhanced Tenaganita's interactions with a range of regionally and internationally based organisations. In the rush to celebrate the emergence of global civil society, feminists must stop to remind themselves that transnationalism does not transcend difference but is embedded within it.

As the two different case studies of the TWC2 and Tenaganita show, for transnational activism to be successful feminists must consciously delineate the boundaries of their engagement, paying close attention to the different situations 'on the ground' in those places where they seek to forge alliances. In some contexts this may mean developing creative responses to the limitations imposed by state forces. Here they can draw on the example of locally-based groups such as the TWC2. In other contexts local groups such as Tenaganita, which seeks to raise the profile of its work at the national level, may welcome limited transnational linkages. But these transnational engagements should proceed in such a way that they do not jeopardise local groups.

Recognising the limitations of transnationalism, rather than celebrating its successes, may thus be the greatest challenge facing the future of global feminism. Since the late 1970s Singapore has turned into one of the major receiving countries of foreign workers in Southeast Asia. With 612,200 foreign workers constituting 29.2% of the total workforce in the year 2000, Singapore now has the highest proportion of foreign workers in the labour force in Asia. About 500,000 of these foreign workers fall under the category of unskilled or low-skilled (of those, currently 135,000 are male construction workers and 150,000 are female domestic workers). Malaysia has historically represented a 'traditional source country' for migrant labour in Singapore, but since 1978 flows have ebbed due to Malaysia's own economic development.

As a result the so-called 'non-traditional source countries', such as such as Bangladesh, India, Indonesia, Sri Lanka, the Philippines and Thailand, began to be resorted to in order to meet persistent labour shortages. In addition, the expansion of the middle classes and women's increasing entry into the labour market has triggered a rise in demand for foreign domestic workers in the context of a lack of state-sponsored child (and other) care facilities. Today, one in seven households in Singapore employs a foreign maid. Singapore is also known for its recruitment of so-called "foreign talent", i.e. professional and highly skilled workers. To manage the fairly large number of foreign workers within its midst, the government of Singapore has implemented clear migration policies with visa categories available for all skill levels. Unlike many other migrant receiving countries, Singapore provides legal employment opportunities not only for skilled, but also for unskilled workers.

Non-governmental concerns for and involvement in migrant labour issues has a relatively short history. Some grassroots activism and service provisioning existed in the late 1980s, and there are numerous (but small) skills centers that have existed for a decade. The plight of foreign workers was for quite some time "off-limits" to socially active citizens because of its association with the "Marxist Conspiracy" case in 1987. In May 1987, 22 people were arrested under the ISA (Internal Security Act) for allegedly threatening the state and national interests. Those arrested included Catholic social workers and lay workers at the Geylang Catholic Center for Foreign Workers. They lobbied for higher wages, social security benefits, job security and employment conditions for all foreign workers. The Catholic Church was seen as a "cover for political agitation" and the Geylang Center was subsequently closed.

This 'historical' incident partly explains the Catholic Church's and other civil society organisations' reluctance to address the needs of foreign workers for many years after 1987. Since 1995, more organizations offering a range of services/ projects as well as advocacy have again appeared. This happened largely in response to the Flor Contemplacion case which triggered the gradual rise of public attention regarding migrant workers' welfare and rights. During the last couple of years, media coverage of various migrant worker issues has also increased. The trade union movement in Singapore has 'historically' (starting in 1969) followed a strategy of acting in partnership with the state.

Since 1969, trade unions no longer confined themselves to collective bargaining for the workers, but also concerned themselves with the overall economic development, productivity, and performance of the society at large. In this sense, it has been argued that the labour movement has transformed itself from a wage-negotiating to a nation- building institution. This report covers existing NGO and trade union activities revolving around migrant workers in Singapore. It relies upon a wide variety of reports and materials originating from non- governmental organizations (local and international NGOs as well as trade unions), academic papers, international organizations (ILO) as well as interviews with key informants/ senior staff at NGOs and trade unions.

COUNTRY'S MIGRANT LABOUR CONTEXT

General Labour Market Situation

Singapore's extraordinary record of growth between 1960 and 2000 resulted in enormous benefits to workers in all sectors. Much of Singapore's economic success is typically attributed to its human resources policies. Changes in its labour law in the 1960s created an extremely flexible labour market, and relaxed regulations on working hours and dismissals, while at the same time it initiated Programmes that provided workers with unemployment benefits and paid medical leave. Its use of educational policy emphasizing training in technology and computer fields helped upgrade skill levels. As of June 2001, out of a total population of 4.02

million, Singapore's labour force stood at 2.12 million, a 27% increase over the last decade.

The unemployment rate was 3.4% (72,900 persons), a 78.95% increase over the course of the decade (ibid.). Educational attainment levels have increased significantly. Singaporean workers with a diploma or degree have more than doubled over the past decade and now account for 27.5 % of the total workforce. The relatively high educational level among the national workforce largely explains the demand for unskilled foreign workers in certain sectors/jobs. The fact that Singapore's workforce is an aging one is another reason for the relatively large non-resident population (now accounting for 18.6% of the total population, or 754,500 persons). Singapore's industrial composition has changed over the past decade.

Whereas the manufacturing sector was once dominant, financial and business services along with community and personal services have grown significantly. This is in line with the prevailing trend towards a knowledge-based economy. With regard to the distribution of employment by sector in 2002, 75% were in services, 24% in industry, 1% in agriculture and fishing; manufacturing accounted for 18%. There was a downward trend in manufacturing but this sector still employed the largest number of workers in 2002 (368,000).

Profile of Migrant Labour

Singapore began to experience a shortage of labour in the early 1960s. This gradually resulted in a demand for foreign workers of all categories. Demand for semi- and unskilled workers have been on the increase since 1984. Initially, a large number of such workers from Thailand and elsewhere were illegal. Since then, the government has revised its migration policies and imposed fines on employers in order to drastically reduce the number of illegal workers.

Malaysians make up the largest nationality group with a total of approximately 200,000. From among the 150,000 foreign domestic workers (hereafter: FDWs), most come from Indonesia (about half), followed by the Philippines and Sri

Lanka. The population of male foreign workers is mostly composed of Southeast and South Asians, with Thais constituting the largest group, followed by South Asians, Indonesians and Chinese. Today, approx. 500,000 to 600,000 foreign workers are employed legally in Singapore, constituting nearly 30% of the total workforce. The bulk is comprised of low skilled and household labourers whose monthly wages are about 14% of the average Singaporean wage.

In the 1990s, nine out of ten construction workers in Singapore used to be migrants (ILO 1999), but this figure has dropped due to a slowdown in this sector. It is now shipbuilding and repair which is experiencing an upsurge in demand for foreign workers. Apart from domestic work, the health sector constitutes another significant employer of foreign women. According to the Singapore Nursing Board's Annual Report of 2003, there were a total of 18,392 Registered and Enrolled nurses, of whom 2818 RNs and 1807 ENs were foreign. They were mainly from the Philippines, Republic of China, Malaysia and others like Myanmar and Sri Lanka.

The numbers have apparently not changed much in the past few years. Nursing homes are mainly staffed by foreign nursing assistants, some of whom may be registered/enrolled nurses in their own countries (email communication, Singapore Nursing Association, July 12, 2005). 2.3 Policy Framework and Issues Singapore's labour management policy is open to migrant workers with professional skills (of whom there are about 80,000, according to the Acting Minister for Manpower, Ng Eng Hen; *The Sunday Times*, September 5, 2004), but it is rather strict vis-à-vis semi-skilled and unskilled workers in the construction, shipbuilding and ship-repair, and other menial labour-intensive industries as well as in domestic services.

The latter enjoy fewer entitlements than the former. Singapore's policy has been described as remaining "firmly committed to ensuring that unskilled and low-skilled foreign workers are managed as a temporary and controlled phenomenon through a series of measures, key among which are the work permit system, the dependency ceiling (which regulates the proportion of foreign to local workers), and the foreign worker levy." For domestic workers, there is also a 'security bond' (S$ 5,000) imposed upon employers to ensure the maid does not 'run away' and leaves the country when her contract expires. The majority of unskilled and semi-skilled workers come through legal work placement agencies on employment contracts for a maximum of two years (subject to a one-off renewal). Their wage is lower than that of Singaporeans and Malaysians (in the 1990s, S$ 450-600 per month for Thais and Bangladeshis, whereby their expenses for daily maintenance per month were S$ 150; Prompiam 1996).

Among domestic workers, there is no standard employment contract and wage levels are linked to national origin, with Filipinos usually being the best paid, followed by Indonesians and then by Sri Lankans. There are three main visa categories available to foreign workers:

1. Semi-permanent residents with semi-permanent work permits who are allowed to take any job anywhere in Singapore (valid for five years);
2. Foreign professionals with annual permits called employment passes which are issued only for specific jobs and for a specific duration (valid for one to five years);
3. Seasonal workers with short-term permits usually valid for two years (subject to renewal).

Foreigners falling within the first category are eligible to apply for citizenship. Just like citizens, they face no restrictions in the labour market and can bring their families (spouses, however, do not have the automatic right to work). Although tied to a specific company, employment pass holders enjoy limitless opportunities to get their permits extended. Work permits are also given to unskilled workers whose salaries are low by local standards but who do not enjoy the same entitlements as professionals. Unskilled migrants are the only group of foreign workers subject to the *Employment of Foreign Workers Act* of 1990 (hereafter: EFW Act).

This Act defines foreign workers as "non-citizens who are looking for jobs or are in employment and who earn not more than $ 1,500 a month" and is designed to control the employment of this category of foreign workers in Singapore. All migrants earning below S$ 1,500 per month are covered by this Act, including FDWs. It is a serious offence for any foreign worker to work or for any employer to employ a foreign worker without such a work permit. A work permit is issued by the Ministry of Manpower to allow a foreign worker to engage in employment in Singapore. It is valid only for the occupation, the employer, the specified worker and for the stated period it is issued for. A police officer or an employment inspector may arrest any person who is working without a work permit.

This being the case, Section 13 of the EFW Act stipulates that a foreign worker must produce his/her permit for inspection whenever necessary, and return his/her work pass through the employer to the Ministry within seven days of stopping work. A work permit holder is not permitted to marry a Singaporean citizen (Frost and Chiu 2003). Section 11 of the EFW Act states that any employer hiring a foreign worker is required to pay a levy imposed by the Minister of Labour. Employers must keep a register of all foreign workers. Section 24 of the EFW Act, however, allows a foreign worker to claim wages and benefits from an employer for the period the employer has hired him/her to work without a valid work pass, if the worker can prove the employer has hired him/her.

Singapore has a general Employment Act covering all un- and lower skilled workers, local and foreign, except for domestic workers and seamen who are explicitly excluded. The explanation for this is the different nature of working environments compared to that of a traditional factory/industrial workplace. There is no minimum wage for foreign workers as is also the case with locals. Wages are given according to productivity and determined by tripartite wage council. The wage levels of FDWs are affected by direct demand and supply factors. Officially, a worker is not supposed to work for more than 44 hours.

A safe working environment is to be ensured. Participation in a half-day health and safety course in the native language of the foreign workers is mandatory as far as the construction sector is concerned. Group medical insurance is to be purchased by employers for foreigners. Employers must also ensure a job before foreign recruitment. A foreign worker levy is imposed to bring the gap between foreign and local skill levels closer through training (but the latter is not provided to FDWs). The Factories Act safeguards workers' health and safety in the workplace and the Workmen's Compensation Act provides for compensation to workers injured at work. Both Acts cover local and foreign workers equally. Health care standards are also the same for local and foreign workers alike.

The Skills Development and Levy Act provides for training for all workers, local and foreign, but there is no training for domestic workers. Workers who register their claims with the MOM will be issued special passes to remain in Singapore while their claims are being settled. *FDWs* Since the infamous Flor Contemplacion case in 1995, the government has become aware of the diplomatic embarrassment maid abuse can cause and blacken its image abroad (a concern in view of losing global investors). It has therefore taken some measures aimed at providing some minimum services to FDWs.

The Ministry of Manpower (hereafter: MOM) provides conciliation services (the Foreign Workers Unit was set up in 1997; a help-line for maids is run from there) in case of complaints from domestic workers. If an issue cannot be resolved in this manner, however, domestic workers do not have recourse to the courts because they are not covered by the Employment Act. In addition, MOM has designed guidelines and a 'training course' for first time employers. Partly in response to increased exposure and rising incidents of 'problem cases', the MOM has made more moves to improve the safety and welfare of FDWs:

- Introduction of a compulsory orientation Programme for all first time employers in April 2004;
- Accreditation as a requirement for employment agencies to get their licenses renewed in June 2004; this is done by two bodies, the Consumers Association of Singapore and Association of Employment Agencies Singapore; certification is meant to maintain standards in an industry

of some 700 employment agencies; the certification is valid for four years;

- Monitoring of employers who change their domestic workers frequently since October 2004; all employers who make five or more work permit applications in a year must go back to the classroom for the employers' orientation Programme;
- Raising of minimum age for FDWs to 23 and introduction of educational pre-requisites in January 2005; FDWs must have proof of at least eight years of formal education;
- Requirement for employers spelled out for the first time in work permit conditions: they must pay an FDW's salary every month and no later than seven days after the last day of that month (February 2005);
- Introduction of multiple-choice entry test in English for all new domestic workers in April 2005; FDWs have to pass the test within three working days of their arrival in Singapore.

Parliament passed an amendment to the Penal Code that mandated more severe penalties for confining or sexually abusing a domestic helper. Warnings to employers of the heavier penalties under the amended Penal Code if they are found abusing their FDWs are clearly outlined in the MOM's *Guide For Employers. Illegal employment* The Government amended the Immigration Act in 1995 in an attempt to curtail employers who are hiring foreign workers who are residing in the country illegally. Due to various measures designed to regulate the employment of foreign workers, such as the foreign worker levy and implementation of a dependency ratio which is adjusted periodically to reflect the supply and demand in the labour market, many employers had resorted to hiring non-registered foreigners, particularly in the construction industry.

The amendments include the following provisions:

- Contractors are now responsible for illegal workers found residing or working on worksites. Unlike the previous situation, they can no longer pass the responsibility to sub- contractors by denying knowledge of the workers' immigration status.

- The onus of proof with regard to the immigration status of workers now resides solely with the employer. Prosecutors are no longer required to prove that employers knew their employees were illegal immigrants. In the past, prosecutions often failed because employers were able to claim that they did not know their employees were illegal immigrants.
- Employers of illegal workers are subject to heavy fines.

Repeated offenders may even be jailed or caned. According to the NTUC's Migrant Worker Forum, in 2004, 521 local employers were prosecuted in Singapore for illegally employing migrant workers.

Political-Economic and Social Issues

Trade union membership is in principle open to foreign workers, but in practice the membership of migrant workers is tied to certain sectors, with domestic workers being totally left out because of their 'non-traditional' employment situation. According to the chairperson of the Migrant Workers Forum at the SNTUC, the key issues and concerns for foreign workers centre mainly upon workplace grievances which can be broadly classified under two headings:

1. Employment related, and
2. Welfare, occupational health and safety issues.

Employment-related issues are mainly about to non-payment or under-payment of wages and unauthorized deductions. Issues to do with welfare, occupational health and safety are concerns pertaining to accommodation, long working hours and workplace hazards. The latter includes work-related injuries and accidents as well as physical/sexual abuse (as encountered by FDWs). One example of non-payment that has reached public attention is the case of 400 Indian workers last year who protested peacefully to claim 4 to 6 months wages owned by their employer (a construction company). A study of Thai workers conducted in the mid-90s listed the following major problems from the viewpoint of the workers:

1. Health,
2. Money related (debts incurred)
3. Labour law and status of illegal worker,
4. Problems related to civil and criminal laws and law enforcement.

Since then, however, the Singaporean government has made improvements to tackle the problem of illegal employment as well as to improve the safety situation of construction workers. The latter might explain the downward trend in the statistics on fatal accidents. The Flor Contemplacion case triggered some awareness of the FDWs' situation in general and of Filipinas in particular. More recently, Indonesian domestic workers have been in the spotlight as a result of reported cases of suicides, fatal accidents, murder and various types of abuse involving their employers and their employers' children. Between 1999 and 2004, 114 Indonesian domestic helpers died (due to accident or suicide) in Singapore, and there were five cases of murder (employer killed by the maid) during the same period.

These incidents point to the serious psychological and other problems some FDWs encounter which are not always directly related to the actual employment situation in Singapore. But these have not been investigated in-depth. Employment-specific problems that all FDWs are subjected to include:

1. Non-coverage by Employment Act (explicit exclusion of "domestic servants");
2. Control through levy and security bond;
3. Orientation Programmes where they are told to be submissive, obedient, not to follow their religious practices and where they were not given information on rights or channels of recourse;
4. No uniform contracts, no uniform wage across all nationality groups, no uniform rules on days off or working hours which results in an ethnic hierarchy among domestic workers with Filipinas usually getting the most preferential treatment.

Unfair dismissal appears to be not uncommon also. There are, e.g. cases of Indonesian domestic workers being dumped on the nearby island of Batam by their employers without having received their wages. It seems as if FDWs' employment may be terminated any time without notice and they are not permitted to use the proceedings under the Employment Act for making salary claims. Until recently (February 2005), they had no right to a regular pay day. Partly related to the security bond imposed by the government, domestic maids are often locked up in the apartments of their employers, have their passports taken away and live in total isolation which has a negative impact on their psychological welfare.

Many of MOM's new policies are directed at immigration status and some measures have been implemented to tackle the problem of non-payment of wages. According to a local newspaper, however, current penalties for errant employers are too light, and no employer has been jailed for not paying up (The New Paper, "Jail and cane them...says one union leader", July 20, 2004). Since then, several employers of FDWs have been prosecuted successfully by the MOM. At least one employer had to pay a fine and serve a default sentence of six weeks in jail (communication with SNTUC, 7 September, 18 October, and 2 November 2005).

Marriage with a local or permanent resident of Singapore is not permitted for any unskilled or semi-skilled foreign worker. From the Singaporean viewpoint, this is meant to avoid social problems. From the migrants' perspective, this might be a source of problems but little is known about this group of migrants' social (and intimate) life while in Singapore. There are no bilateral or multilateral labour and social security agreements between Singapore and the sending countries of its foreign workforce.

MIGRANT LABOUR ORGANIZATIONS

The organizations in this section are understood as referring to collectives of/organizations run by migrant workers themselves as opposed to NGOs set up by Singaporeans. There are strict rules governing the formal registration of NGOs and the state takes a strong interventionist stance. All registered organizations are expressly prohibited from engaging in "political activity". In addition, foreign-based NGOs find it difficult to become formally registered in Singapore, and without registration they cannot operate locally. This explains the very small presence of international NGOs. Because of the strict regulatory rules of the government, it is sometimes not quite clear whether an organization has formal NGO status or not. Formal organizations run by migrant workers do not exist. The Societies Act as such does not prohibit non-citizens from forming organizations – and in fact many expatriates have set up groups (like the American Club).

Prompiam (1996) also writes that the setting up of such an organization is generally speaking not against Singaporean law, however organizing among workers is illegal. Any group that intends to advocate issues of rights has to go through a lengthy registration process and it is presumed that citizenship would be an issue. The case of the women's organization AWARE provides an example: when it was registered, foreign citizens could only become associate members without the right to vote at AGMs or to hold office. Any entirely non-citizen group attempting to register a rights-based organization is unheard of – this could be a good test case for the future.

NATURE OF MIGRANT ORGANIZATIONS

The few 'organizations' identified as relevant for this section can be classified as:

1. Training centres,
2. Informal networks.

Training Centres Bayanihan Centre

The Bayanihan Centre is the second of its kind run by the Filipino Overseas Workers Association (the first is in Hong Kong). It was first mooted in 1998 and officially opened by President Arroyo in 2001 as a training/enrichment centre for FDWs. It is currently located on a former primary school compound and has ample facilities with proper computer labs.

The monthly rental is half funded by the Philippine government with the equal share being provided by the Singapore government. The day-to-day operations and Programmes are mainly supervised by the Philippine Embassy in Singapore. The Philippine Bayanihan Society, comprised of Filipino and Singaporean professionals, is active in fund raising for the running of this centre.

Other

There is also the 'Go Forth' training centre, located in Lucky Plaza, as well as the 'Holy Family' (church-based in the East of Singapore) which offer training courses to Filipino domestic workers. The Embassy runs courses free of charge once a month (every third Sunday) on its premises for Indonesian FDWs. These revolve around language training (English, Mandarin), religious guidance, and skill enhancement sessions such as sewing. About 200 to 300 maids normally turn up for the English and Chinese language classes, religious lectures and the occasional talk by maid agencies on how to work and communicate better with their employers. The Embassy also provides a temporary shelter for Indonesian domestic workers who encounter serious problems such as salary disputes or physical/sexual abuse.

Informal network Indo Family

There is in fact one informal network run on a volunteer basis by Indonesian domestic maids for fellow domestic helpers in Singapore, a helpline called *Indo Family*. This was started by Nurifah Rasidi, a domestic worker herself who has been working in Singapore for eight years (by the year 2005). She is currently assisted by eight other maids who attend to the problems of newly arrived compatriots by 'counseling' them via their hand-phones or by paying a visit to the domestic helper in need during their spare time.

The type of questions they are asked by newly arrived Indonesians usually pertain to communication problems they have with their Singaporean employers. In a newspaper article, Nurifah Rasidi is quoted as saying that during the last two years, she listened to 180 maids who have had to endure everything from beatings to deprivation of food, salary and human contact. The root cause of many problems is the language barrier, with the FDWs not understanding instructions and employers getting frustrated and angry.

Programmes and Services

The informal network of Indo Family assists with the everyday problems newly arrived domestic workers from Indonesia encounter, helps them settle into their jobs and eases communication problems with employers by translating or mediating between them. Considering that Indonesians make up the largest number of FDWs in Singapore, it is unclear whether the relatively low number of cases (180) this network received during the last two years is an indication of their network not being widely known among Indonesians or there simply not being more 'problem cases'.

The training courses set up by the Filipinos for their compatriots seem to be aimed at improving domestic workers' skill levels in preparation for their return rather than at addressing problems in Singapore *per se*, whereas the Indonesian embassy's is more directed at making life in Singapore easier (language skills) and offering a venue for socializing. All of these initiatives serve to create a sense of 'community' and social space for their 'clients' who are all FDWs. There are no migrant organizations serving migrants in other sectors.

NGO INVOLVEMENT IN MIGRANT LABOUR

Key Migrant NGOs in the Country

The existing groups (NGOs set up by Singaporeans) can be clustered in three groupings:

1. Faith- based;
2. Training centres;
3. Shelters/counseling;
4. Advocacy NGOs.

Faith-based organisations *Archdiocesan Commission for the Pastoral Care of Migrants & Itinerant People (ACMI)* Instigated by a Filipino priest, the Catholic Archdiocese of Singapore established the Commission for Migrants & Itinerant People (ACMI) in 1998 with the aim of reaching out to migrant workers/students/travelers and providing support for them. It is a registered Volunteer Hosting Organization (VHO) with the National Volunteers and Philanthropy Center (NVPC). In the beginning it operated with the assistance of volunteers, among them domestic workers themselves. Since 2000, there have been two full time staff, one of them a Filipina.

From the beginning the ACMI has worked with the MOM to run workshops for employers on how to establish harmonious working relationships with FDWs. Other activities include skills training/enrichment courses, free takeaway meals, 24-hour hotline/counseling, shelter. The ACMI has also been active in fund raising activities to assist migrant workers diagnosed with cancer or injured in workplace accidents (source: SNTUC leaflet). The ACMI collaborated with the Community Development Council (CDC) and Heartware Network (youth NGO) to jointly organize a "Best Employer of a Foreign Domestic Helper Contest" in 2001.

The awards presented by the Minister of State/Law and Home Affairs served to remind both local employers and migrant workers about the importance of harmonious working relations and the contribution to Singapore's development and growth of migrant workers. With the support of the Catholic Lawyers Guild the ACMI receives legal assistance on a pro bono basis for its cases. No information was available on how many cases have been dealt with so far and the nature of these cases. The ACMI runs the Madonna Grotto, a crisis home, to house migrants in need of abode for an interim period.

The activities at the Grotto include bible study, rosary recitation, helping at the soup kitchen and preparing other foods. One respondent (personal interview, June 2005), however, mentioned that the shelter run by the ACMI has been closed down. In May 2003, the Hope Haven was launched. It is a counseling service for migrant workers with outreach helpdesks at Lucky Plaza and Little India. These desks are manned by volunteers every Sunday.

An-Nisa (Sultan Mosque)

An-Nisa was started in 2000 by the Women's Committee of the Sultan Mosque as a support group mainly for Indonesian FDWs. They have facilities for gathering and provide religious classes, skills workshops (English, flower arrangement and handicraft lessons). These classes take place every second and fourth Sunday of the month and are said to attract about 600 maids. Embassy staff members have been invited to jointly celebrate Hari Raya Puasa and have in turn offered support in organizing future activities. An-Nisa has participated in fun fairs (selling handicrafts made by FDWs) organized by the Indonesian Embassy in conjunction with Indonesia's Independence Day and Singapore's National Day.

Madonna/Laksetha Skills Centers

These Livelihood Skills centers cater to FDWs of various nationalities. At the Madonna Center, domestic workers can learn basic computer training, cooking, hairstyling, dressmaking and tailoring, English language, nursing aide/ care-giver and music playing. The Laksetha Skills center is managed by members of the Sri Lankan Catholic Community but invites FDWs from different countries to take part in similar courses as offered by the Madonna Center. Volunteer teachers include Singaporeans and non-Singaporeans. Together the two centers are said to provide livelihood skills training for more than 200 students a year.

Marymount Convent/Novena Skills Training Centre

This centre is run by the Good Shepherds Sisters. It started out as a fairly large centre but has begun to phase out its services.

Franciscan Missionaries of Mary Convent

This Franciscan Missionaries of set up a training centre called FILODEP for Filipino FDWs.

St. Francis Worker's Centre

The present set up of the SFWC started in 2000. It serves the needs of workers, especially migrant workers, in the Jurong area. The objective is to assist mainly industrial workers (both local and foreign) with finding solutions for their work-related problems (non-payment of salary, industrial accidents, claims of workmen compensations, living in dormitories, budget and saving schemes) by helping them understand the labour laws, and the use the official channels and mechanisms available (i.e. the MOM complaints and claims departments). It also provides space for the workers to gather, share their problems, celebrate cultural events etc.

The staff consists of (unpaid) volunteers. They provide specific Programmes, for example, for workers to overcome alcoholic addiction, Programmes on budget and saving schemes, and awareness raising about labour laws to claim wages, overtime and compensation for accidents. They are especially frequented by Thai and Indian workers. Counseling is also provided as well as assistance with email communication. The Centre has contact with individuals in the Catholic Migrant Commission, HOME and TWC2 as well as individual contact with the chairperson of SNTUC's Migrant Worker Forum. But there are no joint activities or Programmes in any formal manner with any of the above. This Centre is a member of MFA (Migrant Forum in Asia), an Asian-wide network of migrant worker organizations that holds regular meetings.

Muslim Converts Association

This association also runs a Programme from the Sultan Mosque which is coordinated by an Indonesian woman who is married to a Singaporean. Shelter/counseling HOME After several years of being the first chairperson of the ACMI, Ms. Bridget Lew left the Commission to launch a new migrant centre known as the HOME (Humanitarian Organization for Migration Economics) in December 2004. HOME runs two shelters, one for men and one for women. She is assisted by two social workers. Ms. Lew continues her good working relationship with the MOM in solving individual cases and trying to influence

MOM's policies by lobbying for changes in the system. HOME has partnered with the MOM and SNTUC's Migrant Workers Forum in providing counseling, assistance and hardship grants to needy migrant workers in Singapore affected by the recent tsunami disaster.

According to Ms. Lew, this was the only real collaboration she has had with SNTUC. The Working Committee 2 (TWC2) emerged in late 2002. It grew out of the women's organization AWARE, Singapore's main feminist organization. Unlike other NGOs, the TWC2 was not formally registered through the Societies Act. It was formed as an ad-hoc group with a one-year life-span to "promote respect for domestic workers through education and secure better treatment of domestic workers through legislation". It consists of society activists, lawyers, lecturers and students formed to raise awareness of FDW issues through public education and advocacy for more structured support. They launched two major campaigns: "Dignity Overdue" and "Sunday Off".

TWC2 focused on three main topics:

1. Reducing demand for (and dependency on) FDWs;
2. Providing standardized employment contracts;
3. Improving the treatment of FDWs by their employers.

Their activities were aimed at (1) drawing attention to the gendered division of labour within the home and finding alternative solutions to Singapore's reliance on the labour of domestic workers; and (2) addressing the abuse of FDWs. In the past, TWC2 had conducted public forums and private dialogues with key stakeholders in exploring possible initiatives to further safeguard the interests of FDWs in Singapore. The TWC2 collaborated with the ACMI to organize an "Out of Love" charity concert as part of fund raising efforts for a shelter to house migrant workers who may be in distress.

Their activities further involve:

1. Conducting of research; collection of information;
2. Dialogue with stakeholders;

3. Information campaign;
4. Community involvement;
    1. Contribution to governance – government bodies; trade unions; embassies; other NGOs (such as the ACMI); accreditation bodies (AEAS and Case Trust);
    2. Documentation.

Their overall aim is to promote respect for domestic workers through education, and secure better treatment through legislation and other means. The follow-up to this one-year ad hoc initiative is the new TWC2 (the acronym now means *Transient Workers Count 2*) which is finally legally registered as a society. In addition to domestic workers, it intends to concern itself with the welfare of transient workers in general in Singapore (such as e.g. construction workers). What TWC2's concrete projects/Programmes are going to be, is yet to be seen.

Think Centre

The Think Centre describes itself as an "independent multi-partisan political non-governmental organization" which was first registered as a business (RCB) in July 1999 and has been registered as a society since October 2001 (under ROS). It aims to critically examine issues related to political development, democracy, rule of law, human rights and civil society. It tries to promote awareness about human rights in general. The Centre's activities include research, publishing, organising events and networking. It engages in lawful lobbying activities such as organizing forums, turning up at ministerial dialogues and letter-writing campaigns by email. The president has also been working on migrant worker related rights issues and taken up consulting and training projects for regional NGOs related to migrant workers and human rights issues. They have 30 members, a website, but no funding for office space.

Other *UNIFEM Singapore* UNIFEM runs a Migrant Worker Project aimed at helping Filipino domestic workers in Singapore plan for a successful return home. Currently most domestic workers spend the best part of their lives working overseas only to return home to the same poverty they left, with no plans or money for their future. This is the angle UNIFEM tries to address by running several training courses for migrant workers, or rather modules making up one course, namely:

1. Managing Family Issues Training,
2. Personal Budgeting and Saving Training,
3. Entrepreneurship Training.

A fourth module consists of a one-day briefing by the Philippine OWWA (Overseas Workers Welfare Administration), the taking of which is a requirement by OWWA regulations for completing the overall course. UNIFEM collaborates with the Center for Overseas Workers in Manila in running an economic reintegration Programme in the Philippines.

Nature of Programmes and Services

Most of the Programmes and services of existing NGOs or community groups are directed at FDWs – especially the training centres but also the advocacy group TWC2 which is not surprising as the TWC2 is rooted in the women's movement and thus focuses on women issues. The new TWC2 claims to include male migrant workers, but so far no concrete action has been taken yet. The training centres also all focus on domestic workers. The only general human rights NGO in Singapore, the Think Centre, are concerned with all types of migrant workers. Purely foreign-run initiatives exist to date only in form of an informal network (Indo Family). Other NGOs do involve foreigners – either former migrant workers themselves or expat compatriots who help out on a volunteer basis. Most existing NGO/ community groups, however, focus on foreign domestic workers. The Filipino community and embassy became active sooner than their Indonesian counterparts, but the latter have also become more involved.

TRADE UNION INVOLVEMENT IN MIGRANT LABOUR

Main Trade Union Groups

The bulk of the unions in Singapore have joined a labour union federation, the SNTUC. In 1979, 94.7 percent of union members were affiliated with SNTUC which grew to 96.8 percent in 1984 and 98 percent in 1986. The vast majority of unions (69 of the 72 registered unions) today are affiliated with SNTUC. There are also three independent trade unions (Air Line Pilots, Transport-Vessels, Film Industrial Employees). About 16% of the entire workforce (338,311 in 2002) is unionized (Labor Rights Report, n.d.). The number of overall employee trade unions has fallen during the last decade (from 83 to 71), despite a rise in membership (around 121,000 or an increase of 35.8 %). Sixty-five of all trade unions are under the SNTUC.

When looking at trade union membership across sectors, all sectors have witnessed growth, many of them significant (especially construction). SNTUC's main concern is the welfare of all workers, including migrants. In a recent background paper (SNTUC 2005), it stated that "the labour movement has always recognized and accepted the need for migrant workers to supplement/complement our limited human resources, and appreciate their contribution to Singapore's development and growth". Migrant workers can join trade unions in Singapore. The overall non-Singaporean/foreign membership is about 17.5% or 74,000 foreign workers of the 500,000 work permit holders. The KFEU (Keppel Shipyard union) has the highest percentage of foreigners at about 70%, followed by the SSEU (Sembawang shipyard union) at about 50%.

The UWEEI (electronic/electrical sector union) is one of the largest unions in Singapore and has an about 40% foreign membership, most of whom are likely to be Malaysians as this sector is dominated by Malaysian foreign workers. BATU's (Building, Construction and Timber Industries Employees Union) overall membership is 22,000 of which 20% are migrant workers. It is possible for migrant workers to be appointed as liaisons or representatives at the branch level. According to *The Straits Times* (8 March 2004), only 2% of union leaders in Singapore are foreigners – and presumably Malaysian but no exact information could be found.

Union Services to Migrant Labour

The trade union movement sees its role as working in partnership with employers and the government. They are also heavily involved in social, educational and recreational activities. As members, migrant workers are said to enjoy the same union protection, services and union benefits as local members (although not those extended to local workers' families). The construction union BATU settles any disputes on a group basis including those foreigners who are members. In some cases, subscription fees for foreign workers are subsidized by their employers to enable them to become members. Migrant workers in Singapore have the opportunity to upgrade their skills and to acquire formal certification of competency in a trade.

Employers are encouraged to offer skill improvement to their foreign workers as the levy is lower the higher the skill level of the individual foreign worker is. According to the SNTUC, in 2002-03, about 9,000 migrant workers (on work permits) had benefited from the Basic Education for Skills Training (BEST) and Work Improvement through Secondary Education (WISE) Programmed administered by the union. Rahman and Fee (2005) report in their study on Bangladeshi workers that "a significant number of migrants had upgraded their skills over time", leaving 52% of migrants unskilled at the time of the interview. These opportunities, however, are only available to workers in certain sectors, such as construction.

According to a recent questionnaire which the ILO sent out to trade unions around the world (to which 42 trade unions responded, among them SNTUC), 16 unions replied affirmatively to the question of whether they have a designated migration officer. Two of these unions are in Southeast Asia: Hong Kong's CTU and SNTUC. The main responsibilities of such migration officers were mostly

1. Training and information, followed by
2. Policy advocacy,
3. Individual assistance and lastly
4. Recruitment of members.

SNTUC's designated migration officer is part of the 'Migrant Workers Forum' (MWF) which was set up in 2002 and chaired by Mr. Yeo Guat Kwang. The MWF consists of nine unions with the key leaders involved. One of the tasks the MWF is involved in is the organization of social events. During the May Day celebration, one day is now earmarked for foreign workers. This year's May Day Outing for Foreign Workers (2005) was attended by ca.10,000 migrants. There are ad hoc, one-off initiatives in times of a specific 'crisis' or event. SNTUC's supermarket chain, Fairprice, for instance donated food to the Indian workers who were stranded after their company collapsed and did not pay their wages.

The NGOs/community-based organisations stated that there is no true working relationship between them and SNTUC apart from ad hoc, one-off activities as e.g. in the case of post- Tsunami relief work. There are no concrete projects or Programmes both types of organizations collaborate on. This might partly have to do with SNTUC being reluctant to get involved in domestic worker issues and many NGOs being concerned with exactly this group of migrants. The more policy- and advocacy oriented NGOs have a very good relationship with MOM in the form of regular dialogue. Those involved in service provision tend to take their cases to the MOM instead of SNTUC.

In fact, the MOM is seen as truly trying its best to solve many of the migrant worker related problems, with dedicated staff. By contrast, NGOs lament that the SNTUC's Migrant Workers Forum is not active and not visible enough. But this is partly related to SNTUC serving a different constituency of workers. NGOs also think that there is very little concrete targeting of employers and that penalties for errant employers are too light. SNTUC's MWF highlighted its cooperation with one specific NGO which has a similar working style/method. It also claims to have offered NGOs to submit concrete proposals for projects/Programmes to the MWF, but to date none of the existing NGOs have come forward.

Trends and Developments: Union Policy Advocacies and Stance

The setting up of a Migrant Worker Forum at SNTUC constitutes an important new development with regard to union's involvement in migrant worker issues. Migrant workers who are members are supposedly treated the same as local workers. More recently, the chairman of the MWF has released a statement about the need to do more to raise awareness amongst migrants on their rights. This statement was made in connection with the official endorsement of ILO's Plan of Action 2004. But to other stakeholders (NGOs/CBOs), the role and strategy of the MWF is not clear.

When it comes to the mediation process, the MOM is seen by NGOs as trying to solve the dispute of non- payment of salary of migrant workers but SNTUC seems rather silent in this regard. According to SNTUC, this however is not correct. With regard to workers in the sectors they represent, they fight as much for migrants' wage payments (for instance when a company goes bankrupt) as they do for nationals. But such cases are not publicized and hence not publicly known.

DYNAMICS OF MIGRANT LABOUR WORK

Strengths and Weaknesses/Gaps of Existing Migrant Labour Work NGOs

The main weakness of NGOs and CBOs is that they tend to be small with little if any regular budgets. Few have full time staff. Except for the SFWC, they do not engage in transnational networking across the region or with NGOs based in the sending countries (the 'new' TWC2, however, is planning to do so). This is partly related to the problem of having very limited resources available. There is in fact no NGO/CBO specifically assisting those types of migrants comprised of male workers due to their type of job (i.e. who do not work as domestic helpers). For some there were no services at all until fairly recently.

One of the recommendations by Prompiam (1996), for instance, was that there should be an organization to assist Thai workers in Singapore. This was in the late 1990s. Since then, however, the SFWC has taken up this issue of assisting migrant workers. Unlike in Hong Kong, there is no foreign worker led-NGO (such as a Filipino NGO led by Filipino activists), apart from the informal network, *Indo Family*. The NGOs' advantage, on the other hand, is that they organize public fora/events and bring issues to the attention of the public and policy makers. This has given some of the impetus to make the MOM and SNTUC take some positive action for the protection of migrant workers. In addition, the service oriented/para-legal NGOs fill an important gap by focusing on FDWs for whom there would otherwise be no non-governmental channels.

The grassroots based groups have a crucial role in channeling cases to MOM which would otherwise never have come to MOM's attention as FDWs and other migrants do not usually approach MOM by themselves. The training centres also fill an important gap as male migrant workers can get training through SNTUC but for FDWs, there would otherwise be no such service. Although how effective the actual training is and how useful it really is to returning FDWs are yet to be tested, the courses most certainly serve at least a social welfare role as a forum for FDWs to meet peers.

Trade Union ICFTU-APRO's most recent (2003) Action Plan regarding migrant worker issues recommends the establishment of a migrant workers' desk or committee which SNTUC has fulfilled. However, migrant workers themselves have no representatives on board. Unions are also supposed to engage in the active recruitment of migrant workers as union members. In Singapore, recruitment of foreign workers as members seems to concentrate on those working for big companies in the shipping and construction industries, but excludes workers in smaller enterprises and in certain sectors, such as domestic work. The active recruitment of members seems to be low on the priority list of SNTUC's MWF – which is quite consistent with many other trade unions according to a recent ILO survey (Johansson 2005).

There seems to be scope for more action on this issue, in Singapore as elsewhere. One area in which SNTUC (with MOM) has made major improvements is the housing and occupational safety situation of migrant workers, mostly in the construction sector. However, SNTUC does not have any concrete projects or Programmes for FDWs other than being involved with MOM's training for employers. Also, male migrants can acquire skills, but for FDWs there is no such skill acquisition Programme offered by the SNTUC. Separate training centres and UNIFEM take care of this on a relatively small scale, and this is an area where trade union involvement would be beneficial. According to ILO recommendations in 1999, trade unions in receiving countries are encouraged to:

- Negotiate for internationally accepted standard employment contracts;
- Make representation for the reduction of fees charged to migrants in view of the complete abolition of recruitment fees.

These two points are not tackled by SNTUC. Recruitment is an area the MWF does not engage with.

Cooperation or competition

NGOs have no sense of competition at this moment in time and would rather encourage trade unions to get more involved. They feel that unions should lobby for changes in employment law and working conditions and should be more active in lobbying for standard contracts. Unlike SNTUC, NGOs argue that maids are not in the position to negotiate a fair contract for themselves. SNTUC has the resources and connections to do more. They could set up a database on violations and abuses, injuries and breach of contracts to really find out what the scale of the problems is. As it stands, the nature of household work is not understood by the SNTUC.

Based on trade unions' larger pool of resources, NGOs also argue that SNTUC should offer free legal services. They should have a general welfare fund and legal services for all migrant workers. If they were to offer proper services to migrant workers, they could justify charging a fee (membership fee). Likewise, whether the levy payments could be used to fund such services should be explored. There is a feeling among the NGO/CBO community that the Migrant Worker Forum was purely set up to create a forum in which questions from the media can be addressed and thus, this would manage and control the sudden interest in FDW and other foreign worker issues.

The SNTUC on the other hand seems to be hesitant in seeking more collaboration with certain NGOs based on their different methods of operation. This lack of exchange between the two types of organizations seems to be at the root of NGOs' non-understanding of SNTUC's workings. There is no trust between NGOs and SNTUC (which is a mutual problem). This, however, would be the basis for cooperation/collaboration. To sum up: NGOs are more grassroots oriented and thus ideal for dealing with concrete cases, whereas trade unions are part of the overall labour movement and thus, are mass organizations. SNTUC has a huge political network and large financial as well as human resources. If trust were built up, the SNTUC's MWF could function as the focal point of a national as well as regional network inclusive of Singapore based NGOs.

Models and New Trends in Migrant Work (in-country)

NGO engagement in migrant worker issues in Singapore seems to follow a similar model as elsewhere in that there are

1. groups catering to one specific type of migrant worker; and
2. groups focusing exclusively on domestic workers.

There are, however, no NGOs (apart from the informal network by Indonesians) catering exclusively to one nationality group. Unique to Singapore (in its role as a receiving country) seems to be the fairly large number of kill training centres for FDWs. The trend now seems to be for migrants themselves to get more involved in the service provision for their compatriots. However, there are no signs yet of the setting up of a formal group or a migrant worker advocacy group but this might not be too far off. Some advocacy groups are also finally thinking about engaging with transnational/ regional networks.

Cooperation with counterparts in the sending countries is still underdeveloped. In this regard, Singapore-based NGOs are behind NGO activities elsewhere in this region. SNTUC, together with Hong Kong, is unique in Southeast Asia for having set up a Migrant Workers Forum. This is a laudable development. But to be more effective and engaged with pressing issues from the perspective of the workers (and not employers), more resources need to be allocated. This might also be an issue of political will.

Models and New Trends in Migrant Work (cross border/ international) SNTUC has links with the Migrant Forum in Asia (MFA). It is hosting the occasional visits of MFA representatives and is gradually getting more involved in regional activities with the assistance of MFA (such as meeting with counterparts and NGOs in the sending countries). As member of ICFTU-APRO, SNTUC takes part in regional meetings and there have been a number focusing on migrant worker issues. There is, however, no concrete cooperation/ collaboration taking place with trade unions in sending countries. This is apparently because of the multiplicity of unions. There are too many, a fact which renders the identification of a suitable and trustworthy counterpart in the sending countries very difficult. In countries like Indonesia, since the fall of Suharto, there has been a mushrooming of union activity without a national centre (or too many unions claiming to be national centres).

The political situation in many sending countries is volatile and unions (being politically affiliated with different parties) are affected by this. Resources are limited for any trade union, but the resources in the origin countries are even lower (personal interviews with SNTUC and ICFTU-APRO, June 2005). Considering this situation, outside assistance by ILO and/or ICFTU is needed to help trade unions identify suitable partners - provided the political will was there. No Singapore based NGO has any sustained, regular cross-border links. In this regard, Singaporean based NGOs do not follow trends elsewhere of being part of transnational networks.

Role of International Instruments and Platforms

The major limitations of existing ILO Conventions are that no country in the Asia Pacific has ratified them except for New

Zealand and Malaysia/Sabah which have both ratified Convention no. Also, the content of these conventions reflects the traditional situation of a male dominated migration system. To overcome the impasse of ILO intervention when Conventions are not applicable, the procedure of "pattern or practice studies" was adopted by the ILO Governing Body in 1997. It is a procedure which trade unions might resort to when other venues are not available (ILO 1999).

To date, no such practice studies have been conducted in the specific area of labour migration for the Asia Pacific region. A recent study on the obstacles to the ratification of the 1990 UN Convention has shown the various problem areas which make ratification by the Singapore government extremely unlikely. The only regional platform that the SNTUC takes part in is ICFTU-APRO. At the ASEAN level, an attempt was made to obtain formal recognition of the ACTUC (ASEAN Trade Union council, comprised of ICFTU affiliates and non-affiliates), but without success so far.

7

Women in Global Science and Technology

The countries of South Asia share much in their cultural, historical and socio-economic backgrounds. The region was once famed for its natural wealth and state of development, although the feudal patriarchal societies were deeply divided by inequalities of gender, caste and social status. Conditions worsened during the several centuries of colonial rule, which left the countries economically debilitated. In more recent times, a complex set of political, socio-cultural and economic circumstances has led to continuing ethnic strife in the region. Until the eighteenth century, indigenous systems of education, based on religion, trade and craft, had been fairly widespread.

The colonial system which replaced them was restricted in scope and coverage. Aimed at training clerks and civil servants, this education placed its major emphasis on languages, especially English, and the humanities: science and technology were all but excluded. Further, the use of a foreign language as a medium of instruction reinforced rote memorization as an accepted method of learning. Since the indigenous scientific and mathematical tradition had long died out, the science education that was introduced in the twentieth century was necessarily derivative. Many contemporary scholars have argued that creative thought in the region has suffered due to this reliance on an alien intellectual and scientific tradition.

The above account is over-simplified, but it captures the central problem in the educational systems of South Asia and they continue to carry an uneasy burden of alienation. The science that is taught in schools often seems 'not their own'. In addition to the problems of formal language and terse presentation, there often persists in the school curriculum an urban middle-class bias. The schools and the education service are run by an elite who are themselves the products of an imperfect system. Nonetheless, much can be, and is being, done. Critiques of western scientific traditions have encouraged the re-emergence in South Asia of interesting indigenous approaches to science, technology and development.

Critical assimilation of these new traditions has provided tools with which to analyze and confront a range of problems. The scepticism of science has often been able to challenge fundamentalism, and it is possible to hope that, in the future, cultural diversity will help to overcome ethnocentricity, providing multiple perspectives while enriching the repertoire of 'scientific' methods. Enough still survives of traditional technologies, crafts and arts, to suggest that they might contribute to relating science and technology to everyday practice.

SOUTH ASIA TODAY

Haq (1997) outlines the South Asian scenario with a series of stark statistics. South Asia, with a population of 1.15 billion, contains 22 per cent of humanity, has 6 per cent of global real income and accommodates 46 per cent of the world's illiterate population. Fifty per cent of all malnourished children live in this region. The populations of the individual countries range from the Maldives with 0.3 million people to India with 1 billion. These are largely rural populations: about 90 per cent of the people in Nepal and Bhutan and 75 per cent of those in India live in rural areas with agriculture as their main source of livelihood.

The rate of economic growth in South Asia is less than 2.5 per cent, but there has been a significant improvement over the years in the poorest: - in the case of Bangladesh, from 0.5

per cent in 1965-73 to 5 per cent in 1973-83. Bhutan saw a 7.4 per cent growth rate in the 1980s. However, inequalities in income distribution remain high. There is a clear urban-rural divide in terms of economic and educational opportunities. In urban areas, the fruits of science and technology are seen in terms of job possibilities and an enhanced quality of life, with the result that parental motivation for education is high. Monetary and intellectual resources tend to be concentrated in urban areas leaving the majority out of the fold of most development efforts.

LITERACY LEVELS

As a result of a sustained effort over the last thirty years, adult literacy has increased substantially, from 32 per cent in 1970 to 55 per cent in 1999, but this is still the lowest literacy rate in the world, lower even than Sub-Saharan Africa. Until the mid-1970s, the literacy rate in South Asia was higher than that of Africa, but by mid-1980s the position had been reversed. Literacy rates vary widely between, and within, the different countries, from highs of 96.2 per cent in the Maldives and 91.4 per cent in Sri Lanka to lows of 40.8 per cent in Bangladesh and 40.4 per cent in Nepal (UNDP, 2001).

Within India, literacy rates range from more than 90 per cent in the State of Kerala to 41 per cent in Rajasthan. Despite an increase in literacy rates expressed in percentage terms, the number of illiterates has increased, while the out-of-school population has remained static (in Bangladesh) or has increased (in India).

ACCESS TO EDUCATION

Since the 1940s and 1950s, when the South Asian countries gained independence, their educational systems have expanded several-fold. However, enrolment rates have not increased proportionately and drop-out rates have remained high. According to an Oxfam report *Education Now*, South Asia has 56 million primary aged children out of school, a figure that accounts for 45 per cent of the global total of out-of-school population of children. As with the literacy rate, there is a wide variation in enrolment and retention within, and between, countries.

Sri Lanka and the Maldives have achieved 100 per cent enrolment in primary schools; India and Bangladesh are approaching 90 per cent but Pakistan, Bhutan and Nepal have fairly low enrolment rates. The primary school completion rates have shown considerable improvement in recent years, but there is still a long way to go for achieving universal education.

Table: Net enrolment and primary school completion rates

Country	Net enrolment rate (%)	Primary school completion rate (%)
Bangladesh	85 (?)	38
Bhutan	53	54
India	87	59
Maldives	100	75
Nepal	64	25
Pakistan	31	48
Sri Lanka	100	85

The UNESCO report on follow-up action towards 'Education for All' puts the blame for high drop-out rates squarely on ineffective school supervision, the rampant absenteeism of teachers, the irrelevance of curricula and the indifference shown by the community (UNESCO, 1992). As for the last of these, the PROBE survey in India, and studies by NGOs in Bangladesh and elsewhere, report that the lack of motivation can often be attributed to the low quality of education on offer.

The corollary is that community mobilisation can lead to a marked improvement in the quality of local schooling. Primary school drop-outs have a high probability of lapsing into illiteracy. The region is therefore caught in a vicious cycle of low enrolment, low literacy, low levels of education among the work force, low rates of economic growth and low standards of living.

INVESTMENT IN EDUCATION

Low levels of literacy and school enrolment were once thought to be a consequence of poverty. This myth has been destroyed by a number of studies, particularly those undertaken by the World Bank (World Bank, 1991). The experiences of Europe, Japan, and Southeast Asia suggest that, rather than being a consequence, universal mass education is probably a necessary prerequisite for economic growth. Education in South Asia is largely State-funded (95 per cent in Sri Lanka and 85 per cent in India).

Even so, public expenditure on education remains low. The percentage of GNP allocated to education is less than 3 per cent in Pakistan, Nepal and Bangladesh, and just over 3 per cent in India and Sri Lanka. The Maldives is an exception, with 8.4 per cent of its GNP spent on education (SURF-UNDP, 2001). Most of the education budget is spent on teachers' salaries, leaving little to improve the infrastructure or raise the standards of teaching and learning.

The investment priorities in most of the region have worked against universalisation, because expenditure has traditionally been skewed towards secondary education. There has thus been a top-heavy growth in enrolment. In India and Pakistan, higher education has expanded rapidly, probably at the cost of primary education. Another neglected area has been technical and vocational education, where not only have budgetary allocations been low but expenditure has also fallen far short of targets.

Traditionally, the need for technological development has been used to justify more spending on higher education. Good research and development requires focused spending on higher education but this should not be at the cost of primary education, since the social returns from investment in primary education are known to be higher than from those from comparable investment at secondary or tertiary level. The UNDP (2001) report recommended more private spending on higher education while retaining public funding for primary education.

The UNDP Human Development Reports have persistently pointed out that education is not at the top of the policy agenda within South Asian countries. India has appointed a series of committees and commissions on education but their recommendations have largely gone unimplemented. A similar situation prevails in Pakistan. These two countries spend around twice as much on defence as they do on education. If only a fraction of this money were spent on primary education, universal education might become a reality.

TWO THORNY PROBLEMS

Before considering issues pertaining directly to science and technology education, it is important to acknowledge two problems that plague all educational reform efforts in developing countries in general and in South Asia in particular. One is the problem of child labour which is endemic in all the countries of South Asia, and especially so in Bhutan, Nepal, Pakistan, Bangladesh and India.

Weiner (1991) argues that child labour in India is not simply a result of poor economic conditions. It is bound up with a deeply ingrained value system, shared by educators, administrators, religious leaders and even social activists, a system which leads to an easy acceptance of inequity in society. This value system has further devastating consequences for the education of girls from the lower socio-economic groups within the population. The second is the problem of governance.

Haq (1999) analyses the political, economic, social and civic dimensions of this issue. The widespread prevalence of favouritism, corruption and inefficiency in public life and the low standards of professional accountability are major barriers to the implementation of educational policies and reforms. Again, in the existing value system in society, this is a state of affairs that is too easily tolerated. An education based on critical, quantitative thinking should aim to challenge these value systems.

NATIONAL GOALS AND EXECUTIVE AGENCIES

The major national goal of the South Asian countries is to provide a quality education for every child of school age. Free primary education is promised by all the governments, although the compulsory nature of the provision varies. In Sri Lanka, education is free and compulsory up to secondary school level. In Bhutan, a limited tertiary education is also provided free.

Bhutan, India, Pakistan and Sri Lanka emphasise national integration, cohesion and harmony (Gyamtso and Dukpa, 2000; National Council of Educational Research and Training, 2000; Asian Network (IBE), 2000; Presidential Task Force, 1997; Karunasinghe and Ganasundara, 2000). Sri Lanka specifically lists the following among the goals of education: - democratic principles, human rights, gender equity and environmental conservation (Presidential Task Force, 1997). Religious education is compulsory in Pakistan, Sri Lanka and the Maldives. Job-oriented technical and vocational education is prominent in the statement of national goals of all the countries.

In all the countries of South Asia, a central agency, within or outside the Ministry of Education, is responsible for interpreting national policy and framing school curricula. In Pakistan, it is the Institute for the Promotion of Science Education and Training (IPSET), in India the National Council of Educational Research and Training (NCERT), in Bangladesh the National Curriculum and Textbook Board (NCTB), in Sri Lanka the National Institute of Education (NIE), in Nepal the Curriculum Development Centre (CDC) of the Ministry of Education, in Bhutan the Curriculum And Professional Support Section (CAPSS) of the Ministry of Health and Education, and in the Maldives it is the Educational Development Centre (EDC) of the Ministry of Education.

In all these cases, the writing of curricula is done by teams consisting of subject specialists from within the agency along with experts from outside. In India, the curriculum developed by the NCERT is not legally enforceable in the individual States, but, in practice, the States either adopt, or closely follow, the national curriculum.

STE - A PRIORITY AREA

Given inadequate and unequal access to education, the high levels of drop-out and the low achievement of literacy and numeracy in schools, it is natural to ask if science and technology education (STE) is a real need for these countries. Are there not more pressing problems to be dealt with? The statements of national policies of most countries acknowledge the role of science and technology in economic development. However, this recognition does not necessarily translate into a commitment to science and technology education (STE) at school level.

Current writing and debate about education in South Asia, together with the policy statements of governments and the priorities of NGOs, give credence to this view by remaining largely silent about the importance of scientific and technological education. Since the early 1970s, science has been taught as a compulsory subject in schools in South Asia. There is an element of 'technology' within these curricula, although it usually amounts to little more than scattered pieces of information on technological applications.

A UNESCO survey of science and technology in school curricula in India, the Maldives, Nepal, Pakistan and Sri Lanka found that, with the exception of the Maldives, the total hours of schooling were higher than the world average, while the time devoted to science teaching was lower. Exceptionally in the Maldives, where the total hours of schooling were found to be less than the world average, the time given to science at the secondary level was more (UNESCO, 1986). As for demand, only 26 per cent of South Asian students at the tertiary level are enrolled in the natural and applied sciences, compared with an average of 30 per cent for all developing countries (SURF-UNDP, 2001).

In recent years, Bangladesh has seen a dramatic decrease in the percentage of students enrolling in the science stream at the secondary school level. The reasons for these trends are not clearly understood, but perception of the relevance of scientific and technological education is surely an important factor. Commitment to such education can come about only in a situation in which it is not isolated from the larger problems of education and of society.

Within this larger context, science and technology education should be seen by people as providing information, methods and tools for their empowerment. It is entirely possible for STE in South Asia to play a supportive role by acknowledging and addressing the basic problems of equity, gender roles, literacy, numeracy, health and environment.

TECHNOLOGY AND EDUCATION

In the Platonic culture of ancient Greece, liberal education intended for an elite was separated from professional and technical education. In ancient India, this kind of separation was institutionalised through the caste system. Today, such attitudes are reflected in the excessive verbal and academic orientation of science education. Given the context of low literacy levels and lack of resources, the outcome is simply the rote learning of the textbooks. Orpwood and Werdelin (1987) have explored the partnership between education, science and technology in support of national development.

They point out that technology, defined in terms of tools, materials and techniques to meet basic human needs and desires, has traditionally been passed down through generations. In history, technology has preceded science while technology education has been independent of science. The partnership between science and technology which developed over the years was not successfully transferred to the classroom, while the partnership between technology and education that existed in traditional cultures did not survive the take-over of education by formal schooling. In the meanwhile, science, which was always a matter of formal schooling, retained its academic orientation.

A meaningful technology curriculum might be one way to challenge this state of affairs. Since the time of John Dewey

(1916) there has existed a strong educational argument for using technology to give meaning to, and provide an effective pedagogy for, a range of academic disciplines, including science. In India, Mahatma Gandhi saw the need for educating the brain through the hand. The facilitative role of technology in learning science continues to be recognised today.

Fairly successful models of technology education exist in different parts of the world, as described in the UNESCO series *Innovations in Science and Technology Education*. Layton (1993) has reviewed some approaches to integrating science and technology in school and offered some examples from the teaching of design and technology in England and Wales. However, technology has only recently found wide acceptance as a component of the school curriculum, partly, it has to be acknowledged, for economic reasons.

Globalisation and the economic restructuring taking place in most developing countries including those of South Asia, have introduced much fluidity into the job market. Changing technologies, the disappearance of familiar occupations and the emergence of new fields of employment, all mean that workers have to undergo frequent retraining. In the industrial sector, jobs are being re-structured in ways that call for multiple skills on the part of the workforce. What is needed in this changing world is not simply disciplinary knowledge but flexibility of thought, a wide repertoire of skills and a capacity to tackle new problems.

Another consequence of globalisation is the increasing technological imbalance between the developed and developing countries. The enforcement of intellectual property rights restricts the flow of information to the developing world, even while taking away local control of indigeneous technologies. Critical sectors like agriculture and the pharmaceutical industry are likely to be controlled in the future by a small number of multinational corporations.

Effective national systems of scientific and technological education, combined with regional exchange Programmes, could enable the South Asian countries to retain access to technologies and to resist being marginalised in the globalisation process. Layton, however, has cautioned against economic instrumentalism as a justification for technology education, arguing that it may lead to inflated, and unrealisable, expectations from technology education. Moreover, an instrumentalist view may distort and diminish the educational potential of technology, not least by ignoring its conative dimensions of technology education and its close involvement with a range of global and environmental concerns.

TECHNOLOGY EDUCATION IN SOUTH ASIA

UNESCO has been active in promoting technology education in both developed and developing countries. The UNESCO Report *Learning to Be* made a convincing case for technology education as a component of basic education. The report was well distributed in the developing world including South Asia. It was abridged and translated into local languages and succeeded in influencing the thinking of many educators. Regrettably, a global survey conducted more than ten years later found that, in South Asia, as in most parts of the world, technology education either did not exist or was confused with vocational subjects or practical arts.

However, the situation is slowly improving, in terms of organisational structures as well as curricula. A few years ago, Pakistan, as part of an organisational restructuring aimed at integrating science and technology education, merged the Institute for the Promotion of Science Education and Training (IPSET) with the National Institute for Technical Education (NITE) to form a new organisation called the National Institute of Science and Technical Education (NISTE).

Sri Lanka, in recent education reforms, has replaced the science curriculum at the Ordinary Level of the General Certificate of Education (Grades X and XI) with a science and technology course. At the Advanced level (Grades XII and XIII), a technology stream has been introduced with a bias towards agriculture, industry, commerce, services and professional fields. The national curriculum framework in India has recommended science and technology education

(NCERT, 2000) as a new curriculum component to be implemented from 2002.

The introduction of science and echnology education in South Asia is facilitated by the generally positive attitudes of students towards science and technology. An international study, which included India, found that students in developing countries considered science to be very important for society, and regarded scientists as heroic, intelligent and caring.

In western societies, in contrast, science and technology were often seen in an unfavourable light, responsible for polluting the environment, depleting natural resources, creating unemployment and producing horrific weapons of mass destruction. There are indications, however, that this positive image of science within South Asia might become less pronounced with wider exposure to, for example, English-medium education.

THE WORLD OF WORK

Though technology education is an innovation in the region, a related subject, namely Technical and Vocational Education (TVE) has long been a mainstay of the educational policy of all the countries of South Asia. Using a slight modification of the terminology introduced by de Vries, TVE in South Asia has generally followed either a 'craft-oriented approach' or an 'industrial or agricultural production-oriented approach'.

Elements of technical and vocational education form part of the curriculum in South Asian countries from about grade 6 onwards. In Sri Lanka, the current education reforms require 'Life Competencies' to be taught in grades 6-9 (the junior stage) and a technical subject to be introduced in grades 10-11. Up to the Junior Stage, students are able to move laterally from general education into technical and vocational streams.

Experience of integrating technical and vocational education with general education has rarely been positive. Mahatma Gandhi's scheme of craft-oriented basic education was tried out in India soon after independence but, in a few years, it was abandoned. Nepal, in its early years of democratic rule, experimented with an ambitious technical and vocational Programme which was integrated with general education until the secondary school level. The Indian and Nepalese Programmes were abandoned for much the same reasons: - a lack of resources, inadequate teacher preparation and a general reluctance on the part of students and parents to depart from an academic-oriented education.

In Nepal, the integrated Programme was replaced in the early 1980s by one that focused on local needs and was directed at students who dropped out of the general system. Under this new Programme, separate technical schools are now provided at three levels: lower secondary, secondary and higher secondary, each of which is a terminal level. In India, vocationalisation of secondary education is still part of official policy and 'work experience' and 'pre-vocational courses' form part of the curriculum. In reality, however, such courses, except in a small minority of 'technical schools', are either non-existent or else completely meaningless. Even in post-secondary schools, where vocational subjects are offered, the choice is usually limited to one or two subjects.

Further, the students who opt for the vocational stream often do so not to secure career-related training but because these subjects are considered to be 'scoring', i.e., they enable one to score high marks in the final examinations. The most positive experience might be in Bangladesh where agriculture is a compulsory subject for grades 6-8, after which it is optional. It is meant to be taught through practical training by field-level experts. Although in Dhaka city this is not practicable, at the village level students do visit fields and use the school back lawn as an area for experiments.

In grades 9-10, basic trade training and technological drawing are optional courses. Technical training certificate Programmes can be taken up after grade 8 and diploma courses after grade 10. Separate streams for technical and vocational education exist at various levels in all the South Asian countries. Given the major shortages of skilled labour in these countries, one would expect a high demand for such education. The reality is quite different. South Asian countries are characterised by low levels of enrolment in technical and vocational education Programmes: 1.5 per cent of the total enrolment at the secondary level compared with 10.5 per cent in East Asia.

The situation is worsened by the high dropout rate from technical and vocational education, around 50 per cent in India, Pakistan and Bangladesh. Paradoxically, although the number of graduates of institutions providing technical and vocational education is small and falls far short of requirements of the labour market, their unemployment rate remains high. The problem of vocational education is intimately related to universal mass education, as Masri (1994) has recognised.

In the early years of mass education, socio-cultural barriers and economic considerations ensured that the majority of students entered the workforce at a young age. Later, a dual system came to prevail within which a privileged few continued their schooling while the majority opted for apprenticeship, on-the-job training or formal vocational preparation Programmes. This stage, which assumes a low level of demand for sophisticated skills, is where most South Asian countries stand today. As the 'bulge' of mass education moves up the educational ladder to include higher age groups, vocational educational solutions have to be found at higher levels.

The process would have to be planned in coordination with an expansion and diversification of the agricultural and industrial base. Masri recommends that developing countries move towards a system in which vocational preparation is integrated with senior secondary education. At present, despite the focused nature of the Programmes in Sri Lanka and Nepal, the unemployment rates of their graduates remain high. In Bangladesh, the employment rates for informally trained workers are higher than those who have graduated from technical and vocational schools. Employers prefer workers who have acquired skills through on-the-job practice.

A lack of coordination between industry and these schools is the most common shortcoming of the curricula that are provided. Another problem identified by a World Bank study (World Bank, 1990) is that the curricula are not designed to promote affective objectives like positive attitudes towards work, discipline and employee-employer relationships. Interestingly, this study claims that the primary reason for the failure of new employees in industry is their lack of affective skills in the workplace. The reasons for the general failure of technical and vocational education are the low social status of, and attitudes to, manual work, which is seen as meant for economically weaker and academically backward students.

In addition, technical secondary education may cost up to ten times more than general education but budgetary allocations are low. However, a survey conducted in Maharashtra, India, by the Ambekar Institute of Labour Studies, suggests that attitudes towards technical and vocational education may already be changing in some regions so that an increasing demand may be expected in the coming years. The technical and vocational education needs of South Asian countries are similar. Dasgupta (1994) has analysed these needs and pointed out the merits of regional co-operation, particularly in research and teacher training.

SOME PITFALLS OF INTEGRATING SCIENCE WITH OTHER SUBJECTS

The growing recognition of the importance of technology has created a favourable climate for integrating technology into school learning. Sri Lanka and India have taken the decision to integrate science with technology and Pakistan is likely to do the same. The rationale for these decisions is not clear but it is relevant to ask whether technology should necessarily be integrated with science in this way. Clearly, technology has close links with science as well as with its pedagogy. But technology has wider implications that extend beyond science to subject areas like vocational education, social studies, art, ethics and value education.

The technology education movement should rightly have some influence on all these subjects. However, given the existing organisational and time constraints of the school system, putting the entire burden of integration on science could have negative consequences for meeting specific learning objectives. Previous experience of attempts at integration certainly prompt a need for caution. In the last thirty years or so, many attempts have been made to integrate science with other curriculum components.

In Sri Lanka, the environmental studies curriculum at the primary level was replaced in 1982 by 'Beginning science' and in more recent reforms science and social studies were combined into 'Environment-related activities'. The NCERT in India experimented with subject-based teaching at primary and secondary levels but in the 1980s replaced physics, chemistry and biology by integrated science. In the current curriculum, science and social studies at the primary level are combined into environmental studies. Educationally, it is important for students to make connections between different subject areas and integration seems to offer a way forward. However, in practice, the integrated curriculum is constructed by experts who are specialists in their own disciplines.

Typically the separate physics, chemistry and biology chapters in a textbook are written by different subject specialists and, especially at higher levels, the integration is entirely nominal. Teachers, too, are reluctant to teach subjects other than their own specialized and training courses do not equip them to handle an integrated approach. As a result, two or sometimes three subject teachers end up teaching their subject specialized within so-called 'integrated science'. The environmental studies textbooks conveniently come in two parts which are easily recognised as the former science and social studies.

In recent years, there has been a trend towards integrating health and conservation issues within the science curriculum. This is expected to lead to a curriculum that is issues-based rather than being built around the concepts and principles of science. The current science textbooks in India contain a substantial components of health, agriculture and environment education. Unfortunately, this has simply led to larger books with additional chapters that contain too many facts. These new components burden an already overloaded curriculum and place increased demands upon the students.

Perhaps in reaction to this overloading, a recent trend has been to place less stress on learning subject knowledge and, instead, move the focus of the curriculum towards the development of 'competencies'. Here, too, the Indian experience has been disappointing. The 'Minimum Learning Levels' approach has led to a fragmentation in teaching and assessment and a tendency to 'teach the competencies' which, in the area of environmental studies, has turned out to be yet another list of facts. Subjects are defined by the distinctive ways in which they establish and structure knowledge and by the methods of inquiry that they employ. It needs considerable skill on the part of curriculum developers to bring about meaningful integration of different disciplines without undermining their core concepts.

TECHNOLOGY IS 'DOING'

An essential aspect of technology education is practical work, including planning, design, construction and experimentation. From the perspective of child development, the first spontaneous approach to experimentation is based on what could be called an 'engineering model'. In simple terms, this says, 'Let's do it and see if it works'. Practice of this approach in time leads to an appreciation of a hypothetico-deductive method and to an understanding of the role of experiments in science.

The introduction of technology into schools can be meaningful only if it provides for practical work. However, such work has been the Achilles heel of science and technology education in South Asian schools. In the current culture of schooling, there is a real danger that technology might be interpreted in a very academic way, as mere information about applications, processes and machines. The Indian policy documents on science and technology education emphasise the importance of practical work but action is needed to ensure effective implementation.

The Presidential Task Force (1997) in Sri Lanka has recommended the setting up of activity rooms in all junior schools (grades 6-9) and laboratories in all senior schools (grades 10-13). The perennial problem is the lack of equipment. While adequate funding is obviously the first requirement, equally important is a realisation that technology is all about the imaginative use of resources. From the curriculum development teams to textbook writers, teacher-Trainors, teachers and students, innovation, improvisation and the building up of ideas and resources are needed at all levels.

SCIENCE AND TECHNOLOGY FOR EMPOWERMENT

It is instructive here to list some of the basic problems in South Asian countries which would benefit from the application of science and technology. At the top of the list are water and food resources, nutrition, sanitation and infectious diseases. The major environmental issues in the region are:

- The pollution of water resources (by industrial discharge, household waste, the inadequate treatment of sewage, and excessive or inappropriate use of agricultural chemicals)
- Deforestation (due to increasing cultivation of land, the large scale use of wood as fuel, and overgrazing)
- A loss of biodiversity (shrinking forests, threatened marine and wetland ecosystems)
- Erosion and chemical degradation of soil due to intensive cultivation and excessive use of agricultural chemicals
- Air pollution and other urban environmental problems caused by unplanned growth.

At every level in the school curriculum, one could incorporate activities related to analyzing and dealing with such problems. In some cases, for example water resource management, simple traditional solutions have been found to be of value; in other cases high technology may be of use. Science and technology education should include information-seeking methods of analysis and the development of skill in using tools. Most of these problems also have social and ethical dimensions and these, too, need to form part of a humane scientific and technological education.

A TREND TOWARDS DECENTRALISATION

Although curriculum development in South Asian countries is largely done at the national level, implementation inevitably depends on the exigencies of the local situation. As regional resources and expertise grow in strength, the idea is gaining ground that curriculum change ought to be a more decentralised process. A case study of curriculum managers in Pakistan recommended a cooperative model of curriculum development to accommodate a wider range of interested parties (the 'stakeholders'), most notably the teachers who are ultimately responsible for effecting curriculum change.

A start has been made at the administrative level. India and Nepal are experimenting with participatory approaches to curriculum development. India has long had State Councils of Educational Research and Training (SCERTs). In more recent years District Institutes of Educational Training (DIETs) were established. In Pakistan, centralised curriculum development has partly given way to a process involving the participation of national as well as regional centres. The Maldives has also expressed a wish to involve teachers in future curriculum reform. However, the journey from administrative reforms to functional and intellectual autonomy may be a long one.

The inclusion of technology in the curriculum provides yet another justification for local initiatives. While the context of science might be described as universal, technology clearly needs to be developed and applied in a local context. A technology curriculum that involves 'learning by doing' will have to take cognizance of factors that range from the availability of human and material resources to ecological features, the epidemiological characteristics of the population and social relations in the locality. Ideally, this requires the collaboration of curriculum developers with local technologists, entrepreneurs and those skilled in craft work, as well as local industries and research laboratories.

Since independence Bangladesh has established a tradition of NGOs working successfully in the field of education. The government has recognised the contribution of these organisations and several fruitful partnerships have developed. An Indian example of a long-standing partnership between a State government and an NGO is the Hoshangabad Science Teaching Programme (HSTP) run by the NGO Eklavya. Over the last 30 years, this partnership has developed and implemented a curriculum for primary and middle schools in rural and tribal areas of the State of Madhya Pradesh. One common obstacle to effective local initiative throughout South Asia is the centralised examination system found in all the countries in the region. Here again, Sri Lanka is showing the way forward with the recent introduction of assessment systems that are school-based.

CULTURAL DIVERSITY

The countries of South Asia embrace a wide range of religions, cultures and ways of life, and educational systems need to take account of this diversity. A number of researchers, however, have suggested something of a mismatch between school science and the wider cultural context of schooling. To try to address this issue, Bajrachrya and Brouwer (1997) have experimented in Nepal with a narrative approach to teaching science that locates the subject within a culturally appropriate context. The problem of a mismatch between textbook science and the informal knowledge of students has been studied in India by Chunawala *et al.* (1996), Natarajan *et al.* (1996) and Ramadas *et al.* (1996).

As an example of their findings, Natarajan *et al.* (1996) found that tribal students' ideas about plants were varied, holistic and rich in ecological content. Textbook presentations, on the other hand, tended to be fragmented and focused on detailed structures. Ironically, in the classroom setting, the tribal students were classified as belonging to disadvantaged backgrounds and their considerable botanical knowledge was routinely ignored or belittled. In the case of the Maldives, where curriculum development, teacher preparation and assessment systems are largely directed from outside the country, the problem of cultural mismatch can be severe. Bhutan has recently begun to prepare culturally appropriate curricula. Pomeroy (1997) has given useful guidelines on how science and technology education can be adapted to accommodate diverse cultural assumptions, practices and norms.

THE EDUCATION OF GIRLS

The South Asian region, with its rich cultural and historical tradition, has witnessed a number of women occupying the highest political positions. Yet, paradoxically, South Asia not only has the lowest literacy rates in the world but also the largest gap between male and female literacy. Gender disparity in net enrolment ratios is also the highest in the world, with twenty per cent more boys than girls enrolled in primary schools. Within South Asia, those regions with low literacy and school enrolment rates also have high gender disparity. Discrimination against South Asian women, which begins early with female abortion and infanticide, is a consequence of poverty and patriarchal values that supports a preference for sons. One indication of the scale of the problem is the highly distorted sex ratio in the region, where there are only 940 females for every 1000 males.

Sri Lanka and the Maldives are exceptions to this generally depressing state of affairs. The Sinhala and Tamil communities in Sri Lanka have traditionally had a comparatively egalitarian set of laws on property ownership. The Maldives, within a strict Islamic framework, provides equal educational opportunities to girls and boys at lower levels of education, although gender discrimination sets in soon after primary school. The overall high literacy rates as well as enrolment ratios in these two countries show minimal gender differences.

Haq and Haq (2000), with support from numerous World Bank studies, see women's education as a necessary prerequisite for the overall development of the region. Female education leads directly to falling birth rates and a rising quality of life. The strategies to promote girls' education suggested by Kazi (1989) and Haq and Haq (1998) include the recruitment of more female teachers, the development of relevant and gender-sensitive curricula, and the provision of culturally appropriate facilities to meet the special needs of girls.

A number of recent governmental and non-governmental initiatives have successfully broken the barriers to girls' education. Examples of such Programmes are the Female Education Scholarship Programme (FESP), the Bangladesh Rural Advancement Committee (BRAC) in Bangladesh, the Mahila Samakhya, the District Primary Education Project (DPEP) and Lok Jumbish in India, the Social Action Programme in Pakistan, the Equal Access for Girls' Education Programme in Nepal and the Community Schools in Bhutan. The curriculum is one area where action is readily possible. A study of literature textbooks in India in the 1970s found a prevalence of sex-role stereotyping and extreme belittlement of women.

In other subject areas, the use of nouns and pronouns excluding women and a biased depiction of sex-roles in textbook illustrations have been common. However, at the national level (but less so at the regional level), there is an emerging sensitivity to the gender roles portrayed in textbooks. The new Programmes directed towards improving girls' education have therefore produced their own textual and supporting materials in which, for example, it has become increasingly common to depict girls in active, rather than passive or supporting, roles. Since textbooks in South Asian countries are produced centrally, this is one area where change can have an immediate impact. It would be helpful if the useful set of guidelines prepared by Kalia (1986) could be updated and given wide circulation.

Gender bias within society is particularly strong in the case of technology, which is generally seen as a male preserve. School technology education therefore carries the risk of reinforcing, and perhaps even deepening, the gender divide. However, a number of recent developmental projects in South Asia have had considerable success in overcoming the sex-role stereotyping of women and technology. Rural women in Bangladesh and India have been trained in occupations ranging from primary health care and fish farming to solar energy installations and hand pump repair. These local examples could form the basis of a technology education Programme. Gender equity within technology education can also be promoted by highlighting the social usefulness and ecological impact of technologies, and by selecting exemplar technologies that are of interest to women and girls.

SUPPORTING LITERACY AND NUMERACY

High drop-out and low enrolment rates reflect the low quality of education offered in the majority of schools in the region. A recent survey in Pakistan revealed that only 34 per cent of children who completed primary school could read with comprehension, and over 80 per cent were unable to write a simple letter. In Bangladesh, only 64 per cent of girls and 57 per cent of boys who complete primary school achieve literacy. Studies in India have found high underachievement even in privileged communities, while in underdeveloped parts of the country the literacy rates of primary school leavers are down to zero. Even in Sri Lanka and Maldives, which are doing better than the other countries in the region, the pass rate at the school leaving examination is only around 50 per cent.

The low quality of verbal and quantitative skills currently achieved in primary schools adversely affects comprehension in all subject areas. Instead of acquiring an understanding of scientific concepts and the processes of scientific inquiry, students memorize facts and procedures that are useful for passing examinations. A lack of language proficiency is one reason for the undue emphasis on factual knowledge at all levels of education. The importance of literacy and numeracy for scientific and technological education is well recognised, but this relationship might, with some advantage, be reversed, i.e., science and other subjects could be seen as a means of supporting the development of language and of reinforcing literacy and numeracy.

From the earliest years, verbal ability can be developed through learning. Instead of demanding the reproduction of passages of text, exercises in science and technology should require students to describe their own observations and actions orally as well as in writing. Creative writing, critical analysis, the building up of arguments, the use of causal connectives, and the framing of appropriate questions, can all contribute to language development while helping the students to learn science. In a parallel way, numeracy can be developed through measurement and quantification in the context of a number of subjects, most obviously science and technology. There is a difference here from the abstract 'word problems' associated with mathematics education, namely that scientific and technological problems presented to students are real problems and involve real-world data and questions.

An example is the Homi Bhabha Curriculum for Primary Science. This introduces students to quantification (prediction and estimation, informal comparisons, seriation, picture graphs, Venn diagrams and geometrical ideas in two and three dimensions) *via* familiar everyday activities. This approach requires co-ordination between the mathematics and science curricula from the earliest years to ensure that the level of mathematical thinking demanded in the science and technology curriculum is compatible with that required by the mathematics curriculum.

INFORMATION TECHNOLOGY

Of all the various aspects of scientific and technological education, it is information technology that has received most attention from policy makers in recent years. Pakistan and Bangladesh have introduced compulsory computer education in grades 9 and 10. In the technical and vocational sector, too, training in information technology has met with much success in India and Pakistan. The Government of Pakistan's *IT Policy and Action Plan* emphasizes human resource development and makes comprehensive, wide-ranging and progressive recommendations for education.

In addition to graduate and post-graduate Programmes, the policy also recommends focused hands-on training in specific areas that are identified by reference to market needs. It recommends the training and employment of women in large numbers in all sectors of the software and telecommunications industry. The provision of IT education to rural and poor segments of society is seen as a strategic priority for social and economic development. The policy also aims to encourage people with special needs to use information technology to allow them to participate more effectively in society.

The implementation of courses in information technology is inevitably limited by the availability and maintenance of computers. Here again, there is an unfortunate tendency for such courses to degenerate into copying and reproducing notes on 'What is a computer?', without actually getting a chance to use it. Nonetheless, computers and the Internet offer tremendous opportunities to South Asian countries. There have been a number of cases of successful connectivity in isolated rural areas to allow, for example, the sharing of meteorological, health and crop information. Such initiatives could be linked with scientific and technological education in rural schools.

RESOURCES OUTSIDE SCHOOL

School science and technology education need to be supported by out-of-school resources meant for children as well as adults. The cheapest and most easily accessed is the print medium, the demand for which increases with rising levels of literacy. Access to printed materials is also important for sustaining literacy in neo-literates. However, the space given to science and technology news and information in mass-circulation newspapers and newsmagazines is typically minimal, although there are creditable exceptions, such as the *Dawn* newspaper in Pakistan and *The Hindu* in India.

In Sri Lanka the science establishment is particularly active in popularising science. Several Programmes and services of the Sri Lanka Association for the Advancement of Science (SLAAS) are directed at school children and the public. In addition to magazines, lectures, quizzes and exhibitions, the activities of the SLAAS include a Media Resource Service (MRS) for science journalists. In India, the media resource services for science and technology are run by two Non-

Governmental Organisations, *Vigyan Prasar* and *Eklavya*. With the spread of the Internet, media resources have become easier to access and such services could be run all over South Asia at a relatively low cost.

In general, however, the availability of scientific and technological literature in the region, especially in the local languages, remains low. Local language publishing suffer from several constraints, ranging from low circulation numbers and a lack of information tools to unfriendly regulations and troublesome bureaucratic hurdles. In Bangladesh, the NGO sector has successfully made use of new information and printing technologies, including desktop publishing, to produce attractive books for their educational Programmes. Ahmed (1997) has suggested a number of ways to strengthen the publishing industry in South Asia, including regional co-operation to publish and market books in common languages like English, Bengali, Urdu and Tamil. He cautions, however, that the countries involved would need to co-operate in de-politicising the content of such books. Where literacy levels are low, the print medium has obvious limitations. Equally obvious is the educational potential of the broadcast media, although these tend to be dominated by commercial interests. The *Kerala Shastra Sahitya Parishad* and various other 'Peoples' Science Movements' in India have experimented with a number of other strategies for promoting scientific and technological education.

These include rural forums, women's forums and 'Sastra Kala Jatha' (a science and art procession or march) which includes music, dance and drama based on social-political, health and environmental themes. In recent years, India has been participating in the International Olympiads. Such participation can influence scientific and technological education at the regional level, motivating students towards science and also building up capacity in the teaching community.

The centrality of gender, participation and governance issues in sustainable poverty reduction has long been recognized by some international development agencies such as the World Bank and the United Nations Development

Programme (UNDP). However, these issues still tend to be treated separately, and it was only in recent years that some attempts have been made, particularly on the part of Management Development and Governance Division of the UNDP, to connect gender, poverty, and governance issues as its contribution to the Beijing +5 initiatives. As Sally Baden notes, "The current literature on governance tends to conflate goals, and assume positive links between, on the one hand, governance and poverty reduction and, on the other, between poverty reduction and gender disadvantage."

Gender and poverty linkages have been re-examined in light of the so-called "feminization of poverty" trend. The "feminization of poverty" could imply any of the following trends. First, that there are a greater number of women who are poorer than men. Second, that the severity or degree of poverty experienced by women is worse than men's. Third, that there is an increasing trend of more women falling below the poverty line because of increased number of female heads of households, etc.

The social relations of gender have been pointed out to mediate the differential experience and impacts of poverty on women and men's lives. Governance and gender linkages have also been articulated mainly, in urban poverty reduction, particularly in the effective delivery of social services and mechanisms of urban administration. Meanwhile, participatory research and development tools identified with Participatory Rural Appraisal (PRA), have been used in poverty assessments to aid poverty reduction efforts.

Governance and participation linkages are clearly made in attempts to conceptualize "participatory governance" as "the missing link in poverty reduction", as well as in the use of participatory development tools in organizational capacity-building and improvement of local governance. Gender issues however tend to be glossed over in participatory development initiatives when Trainors and project planners ignore the social differences and inequalities arising from gender, class, ethnicity, and other factors.

The relationship between gender planning, good governance, and poverty reduction efforts in Southeast Asian states is explored in this study, using Vietnam and the Philippines as case studies for the period 1986 to 1998. It examines a relatively unexplored question on women and change in comparative Southeast Asian studies: How do state bureaucracies that operate in different political, and ideological environment integrate women and gender considerations in their official plans and Programmes for poverty reduction?

In turn, how do women relate to bureaucratic politics when state bureaucracies do (or do not) target them as beneficiaries of poverty reduction policies and Programmes? This chapter mainly outlines some of the general issues and comparative insights at the level of national state bureaucracies emerging from a much larger research that explores more systematically the differences and similarities in the way state bureaucracies in Vietnam and the Philippines implement poverty reduction Programmes and plans. Three sets of research questions that are addressed in the larger project relate to the processes and strategies, as well as the substance and outcomes, and women's responses to these, of the integration of gender issues in poverty alleviation:

A. Processes and Strategies:

1. In what institutions or bureaucratic locations in Vietnam and the Philippines do women's Programmes on poverty reduction exist?
2. What authority do these women's Programmes command, what power do they have at their disposal and what resources do they control? How do bureaucracies tap the existing social capital in the local communities and use synergistic efforts by aligning with other government units, women's groups, universities, etc.? What strategies do they use to encourage women's participation and get the support of women's organizations?
3. What are the orientations, types, approaches and priorities of such Programmes? What measurements or indicators do bureaucracies use in integrating women and gender in their Programmes?

4. Do political orientation and policy environments matter in official planning for women? How is this validated in the comparative analysis of the processes and strategies of gender planning in the Philippines and Vietnam?

Substance and Outcomes:

1. What outcomes or results are produced by the integration of women and gender concerns in local poverty reduction Programmes of the state? How these outcomes are measured, monitored and evaluated?
2. How are the outcomes of state-organised poverty reduction efforts affected by market reforms, for example, the decollectivisation of agriculture and emergence of private enterprises in Vietnam, and structural adjustment in the Philippines?
3. What combination of ideological inspiration, policy orientation, and bureaucratic practices produce outcomes which address women's practical (access-related) and strategic (empowerment-related) gender needs?
4. Are these countries affected by the observed shift in development discourse from "integrating women" to mainstreaming gender? And if so, what outcomes have been produced by such shift?

Women's Responses:

1. How do organised women, respond to the state's call for the integration of women in development planning in general and in poverty reduction Programmes in particular? How do they respond to the above strategies and approaches used by state bureaucracies to enlist their participation and support?
2. What strategies do women used vis-à-vis state bureaucracies? How do they tap the existing social capital to produce outcomes similar to or different from those desired by bureaucracies?
3. How do organised women respond to the outcomes of bureaucratic attempts to alleviate poverty?

How did they respond to the shift in discourse and policy emphasis from the "integration of women" to the "integration of gender"? To what extent are policy networks, government bureaucracies and women's organizations in the Philippines and Vietnam affected by this shift? Are there differences and similarities in the way organised women in each of these countries respond to this shift? This chapter focuses mainly on the processes, strategies and substantive outcomes of integrating gender considerations in poverty alleviation plans within the bureaucracy at the national and provincial levels.

Hence, it does not present detailed data on the interplay between state bureaucratic politics and processes, policies and policy context, on the one hand, and gender-aware planning and women's responses, on the other at the village or community level, and women's organisations. In the larger research, macro, meso and micro levels of analysis combine with feminist participatory research techniques such as participant field observation, key informant interviews, focus group discussions, and women's life history in three communes in Vietnam and three villages in the Philippines.

Critical issues addressed are: How do states govern when they mainstream gender and women's concerns in poverty alleviation efforts? How do women relate and respond to such efforts of state bureaucracies? How are participatory governance and strategic gender planning towards women's empowerment integrated in poverty reduction efforts? What does participatory governance have to cffer both gender and development planning and planning for poverty reduction? How does gender analysis enrich our understanding of the participatory governance component of poverty reduction?

Poverty reduction is understood here not as an individual problem but as a community problem, and a function of building social capital and participatory governance mechanisms. It is by definition different from mere poverty alleviation, which does not imply the reduction of the number of people who are poor, but only the lessening of suffering by the poor, or slight improvement of the conditions under which they live.

Sustainable poverty reduction therefore refers to the systematic or Programmatic attempts to increasingly the number of people who are able to get out of poverty, and sustain that success over long periods of time for the eventual goal of poverty eradication or elimination, the ultimate target of human development. On the other hand, gender planning refers to the institutional framing and implementation of policies, Programmes and projects at various levels of society that contribute to the re-ordering or reconstruction of gender identities and relations between women and men. Strategic gender planning is the attempt to develop a comprehensive Programme that will empower women for long-term success in improving their situation *vis-a-vis* men and eventually, in eliminating poverty.

Both sustainable poverty reduction and strategic gender planning would require the cooperation between government, organizations of poor people, non-government organizations, and the rest of civil society. In feminist literature, this cooperative relationship has been called "triangle of empowerment" involving women's movements, feminist politicians and feminist public administrators or femocrats. Hence, the governance component of poverty reduction refers to how the relationship between government, civil society, and poor people is altered or maintained in the course of governments' poverty reduction efforts.

Participatory governance, as understood here, goes beyond the framework of accountability, as it also refers to the transformation of relationships between rulers and the ruled in ways that recognise and respect women's choices and autonomy, and that include more accountable, participatory-based, and egalitarian political practices. This research is interested in the theoretical and strategic implications of integrating gender analysis into participatory governance mechanisms as a vital component of poverty alleviation, beyond the simple mobilisation of women based on their characterisation as beneficiaries of aid.

GENDER AND GOVERNANCE REFORMS IN VIETNAM AND THE PHILIPPINES

Women's empowerment and well-being in most developing countries in the South are affected by rapid political and economic changes taking place at local, national, and global levels. Both the Philippines and Vietnam have experience high economic growth rates in the 1990s, partly owing to the influx of portfolio foreign investments and venture capital from the East Asian NICs (newly industrialising countries).

Hence, current state- initiated efforts for gender planning and the concomitant responses of NGOs and women's groups must be understood in the context of the current processes of economic liberalisation (marketisation), pressures towards political liberalisation (democratisation), and increased awareness of women's and gender issues (gender mainstreaming) on the part of government and civil society forces. They must also be analysed in the context of how both gender mainstreaming and poverty reduction have become part of the dominant discourse within the international development, from the World Bank to USAID and other development ministries of OECD countries.

The end of the Cold War in 1989, and the widespread opposition to the harsh impact of structural adjustment Programmes on the poor, particularly poor women, has set the stage for shifts in international development discourses and interventions. There has been an increased emphasis by international agencies, NGOs, including women's organizations, on capacity-building, participation, social capital, good governance, gender mainstreaming in public management, and wider capacity development to accompany the wider goal of social development. International development agencies have begun to realize that too much emphasis on financial restructuring has led to the lack of emphasis on building local institutions and capacity for development, shifted their emphasis on "capacity development" in its Programmes and projects based on increased North-South dialogues and partnerships.

Both the Vietnamese and Philippine governments have therefore aligned their national development plans with these dominant discourses. In the Philippines in particular, the comprehensive national plans under the Aquino and Ramos governments have informed by the latest development buzzwords on environmentally sustainable development, human social development, gender equity and empowerment, and capacity building. These discursive buzzwords are interpreted and operationalised in Programmes and service delivery that occur in the context of the devolution and decentralization of powers.

This has occurred more swiftly in the Philippines than in Vietnam with the framing of the 1991 Local Government Code. The Philippines and Vietnam represent two interesting cases with differing policy contexts, political- ideological environments, bureaucratic cultures, and levels of economic industrialisation. Thus, they offer contrasting insights on the intersection between gender and state bureaucratic politics, especially in the period after 1986. The Philippines has, since 1986, undergone a formal liberal democratic transition from authoritarian rule, marked by a liberal economic policy regime under a weak but patrimonial state.

This political transition started under a woman president (Aquino) whose candidacy was given widespread support by popular women's groups. Her administration, and her successors, emphasised mainstreaming women's concerns in development plans. This was accomplished through government line agencies and the reorganised National Commission on the Role of Filipino Women (NCRFW) that brought feminist activists and advocates into government service. Likewise, since the consolidation of socialism in Vietnam, chapters of the Women's Union have been established at every level of government, and the National Committee for the Advancement of Women (NCAW) was given much broader scope and powers.

Vietnam, like the Philippines, is aspiring to become a newly industrialised country through market reforms started in 1986 under *doi moi* (change or renovation), guided by socialist state ideology. The pace of pace of such reforms have been much slower in Vietnam compared to the Philippines, due to the dominance of more conservative elements within the Vietnamese Communist Party and National Parliament compared to the pro-reform group. Nevertheless, Vietnamese people in both the urban and rural areas have been experiencing both the harsh and the positive effects of market reforms, from the influx of foreign investments, de-collectivisation of agricultural production, increased use of cost-recovery schemes such as user fees, and privatization of some state companies.

Market reforms in both countries have been accompanied by rapid increase in relative poverty, and deterioration of social services. Trade liberalisation, privatisation, currency devaluation, cutbacks in social services and tax reforms that accompany market reforms are intended to "get the prices right" and to further open up the economy. These trends associated with structural adjustment and global restructuring, have been found to disproportionately affect women, the poor, and other disadvantaged groups.

It has been documented in several studies in developing countries that, in the aftermath of economic restructuring, women tend to have higher rates of unemployment and poverty than men. Women's unpaid household work, farm labour and informal sector work intensify as male-female wage and salary differentials widen. Increased rates of anemia among adult and pregnant women are noted along with the deterioration of girls' health and education levels. More women especially from the poorer classes experience greater stress in making ends meet and keeping the family together, while others experience domestic violence in the midst of poverty, insecurity, and social frustrations.

More women family members become single household heads as domestic or household structures change, especially due to divorce, male abandonment or migration. Parallel studies in Vietnam and the Philippines also indicate that the effects of market reforms or structural adjustment are harsher on women and children. These have created more poverty, austerity, and added demands and burdens on women, especially in poor rural households.

Hence, when market reforms and development plans are found to produce "persistent inequality" for women, feminist scholars, planners and advocates examine the conditions and causes of this "gender bias" in the "development" process. They trace the causes to a combination of factors. Among these are the prevailing neo-classical economic assumptions on the elasticity of women's labour. There is also the complicity of adult women and men in the socialisation of inequalities and differential entitlements in resource allocation, as well as the lack of investment in human capital of women and girls.

The poor conditions of women's participation in technological and educational developments are further compounded by shifts in corporate strategies to reorganise production and gender relations. At the levels of national and international development bureaucracies, both government and non-government, there are persistent problems in mainstreaming gender principles and institutionalizing gender equity or "getting institutions right" for women and not just for market efficiency.

Moghadam asked a critical question: "what should be done to attenuate the adverse effects of crises and adjustment and to enhance women's participation in the changing political economy?" Addressing this question seems even more important since gender planning, whether carried out by governments or international development agencies, has been framed on the argument that market-oriented strategies work best for women who are often assumed to be not fully integrated into the market economy.

GENDER PLANNING AND POVERTY REDUCTION IN THE PHILIPPINES AND VIETNAM

Successive governments in the Philippines and the socialist government in Vietnam have given attention to poverty reduction as the centerpiece of their respective official development planning, e.g. the 1987-1992 and 1992- 1998 Medium-Term Development Plans of the Philippines National Economic Development Administration and Vietnam's Hunger Eradication and Poverty Reduction Programme (HEPR).

The role of women in poverty reduction has been given special mention within official development plans. However, it is not clear how such roles would be enhanced under restructuring as national government bureaucracies do not appear to have fully considered both in their plans and Programme delivery the gaps and contradictions between larger market reforms and the goals of economic efficiency and social equality. The assumption that market-oriented strategies work best for women goes along with the view that women (and other marginal social groups such as disabled peoples and ethnic minorities) are not as productive and fully integrated into the market economy.

This explains the popularity and dominance of the Women in Development (WID) framework in most poverty alleviation and development plans, despite the official shift from "women" to "gender" in development planning focus since the late 1980s. The shift has been a response to the limitations of the earlier Women-In-Development (WID) framework's attempt to integrate women in development processes. However, there remains a stubborn conflation of women and gender, a persistent exclusion of the consideration of men, male identities, and masculinities in gender and development discussions, as well as difficulties experienced by front-line government workers in operationalizing gender in their community-based Programmes and projects.

Although both countries have created an open environment for international cooperation and put increased emphasis on mainstreaming women's concerns in official development plans, they differ in terms of their bureaucratic operations and relationships between their governments, civil society and international NGO community. This stance of national governments towards women's issues began, in the case of the Philippines, as a response to the United Nations' International Women's Decade. In the case of Vietnam, it was a political imperative of the orthodox Marxist approach to addressing the "woman question" within the context of class and national liberation from French and American colonialism.

The understanding of the gender dimension of poverty reduction therefore must begin from the analysis of how poverty reduction has been influenced by both nationalist discourses and international development agenda, particularly in how poverty reduction and gender inequalities have been tackled in national development Programmes. Income-Based and Outcome-Based Measures of Poverty Both the Philippines and Vietnam have elaborate ways of defining and measuring poverty based on dominant economic and income-based measures of relative deprivation and need. Income-based measures such as the construction of poverty lines and official poverty thresholds are commonly used in both countries.

Poverty lines could measure poverty incidence (head count of the number of poor people or poor families and households), depth (poverty gap: average distance below the poverty line as a proportion of the line) and severity (Distribution-sensitive measure is the weighted average of the squared distance of the incomes of the poor from the poverty line as a proportion of the line). For example, the Philippine government's official approach to poverty line identification begins with the construction of representative food menus for rural and urban areas of each region, prepared by the Food and Nutrition Research Institute which considers local consumption patterns and a minimum nutritional calorie requirement of 2,000 kilocalories per person per day, with 80-100% of recommended daily allowance for vitamins and minerals.

In Vietnam, the poverty line is measured by the amount of monthly rice consumption, which roughly translates into the caloric daily requirements of an average person. As another income-based poverty measure, both Vietnam and the Philippines also utilize for international comparative purposes the World Bank's $1 per day person (at 1985 purchasing power parity). This is the income needed for a family of five to be considered no longer poor. A $1 US per day income roughly translates into 6,000 pesos per month, with median monthly food expenses at 3,000 pesos.

In Vietnam, the same measurement is roughly equivalent to 520,000 Vietnamese dong monthly income for a family of five. There are serious comparability and consistency problems in the use of official poverty lines, leading analysts in the Philippines to develop the Fixed Level of Living Lines (FLOL). The poverty lines obtained are often not consistent and comparable across regions since the menus for one year may be based on the Food Consumption Survey done in previous years, and estimates of food thresholds for richer regions tend to be higher than for poorer regions. Thus, Balisacan proposed the use of an indicator of household economic welfare (loosely referred to as living standard) based on "cost of basic needs" approach.

The indicator is derived from first obtaining a national reference food bundle which satisfies the minimum requirement of 2,000 kilocalories per person per day. The bundle costs may be adjusted to account for regional cost-of-living differences. Then the nonfood component may be estimated from the consumption patterns of households where the total incomes or expenditures are just enough to meet the food threshold.

The government's official measures show that 37.4% of the population was below the poverty line when the 1997 Asian financial crisis occurred. This was lower than the 40.6% figure in 1994 but it is still high compared to other countries in the region, with the exception of Vietnam which registered 50% of the population below the poverty line in 1994. The depth of poverty or average income shortfall of the population was 12.5% of the poverty line while the weight or severity of poverty was 6% of the line in 1997. As macro-based measures both the official poverty line and FLOL are unable to capture gender income and consumption differentials which are taken into account in other outcome-based measures of poverty and well-being.

Outcome-based measures of poverty and well-being are also used internationally and in many countries, including the Southeast Asian Region. There is the Human Development Index (HDI) which is a more comprehensive measure that focuses on non-income indicators. It is a composite index reflecting three basic outcomes: health as proxied by life expectancy; knowledge as proxied by functional literacy, and standard of living as measured by real per capita income (UNDP, 1999).

The HDI ratios range from 0 to 1 with 1 indicating the perfect condition. The Human Poverty Index (HPI) is the obverse of the HDI which provides a multidimensional composite index of deprivations in health, knowledge, economic provisions and social inclusion. The index measures short life (proxied by people expected to die before age 40), lack of education (proxied by percentage of illiterate adults), and lack of access to public and private resources (proxied by the percentage of people without access to health services and safe water and percentage of underweight children under 5).

The Capability Poverty Measure (CPM) focuses on people's lack of capabilities. It is a simple average of three basic indicators that reflect the percentage of the population with capability shortfalls in three basic aspects. These are living a healthy, well-nourished life (indicated by the percentage of underweight children under 5; having the capability of safe and healthy reproduction (the percentage of births unattended by health personnel) and being literate and knowledgeable (percentage of women age 15 and over who are illiterate) The integration of gender-relevant indicators in both the HDI and HPI has been done with the creation of the Gender-related Development Index (GDI).

The GDI is the HDI adjusted for gender inequality, which compares male and female literacy, educational, health, and income levels. The Gender Empowerment Measure (GEM) indicates the participation of women in economic and political life, including the number of women in key national government, legislative, and executive positions. Vietnam and the Philippines fared quite well in terms of human development and gender-related indicators despite their lower GDP. The Philippines scored particularly high because of its .90 ratio for education. This score however does not reflect the quality of education in the country, as well as regional and geographic differences in educational quality and access.

Another outcome-based measure is the Minimum Basic Needs (MBN) which integrates non-income indicators into the formula. Using the Minimum Basic Needs (MBN) framework, the government has identified 33 MBN requirements grouped under 3 three categories: survival, security, and enabling needs. The delivery of "quality social services" would use structures and mechanisms such as women's centers, day care centers, schools and scholarships, and women's associations and cooperatives. Disadvantaged women that cut across all sectors are highlighted as one of the "target groups" for SRA.

The MBN score is based on whether the family has income above a subsistence level; access to potable water, has a sanitary toilet, employed household heads and members above 18, members involved in at least one people's organization, children between 3 and 5 years old who are in daycare facilities, housing that can last for at least five years; no severe or moderately underweight children under 5 years old and couples practicing family planning. The Ramos administration's integrated anti-poverty Programme, dubbed as the Social Reform Agenda (SRA), depended on nationwide consultation with grassroots organizations and NGOs, some of which were drawn into the leadership of Social Reform Council (SRC).

This consultation was facilitated by the SRA's broad political support base, and the participatory mechanisms, though limited in many ways, created by the Local Government Code. The SRA has all the current buzzwords in its three components: "access to quality basic services (imperatives to survival); sustainable development of productivity resources, and access to economic opportunities (means to work and earn a living); and institution-building and participation in governance (towards self-governance)".

The MBN was developed as an outcome-based poverty measure during the Ramos administration as part of its implementation of the Social Reform Agenda or SRA. The MBN is an integral part of a Community Based Indicators Monitoring System that has been installed in 5th and 6th class municipalities in pilot provinces. The MBN under SRA was adopted in at least 1154 poor *barangays* in 432 municipalities in 77 provinces. Initial confusion regarding the indicators resulted in efforts to refine the measures as well as implementation of the monitoring system.

The Politics of Gender and Poverty Reduction Gender mainstreaming has now been accepted as part of the official imperatives of government agencies in Southeast Asia. Efforts in gender mainstreaming however remain uneven largely due to the relative weak political clout and limited resources of national women's ministries in influencing the bureaucracy and policy directions. The NCRFW in the Philippines and NCAW in Vietnam are only policy recommending bodies, with neither executive nor legislative powers.

Much of their activities are focused on national policy advocacy, lobbying and doing gender training for government and non-government front-line workers. Hence, there still seems to be a lack of cross-fertilization between gender development planning and poverty reduction. While not all gender issues are poverty- related issues, and vice-versa, gender and poverty issues tend to be treated separately as mainstream poverty reduction plans and Programmes often make mention of gender and women's contributions only as another "input" to be added. The succeeding discussion outlines some of the main political and bureaucratic factors that have shaped gender mainstreaming in poverty reduction in the two countries under study.

Vietnam's experiences with gender mainstreaming are circumscribed by the solid legal foundations for gender equality under Vietnamese laws since socialist reconstruction, and official recognition of the Women's Union as a quasi-state, quasi-NGO mass organization working for women's empowerment. However, these legal foundations are subject to interpretation, negotiation, and contestation based on deeply rooted adherence to Confucian value system which accords a subordinate position to women.

This value system is also open to contestation, negotiation, and hybridity, as it interacts with the increased marketization of the economy and social relations, and informal institutions that emerge outside the parameters of legal and bureaucratic frameworks. The Vietnamese National Parliament, for example, has a high percentage of women at 26% in 1997 and easily one of the highest in the world. The relative influence of women parliamentarians in critical policy areas such as the national budget and finance, defense and fiscal policy, and their marginalization from key cabinet and parliamentary committee positions are also open to questions.

What is rather odd in the Vietnamese case compared to other Southern developing countries (but perhaps not to former Eastern European countries) where female political representation looks like a pyramid - the number of women thin out as you get to the top —, is that there are fewer women in provincial and district governments and local commune-level People's Committees than at the national level. Such trend could be explained either in terms of the greater room for political maneuverabillity at the local level, or in terms of much well- entrenched cultural value on sex-role complementarity at the family and community levels, manifested in women playing less active roles in community political affairs.

The Hunger Eradication and Poverty Reduction (HEPR) Programme is perhaps the most comprehensive attempt of the Vietnamese government to tackle poverty. In the official letter of the Programme, there is very little mention of women and gender considerations as the Programme details tend to assume gender parity and/or gender neutrality in the course of poverty reduction efforts. The implementation of HEPR is also very sporadic and uneven, and highly dependent on the political will, initiative and interests of provincial and district officials in accessing national and international funding to support the Programme.

The limited availability of external development funds, as well as international disaffection with the "hidden costs" (corruption, bureaucratic failures, political risks, etc) in doing business and development work in Vietnam have also contributed to the slow pace of implementation of HEPR. A more comprehensive analysis of poverty reduction in Vietnam would have to go beyond the analysis of HEPR, and discuss the operations of the implementing line government agencies such as the MOLISSA (Ministry of Labor, Invalids and Social Services Administration), the MARD (Ministry of Agriculture and Rural Development), Ministry of Resettlement, the Ministry of Education and Training (MOET), and the MPI (Ministry of Planning and Investments), among others.

These ministries' operations will have to be discussed along with agencies such as the Bank for the Poor and quasi-state mass organizations such as the Women's Union, Farmers' Union, Home Gardens' Association, and War Veterans Association. Perhaps the Vietnamese Women's Union is the most important quasi- state mass organization (some reports call it an NGO) that is playing a critical role in the improvement of women's status in Vietnam and in poverty reduction. The reach of the Women's Union is impressive.

It has chapters at the national, provincial, district and commune levels, with representatives sitting on the People's Committee at every level of government. While Women's Union chapters often boast of huge membership, ranging from 200 to 2,000 paying members at every commune, many chapters are in dire need of revitalization. Although there are a few "showcase chapters" that have been very effective in implementing successful Programmes and projects at the community levels, in most cases, only a few key members are active and fully informed of ongoing activities of the organization. In places where there have been opportunities to access international and national development funds, the Women's Union leadership and key active members are often tied in strong familial or kinship and crony relations with the local, district, or provincial leaders.

The typical poverty reduction projects of the Women's Union are reminiscent of the WID approach to women's welfare, such as micro-credit, micro-enterprise, literacy, health and hygiene, and family planning education. In most cases, these projects meet breaking points at which they are either terminated or remain unsustainable. There are also problems in replicating their success and scaling up their operations.

Likewise, a thorough analysis of bureaucratic spaces where women and poverty Programmes exist would require an examination of the government's overall framework on poverty reduction, such as the Social Reform Agenda (SRA) of the Ramos administration, and al government line agencies responsible for social service delivery, such as the Department of Social Welfare and Development (DSWD), Department of Agriculture (DA), Department of Health (DOH), Department of Agrarian Reform (DAR); Department of Labor and Employment (DOLE), and Department of Education, Sports and Culture (DECS). Some poverty-related Programmes in these agencies are carried out in cooperation with other agencies such as the Department of Trade and Industry (DTI), Department of Public Works and Highways (DPWH), Department of Environment and Natural Resources (DENR); Department of Science and Technology (DOST), Department of Finance (DOF); and the Department of Interior and Local Government (DILG). Such an analysis, however, is beyond the scope of this chapter, which only aims to provide a broad sketch of issues emerging from preliminary research findings.

The Philippines efforts to integrate women's issues and gender considerations took off after the demise of the Marcos dictatorship in 1986 and the democratization process started under the Aquino government. Under the leadership of the NCRFW in the late 1980s and early 1990s, feminist activists and academics trained in the politics of the women's movement collaborated on the mainstreaming of gender concerns within the civilian bureaucracy, especially the executive and legislature.

These efforts has resulted in a number of important documents that have potential impact on the government's poverty alleviation agenda: the *Philippine Plan for the Development of Women*, 1990 to 1995, and the 30-year *Philippine Plan for Gender-Responsive Development* (PPGD), 1995-2025, which guide government agencies in responding to Gender and Development (GAD) issues. These documents embody the Philippine government's international commitment to the implementation of the Beijing Platform of Action (BPA) and the UN Convention on the Elimination of the All Forms of Discrimination Against Women (CEDAW). The NCRFW was given support by various international development agencies such as CIDA, UNIFEM, UNFPA, etc. in its internal capacity-building and policy advocacy work.

Gender mainstreaming has thus officially become an important agenda of the national and local governments. On the last year of the Aquino administration, RA 7192 or the "Women in Development and Nation Building Law" was passed and was given added impetus by the Ramos administration with the signing of Executive Order 273 which approved and adopted the PPGD. EO 273 directs all government agencies at the national, regional and local levels to implement the policies, Programmes, projects and strategies outlined in the PPGD; incorporate gender concerns in their respective annual plans and inputs to national development plans, otherwise know as the GAD Plan; and include GAD in their annual budget proposals and financial and work plans, otherwise known as the GAD budget.

The GAD budget may be used in the areas of gender-responsive advocacy and training to equip development workers with skills required for gender mainstreaming; Programme planning to ensure that gender-responsive plans are drafted and implemented; development of a gender-responsive data and information system; and setting up of institutional mechanisms such as GAD Focal Points, Technical Working Groups, and Trainors' Pool to ensure that GAD concerns are recognized and addressed. In the first year of the GAD budget implementation, the 1995 General Appropriations Act allowed agencies to determine how much of their annual budget should be allotted to the GAD plan, but few agencies came up with their GAD budget.

To ensure that all agencies would comply, the 1998 General Appropriations Act and the Local Budget Memorandum directed all national and local government units and other agencies to set aside a minimum of 5% out of their 1998 appropriations for Programmes, projects and activities in accordance with the Women in Development and Nation Building Law. RA 7192 also directs agencies and LGUs to use up to 30% of their official development assistance for GAD on top of the 5% GAD budget provided for under the 1998 Appropriations Act.

The GAD budget may be taken from the agencies' regular budget, and its special project fund and from the Priority Programme/ Project Fund to undertake new "GAD investments" such as baseline research to identify gender issues; counterpart Philippine government fund for foreign funded GAD projects; and expansion of GAD advocacy and technical assistance down to the local levels.

Philippine women's NGOs, on the other hand, straddled between the continuing emphasis on women's organizing, gender sensitivity training, gender advocacy within and outside government, and the integration of gender concerns within government Programmes Government service delivery in the Philippines and Vietnam is often hampered by the lack of coordination, and inability to tap into the ongoing initiatives of women's organizations, particularly the growing NGO community. Such problems are most acute in the case of the Philippines, where the personality-oriented political culture works against continuity in bureaucratic Programmes and service delivery.

For example, the continued implementation of the Comprehensive and Integrated Delivery of Social Services (CIDSS) Programme, under SRA is threatened by the lack of political will on the part of the Estrada administration to continue the Programmes identified with former President Ramos. Thus instead of simply strengthening the SRA implementation, the government of President Estrada came up with its own poverty alleviation strategy through the *Lingap Para sa Mahihirap* Fund and the identification of the 100 poorest families in every municipality for targeting purposes.

The Philippine government also created a policy advisory body called the National Anti-Poverty Commission (NAPC), which from the onset has been saddled with controversy around the issue of partnership between the government and civil society organizations who are involved, and not involved, in the Commission. Many NGOs and people's organizations who were supportive of the Aquino and Ramos administrations and those identified with the national democratic movement are conspicuously absent from the composition of NAPC and its supporters.

The Commission also lacks the necessary resources, human and material, as well as the political powers and credibility needed to make it not just a policy advisor-overseer but also as a permanent implementing agency. On the positive side, the elected Vice-Commissioner for non-government sector of NAPC, Princess Nemenzo, is a well-known feminist advocate who is active in the women's movement.

There is also increased interest on the integration of gender concerns in poverty reduction efforts among the women members of NAPC, the women's organizations, and broad coalition networks within the Commission, which could lead to the introduction of a gender framework within the government's poverty alleviation plan. Vietnam is in a way fortunate to be able to avoid the pitfalls of a weak liberal democratic state and a political culture that is fixated in legal battles and personality-oriented electoral exercises.

Vietnam is often characterised rather inaccurately as having as a strong, over-bearing, over-centralised state with a bloated bureaucracy that values hierarchy, authority lines, and top-down planning. However, the State's effective control has continuously been challenged and/or supplemented by local informal institutions especially in areas of social and economic life where the state has abdicated its responsibility, as in social safety net provision, disaster relief and rehabilitation, and job creation.

This explains why the state, despite its characterisation as strong, has not been able to utilize its power in expanding the national revenue base, particularly those emerging from the informal economy and business sectors, in order to fund its job creation schemes and social Programmes. This also explains why despite the overall seriousness of the Vietnamese State in responding to the needs of peasants and workers, we are seeing examples of collective action among their ranks which challenge the lack of consultative mechanisms and processes in the course of implementing urban and rural infrastructure development projects.

Another critical area where both the Vietnamese and Philippine governments have largely failed is in improving the plight of minority peoples, especially of women and girl ethnic minorities. This tends to be a blind spot for the state leadership in both countries which are dominated by dominant ethnic, religious, and linguistic groups. This explains why the poor among ethnic minorities in the rural areas fare worst than the poor in dominant majority groups in both rural and urban areas.

This study has examined the relationship between gender planning, governance, and poverty reduction efforts in the Philippines and Vietnam which have differing policy contexts, political ideological environment, bureaucratic culture, levels of economic growth and industrialisation, and activities of women's organisations and NGOs. It provides contrasting insights on the integration of gender in state bureaucratic politics in the framing of poverty alleviation plans. There are at least four general conclusions emerging from the above discussion.

First is that the implementation of gender-aware Programmes related to poverty reduction is still scattered, sporadic, and piecemeal, despite some deep and subtle differences in their levels of gender mainstreaming within government bureaucracies. Government line agencies in both Vietnam and the Philippines have yet to develop a clear and comprehensive framework for understanding and addressing the close linkages between gender and poverty concerns. In the absence of such framework, government agencies with more established turf and weight to pull could enjoy additional funding allotment for general and Gender and Development (GAD) related Programmes compared to women's ministries and mass organizations or NGOs.

However, these government agencies tend to only continue what they have been traditionally doing without infusing an integrated and holistic social approach, and a more profound analysis of gender and poverty issues in their Programmes. Second, the absence of a clear and comprehensive framework for the analysis of gender and poverty linkages is reinforced by the rather compartmentalized and fragmented approach of government line agencies to addressing women and gender concerns.

This is confounded by the great difficulty among front-line government workers, implementers and planners, as well as feminist NGO advocates, in shifting from the original women-focused interventions under the Women-in-Development (WID) to the Gender-and-Development (GAD) frameworks that focuses on gender equity and empowerment principles. Hence, many projects that simply target women as beneficiaries and/or participants for the sake of project efficiency and cost-saving measures, are uncritically accepted as a form of GAD intervention.

The conflation of women and gender, and the treatment of WID as GAD, create problems in getting the support of both male and female elected city officials who approve budgetary allocations. In the Philippines, for example, the allocation of the GAD budget in many cities and municipalities is threatened by the lack of support by local politicians, and the parallel weakness on the part of city-based women's NGOs and other advocacy groups to lobby and get public support. GAD plans, projects and budgets are still generally understood by the public, government elected officials and civil servants, NGOs, and women's organizations, as mainly targeting and benefiting women, and not addressing gender relations and equity issues.

The conflation of women and gender, and WID and GAD, is clearly demonstrated in the way the Vietnamese Women's Union and the Philippine Department of Social Welfare and Development (DSWD) has carried out women's Programmes subsumed as gender-sensitive interventions. Like the Women's Union in Vietnam, the DSWD is perhaps the best well-known government agency in the Philippines that has a strong women's Programme in its poverty alleviation efforts.

In its range of Programmes and services, the women-focused ones are those under the Women Welfare Programme, i.e. Social Communication Skills Development, Maternal and

Child Care, Self-Enhancement Skills Development, Community Participation Skills Development, Practical Skills Capability Building for Disadvantaged Women and Special Project for Women in Especially Difficult Circumstances. Both the DSWD and Women's Union projects are earmarked as Programmes for women only, and these are the very same Programmes that are understood as gender-related and leading to gender empowerment.

There is however, little attempt to integrate a gender framework which necessitates the creative integration and problematization of men and masculinities into mainstream Programmes on family welfare, credit provision, job creation, community capacity-building, and disaster relief and rehabilitation. Third, the integration of women into poverty alleviation projects and Programmes that see them primarily as mothers, homemakers, and dependents of men has resulted in their domestication and so-called "housewification", which prevent them from challenging the distribution of power and decision-making within their households and communities.

The Philippine government's centerpiece livelihood Programme for women is still the Productivity Skills Capability Building for Disadvantaged Women (PSCB) which mainly train women in traditional female skills such as sewing craft, toy craft, food preparation and preservation, and baking. This Programme, as well as many of the Women's Union income-generating projects, tends to reinforce the domestication of women, and the view that women are only secondary breadwinners. These income-generating activities designed primarily for women are likely to be unsustainable, given the saturated market, intense competition, low profit margins, and lack of access to credit. They also tend to overlook the workload implications for women who have many domestic and community-related responsibilities.

The role of women and households as social safety net providers ought to be supported by appropriate policy and bureaucratic interventions that complement and strengthen, rather than substitute and undermine, people's own initiatives.

Policies that discourage people's informal sector activities, such as laws against street vending and home-based businesses, must be reviewed and balanced against the need to create strong regulatory environments, while providing and enabling policy environment for the poor to help themselves. Lastly, female embodiment, participation, and representation in state agencies do not necessarily lead to the attainment of feminist goals or to the adequate handling of gender issues, which consider women's and men's concerns, and other factors of social differentiation such as disability, ethnicity, age, and sexual orientation.

The representation of women in government bodies, their participation as beneficiaries and managers of poverty alleviation projects, and their role as government service providers is good, and sometimes effective means to attain women's empowerment. However, they are neither feminist ends in themselves, nor necessarily expected to lead to feminist outcomes. Women's representation in local government units and other decision-making bodies under the Local Government Code in the Philippines are already limited.

And even if its provisions are well-used by women's organizations, mere female representation is not a guarantee that women representatives are capable of addressing gender problems, and the political, cultural and social constraints in doing so. Likewise, it is not realistic to expect that gender relations are improving, or that women's empowerment is occurring, just because women are targeted as participants or beneficiaries of poverty alleviation projects and Programmes, or just because women planners and executives are the ones who design and implement them. This is most clear in the Vietnamese case where increased female political representation at the national level has not been accompanied by similar trends at the local level, or by any significant policy changes to improve gender-related conditions and Programmes.

To be truly effective, social policies and Programmes must incorporate feminist visions and goals. At the same time, male and female civil servants and service providers at all levels of the bureaucracy need to understand more clearly the feminist values and principles of gender equity and empowerment and how they can effectively bring these into their service work, advocacy roles, and work environment. They also need to ensure that such values, principles and goals are clearly understood by the local people, women and men, in the communities that they serve.

Bibliography

Noeleen Heyzer. *Daughters in Industry: Work, Skills, and Consciousness of Women Workers in Asia*. Kuala Lumpur: Asian and Pacific Development Centre, 1988.

David Wigg ; foreword by H.E. Dame R. Nita Barrow. *In a Class of Their Own: A Look at the Campaign against Female Illiteracy*. Washington, D.C.: World Bank, c1994.

My Rights, Who Control[S]? : A Report of the Regional Consultation, Asia Pacific Women's Issues, Law and Development ... Kuala Lumpur: Asia Pacific Forum on Women Law & Development, 1989.

Kate Young. *Serving Two Masters: Third World Women in Development*. Ahmedabad: Allied Publishers, 1989.

Betty Jamie Chung, Ng Shui Meng. *The Status of Women in Law: A Comparison of Four Asian Countries*. Singapore: Institute of Southeast Asian Studies, 1977.

San Juan. *Women Empowering Women: Proceedings of the Human Rights Conference On The Trafficking Of Asian Women*, April 2-4, .../ Metro Manila : Coalition Against Trafficking in Women-Asia, 1993.

Barbara E. Ward. *Women in the New Asia; The Changing Social Roles of Men and Women in South and South-East Asia*. Paris: UNESCO, 1963.

Rekha Dayal. *Women in Health and Development in South-East Asia*. New Delhi: World Health Organization, Regional Office for South-East Asia, 1985.

Lynne Brydon and Sylvia Chant. *Women in the Third*

World: Gender Issues in Rural and Urban Areas. New Brunswick, NJ : Rutgers University, 1989.

Penny van Esterik. *Women of Southeast Asia.* De Kalb, IL: Northern Illinois University, Center for Southeast Asian Studies, c1996.

Yayori Matsui. *Women's Asia.* London; Atlantic Highlands, N.J. : Zed Books, c1989.

Committee on Women's Studies in Asia. *Women's Studies, Women's Lives: Theory and Practice in South and Southeast Asia.* New Delhi: Kali for Women, c1994.

R. Lund and S. M. Panda. Asian Financial Crisis, Women's Work and Forced Migration. *Norsk Geografisk Tidsskrift, v. 54:3, 2000, p. 128-133.*

Darunee Tantiwiramanond. Changing Gender Relations in Southeast Asia and the Contribution of Women's Organizations. *Southeast Asia Studies Bulletin, Oct 1997, p.18.*

Richard Leete. The Continuing Flight from Marriage and Parenthood among the Overseas Chinese in East and Southeast Asia: Dimensions and Implications. *Population and Development Review, v. 20:4, Dec 1994, p. 811 (19 pages).*

Barbara Watson Andaya. From Temporary Wife to Prostitute: Sexuality and Economic Change in Early Modern Southeast Asia. *Journal of Women's History, v. 9:4, Win 1998, p. 11 (24 pages).*

Wazir Jahan Karim. *Gender Studies in Southeast Asia. Southeast Asian Journal of Social Science, v. 21:1, 1993, p. 98-113.*

Gavin W Jones. Modernization and Divorce: Contrasting Trends in Islamic Southeast Asia and the West. *Population and Development Review, v. 23:1, March 1997, p. 95 (20 pages).*

Parvati Raghuram and Irene Hardill. Netgitiating a Market: A Case Study of an Asian Woman in Business. *Women's Studies International Fourm, v. 21:5, Sept 10, 1998, p. 475-483.*

Purification V. Quisumbing The Position of Women Under Labor Laws in ASEAN. *Philippine Journal of Industrial Relations, v. 8:2 & v. 9:1, 1986-1987, p. 138-144.*

Robert Weissman. Repression to Cooptation: Challenges for Women Workers in Southeast Asia. *Multinational Monitor, v. 14:11, Nov 1993, 20 pages.*

Spinder Dhaliwal. Silent Contributors, Asian Female Entrepreneurs and Women in Business. *Women's Studies International Forum, v. 21:5, Sept 10, 1998, p. 463-474.*

Judith Nagata & Janet W. Salaff. Strategies for Survival: Lives of Southeast Asian Women. *Southeast Asian Journal of Social Science, v. 24:1, 1996.*

Barbara Watson Andaya. Women and Economic Change: The Pepper Trade in Pre-Modern Southeast Asia [On Sumatra]. *Journal of the Economic and Social History of the Orient, v. 38:2, May 1995, p. 165-190.*

C. Shan Beyrer. Women and Girls and the Sex Industry in Southeast Asia; Political Causes and Human Rights Implications. *Social Science & Medicine, August 2001, v. 53:4, p. 543-550.*

Laura Sanchez. Women's Power and the Gendered Division of Domestic Labor in the Third World. *Gender and Society, v.7:3, 1993, p.434-59.*

Jan Jindy Pettman.Women on the Move: Globalization and Labor Migration from South and Southeast Asian States. *Global Society, v. 12, Sept 1998, p. 389-403.*

Jurgette Hondulado. Women Workers in Southeast Asia: Issues, Demands and Participation in Trade Unions. *Philippine Journal of Industrial Relations, v. 8:2 & v. 9:1, 1986-1987, p. 161-172.*

Tania Murray Li. Working Separately but Eating Together: Personhood, Property, and Power Inconjugal Relations. *American Ethnologist, v. 25:4, Nov 1998 p. 675-676.*

Index